# Bessie Smith
## 1894–1937

"She showed me the air and taught me how to fill it."  —*Janis Joplin*

"Bessie was my favorite, but I never let people know I listened to her. Mamie Smith, the other famous blues singer, had a prettier voice, but Bessie's had more soul in it. She dug right down and kept it in you. Her music haunted you even when she stopped singing."  —*Mahalia Jackson*

"Bessie Smith, she was the best blues singer there was, but that trouble was inside her and it wouldn't let her rest."  —*Sidney Bechet*

"Had she lived, Bessie would have been right there on top with the rest of us in the Swing Era."  —*Lionel Hampton*

"It was Bessie Smith, through her tone and her cadence, who helped me to dig back to the way I myself must have spoken when I was a pickaninny, and to remember the things I had heard and seen and felt. I had buried them very deep. I had never listened to Bessie Smith in America (in the same way that, for years, I would not touch a watermelon), but in Europe she helped to reconcile me to being a 'nigger.' "  —*James Baldwin*

"Even though she was raucous and loud, she had a sort of a tear—no, not a tear, but there was a misery in what she did. It was as though there was something she had to get out, something she just had to bring to the fore."  —*Alberta Hunter*

"She was a woman who loved life—period."  —*Ruby Walker*

Bessie. *Photo by Carl Van Vechten, 1936.*

# Bessie

## Chris Albertson

STEIN AND DAY/*Publishers*/New York

Cover photo: Collection of American Literature, Beinecke Rare Book and Manuscript Library, Yale University/Courtesy of the Estate of Carl Van Vechten, Joseph Solomon Executor.

A STEIN AND DAY REISSUE
THIRD STEIN AND DAY PAPERBACK PRINTING 1985
*Bessie* was originally published in hardcover
by Stein and Day/*Publishers* in 1972.
Copyright © 1972, 1982 by Chris Albertson
All rights reserved, Stein and Day, Incorporated
Designed by David Miller
Printed in the United States of America
Stein and Day/*Publishers*
Scarborough House
Briarcliff Manor, N.Y. 10510


**The Library of Congress has cataloged the first printing of this title as follows:**
   **Albertson, Chris.**
      Bessie. New York, Stein and Day [1972]
      253 p. illus. 24 cm.
      "Selected discography": p. 239–242.
      Bibliography: p. 243–244.

   1. Smith, Bessie, 1898?–1937.   I. Title.
ML420.S667A7          784'.092'4          79-163353
ISBN 0-8128-1700-1 (pbk)    [B]                    MARC

Library of Congress          73[74]                    MN

Bessie died long before I was even born, but the way Daddy's stereo sent her forth on my fullest childhood Sundays, I couldn't believe it.

> *"Twenty-five cents . . . huh!*
> *No, no, I wouldn't pay twenty-five cents to*
> *go in nowhere . . ."*
> *and I said, "Me neither."*
> *Thought she was talkin' 'bout the P.T.C.*
> *until my momma told me what a "speak" was.*

> *Sunday morning in 1959*
> *our church hymn was "Weeping Willow Blues"*
> *and Bessie belted out them words without pretending.*
> *By the time the cornbread was done, she'd be draggin' out*
> *"Luv, oh luv oh careless luv . . ." and that was grace.*

To some she could've looked like any old nappyheaded, drunken, negligent mother off of South Street; to me she was the Ghost Lady-with-a-perpetually-broken-heart. My introduction to Miss Bessie was a gaze back at the green, lavender, blue, and orange smoky-filmy photos on volumes one through four.

Bessie Smith, subject of a family tradition, is alive and well on Philadelphia Sundays, and in my soul.

—Sheila F. Waters
Philadelphia, 1972

# AUTHOR'S NOTE

Reviewing for *down beat* a 1970 children's biography of Bessie Smith, I lamented the superficial treatment generally afforded her and pointed out the need for a comprehensive, factual biography that not only documented the great singer's performances and recording activities but also revealed something of the woman herself. I ended my review by stating that I wished I could write such a book, but that it would take more insight than I had at the time.

Considering her importance, published data on Bessie Smith are far from voluminous, but what does exist—at least two biographical books, numerous chapters, and hundreds of magazine and newspaper articles—contains such repetition of material that it could boil down to ten or fifteen pages of print without significant omissions. Wherever she went, Bessie Smith's personality drew as much attention as her music did, but we could read everything that has been written about her and still not know why.

One reason treatments of Bessie's life have been so sketchy is that the early jazz writers—who wrote their chonicles in the late thirties and the decade that followed when sources of information were still abundant—had so much ground to cover that they either concentrated on the then contemporary activities of the big swing bands or dealt in very general terms with the history and development of Afro-American music. When the writers focused their attention on an individual performer, they concentrated on his developing career and an analysis of his music rather than on his personality and private life. As they have in the case of Bessie Smith, writers and interviewers most often make the mistake of seeking their information from fellow star performers rather than the unknown chorine or stage hand who—having fewer distractions and a more intimate working relationship with the subject—are usually the most perceptive observers.

A wealth of valuable information is contained in the efforts of the music's early chroniclers, but one must spend a great deal of time sifting fact from fiction, and the very fact that it is possible to write a book about Bessie Smith in 1972 and include so much hitherto unpublished material regarding her character and career clearly illustrates the neglect of which I speak. This is, of course, not to say that everything contained in this book is gospel truth—it is quite possible that I have failed to detect an occasional embellishment—but, on the whole, I believe my account captures the essence of this remarkable woman's life, and that the margin of error is a thin one.

I did not want to write a rehash of previously published material: too many questions had been left unanswered; too many gaps needed to be filled. The missing material could be obtained only from press clippings that had escaped the eyes of previous researchers, and from the memories of Bessie's few surviving associates. The clippings would of course always be there, memories would not; each passing hour could easily represent a loss of valuable material.

Few living persons knew Bessie Smith as well as Ruby Walker, her niece by marriage. Ruby spent many years with her famous aunt, as a performer in some of her shows and as a close companion during the last fourteen years of her life. It was only after Ruby agreed to share with me her recollections of Bessie Smith that I felt it possible even to begin writing this book.

As Ruby's remarkable memory poured into my tape recorder hour after hour, I began to realize how little we have known about Bessie Smith. Ruby's vivid descriptions of events and the daily routines in her aunt's life brought a blurred portrait to sharp focus. Equally helpful were the names and places woven into Ruby's recollections; often the casual mention of a person once associated with Bessie but long since retired into oblivion led me to new sources of information.

One of the many persons mentioned by Ruby was Jack Gee, Jr., Bessie's son, adopted in 1926. Now in his early fifties, he was one of the most important people in Bessie's life, and his recollections added a new dimension to his mother's biography. It was Jack, Jr., who led me to Lionel Hampton (who would have thought there would be a link between Hampton and Bessie!), and to Maud Smith, widow of Bessie's brother Clarence. Mrs. Smith toured extensively with her sister-in-law and proved to be extremely helpful in substantiating information already learned from Ruby Walker, and in adding details regarding Bessie Smith's childhood and her relationships with Jack Gee and Richard Morgan. Oddly enough, while Jack Gee, Sr., has spoken to numerous writers over the years, neither Ruby Walker, Jack, Jr., nor Maud Smith—with whom Mr. Gee maintains regular contact—has been approached before. The reader can draw his own conclusions as to why Mr. Gee has neglected to lead writers to these valuable sources of information, but I believe the explanation is contained in this book.

Augmenting the many interviews that help make up this biography were black newspapers and periodicals from 1915 to 1937. They yielded some three hundred relevant—if not always reliable—items, often bearing out information obtained through interviews. It should be pointed out that the black press of that period relied heavily on volunteer writers—sometimes people who were performers themselves—and that these writers were at times paid by the theatre owners or the performers whom they reviewed. A glowing review was therefore not always a reflection of the writer's candid opinion.

Unfortunately not all the gaps could be filled. Although I am able to shed some new light on Bessie's activities in her formative years, information regarding that period of her life is still so scant and vague that we may never know the whole truth. We know a great deal about Bessie's personality in her last fifteen years, but we can still only guess what shaped it.

Jazz critic Rudi Blesh has recalled how close he came to writing a Bessie Smith biography in the late nineteen-forties, when the available sources of information were more numerous. Bessie's sisters, Tinnie and Viola—then still alive, living in Philadelphia—had agreed, along with Jack Gee, to cooperate in piecing together Bessie's life. The two sisters had a trunk full of rare photographs, letters, sheet music, and other items that had belonged to Bessie. The three relatives made a financial arrangement with Blesh, and a major publisher drew up a contract: but just as the work was to begin, Jack Gee decided he wanted more money. His unrealistic demand made the project impossible, reignited his long-running feud with the two sisters, caused them to withdraw, and led to the complete disappearance of the trunk and its valuable contents.

A similar frustration befell me during the two years I spent preparing this biography. An engineer at Columbia Records told me that he had stumbled on the company's files of artists' contracts and correspondence from the nineteen-twenties and -thirties. This file, which included all the interoffice memoranda of the period, would certainly have told us much about the relationship between Bessie and Frank Walker, Columbia's director of "race" records; it probably would have documented the company's attitude toward its "race artists" at the time. Fortunately the engineer picked up a ledger containing an account of payments made to black artists—including Bessie—and details of their recording agreements, but the rest of his find, gathering dust in the corner of an air-conditioning room at the Thirtieth Street studio, had been thrown out as "old junk" just before we got back to it.

As the pieces of Bessie's character and career were amassed, it became clear that *Bessie* could not be another book for the jazz enthusiast alone; the extraordinary life-style and personality of this woman contributed as much to her renown as her voice did. *Bessie* had to be more than the story of the world's most famous blues singer; it had to be the story of a woman who was black and proud long before that became the acceptable thing to be. Its candor may offend, its dispelling of myths may disillusion; but a biographer is obligated to document his subject's whole personality, and I did not feel that I should be inhibited by the fact that I am white and Bessie Smith was black—the fact is that no writer, black or white, had undertaken a serious, researched biography of Bessie, and time was running out. In the final analysis, Bessie's life-style will shock or offend only those whose precepts are based on outmoded, puritanical values.

There are many incidents in this book that show Bessie Smith in an unfavorable light; others are either favorable or unfavorable, depending on the reader's attitude. I included them because they reveal aspects of her personality that seem essential to an under-standing of her. Other incidents, far more sensational, have been left out because they did not contribute to this understanding. Bessie Smith cared remarkably little for the good opinion of others; she sought acceptance as a human being, but she would not alter her ways in order to gain it. Always outspoken, she would, I believe, have been more than candid had she been able to tell her own story.

My own interest in Bessie Smith dates back to the late nineteen-forties, when, as a teenager in Copenhagen, I heard her big voice testing the tiny speaker of my radio. I didn't understand the words; I didn't even know what kind of music I was listening to. I did know that I had to hear more. New records were hard to find in postwar Denmark, so I began to search through countless bins in secondhand record shops and made trips to the United States Information Service library, where I borrowed books about the blues and Afro-American music in general. Typically, the U.S.I.S., although it boasted a sizable record library, offered as samples of black music only a handful of Library of Congress field recordings—not a single jazz or blues record.

In January 1970, when Columbia Records decided to reissue Bessie Smith's total output, I thought I knew a lot about Bessie. I had listened to all her recordings at one time or another, but never as intently as when Columbia engineer Larry Hiller and I began production work on the reissues. We must have played each of Bessie's 159 recorded selections at least twenty-five times during the first year and a half of nightly studio sessions, and I learned more as I did research for the notes accompanying the first three album releases.

The National Academy of Recording Arts and Sciences awarded me the Grammy for the best liner notes of 1970. By then I had begun work on this book and discovered, ironically, that my album notes perpetuated much of the misinformation that has characterized most writing about Bessie Smith.

A thin line separates misinformation and conjecture. Therefore, lest the reader interpret the dialogue in *Bessie* as conjecture on my part, I should point out that all dialogue included in the account of incidents is taken verbatim from firsthand recollections; it may not give the actual words spoken, but I believe it captures the essence of what was said. In some cases, such as the Carl Van Vechten party incident, two eyewitnesses—interviewed separately—recalled an almost identical exchange of words.

There are many important figures in black music's past, like Bessie, whose true stores remain untold. One reason is the understandable reluctance on the part of black people to speak freely to a white interviewer—and the great majority of jazz writers are white. Regrettably, control over the commercial aspects of black music (and sometimes over its creative aspects as well) is mostly in white hands, and it is not uncommon for an outspoken performer to face closed doors. We usually hear only of the events that take place, not of those that have been prevented from taking place. That situation is changing: the old clique of writers, club owners, record company officials, and impresarios who for decades literally ruled over the world of black music is gradually breaking up. Performers themselves are filling some of the vacated spots, and we see the emergence of a new breed of writers, black and white, whose concern is social as well as musical. This changing of the guards, and the new literary freedom that has resulted from it, must now be combined to produce the true account of Afro-American music and its creators. To do so, one must also delve into concurrent events, attitudes, and social habits—important ingredients that jazz writers tend to leave out of their chronicles.

In *Bessie*—seeking to paint a picture of Bessie Smith's times as well as of her personal life and career—I often caught myself getting carried away with historical and sociological asides, and I soon realized that an adequate social history of black Americans in the first four decades of this century is yet to be published. Frederick Lewis Allen, in his otherwise excellent books on America's twentieth-century growing pains, all but left out black Americans, treating them rather naïvely when he did; Gunnar Myrdal's *An American Dilemma* reveals a far deeper understanding of the plight of Bessie Smith's generation in a racist society, but in such scholarly works the nitty-gritty of black life gets buried in explanation of a social phenomenon's broader consequence.

A case in point is the phenomenon of the "buffet flat," which the nature of this book allowed me to touch upon only briefly. Sociologists have dealt with numerous consequences of these establishments, but nowhere does one find a book that explains what a buffet flat was or how it was operated. In Claude McKay's *Home to Harlem* and other works by black writers of the period one finds numerous references to buffet flats, but—due to a combination of literary taboos and the fact that most readers of that time knew very well what the notorious flats were—one looks in vain for details.

Buffet flats, speakeasies, white Hollywood goddesses, and a Florida real estate boom may seem like incidentals when speaking of Bessie Smith, but it would be hard to imagine a future biographer of a fifties rock-and-roll star leaving out teenage gang wars, motel romances, or skinnydippers and panty raids.

Bessie Smith's story forms only a small part of the history of Afro-American music. It is not complete as told in this book, but—thanks to the people named in my acknowledgments, and a few who wished to remain anonymous—I do believe this biography to be the truest and fullest account of Bessie Smith, the woman and the artist, that can be written at this time. Hers was the voice that opened the door, led me to the music of black Americans, filled my head with sounds that memory may dim, but never fade away completely, and ultimately led me to America. I can never repay my debt to Bessie Smith, but I hope I have done her justice and that this book may inspire similar efforts to tell us what we ought to know about other major figures in black music.

Chris Albertson
New York City, July 1972

# ACKNOWLEDGMENTS

For giving their recollections and putting up with questions that sometimes were personal, and often naïve; for contributing the dialogue that appears in the book, my special thanks go to Eubie Blake, Demas Dean, Thomas A. Dorsey, Brick Fleagle, Juanita Green, John Hammond, Lionel Hampton, Katherine Handy, Alberta Hunter, Eddie Hunter, J. C. Johnson, Jo Jones, Allan McMillan, Irvin C. Miller, Isabel Washington Powell, Gertrude Saunders, Frank Schiffman, Zutty Singleton, Elmer Snowden, Earle Sweeting, Leigh Whipper, and Sam Wooding. I also acknowledge the reminiscences passed on to me before their deaths by Lil Hardin Armstrong, Lovie Austin, Ida Cox, and Lonnie Johnson.

For many hours spent scrutinizing the fine, faded print of hundreds of newspapers and periodicals I thank Henri Berrings, Anthony Davis, Lloyd Peerman, and Sheila Waters; for performing the tedious job of typing and retyping manuscript and for many helpful suggestions I am grateful to Harold Hanson; for detective work in Philadelphia I thank my faithful friend of many years Bertha Waters; for clues and phone numbers I am grateful to Linda Kuehl; and for his extraordinary insight and social analysis—from which I confess to have borrowed freely—I am indebted to William Dufty.

I also wish to acknowledge the cooperation of Walter C. Allen of the Institute of Jazz Studies at Rutgers University, Newark, New Jersey; the staffs of the New York Public Library's Schomburg Collection and the Lincoln Center Research Library of Performing Arts; Valdo L. Freeman of the Negro Actors' Guild; the American Federation of Musicians, Local 802; Ernest F. Dyson of Federal City College, Washington, D.C.; Jerome A. Ford of Barber-Scotia College, Concord, North Carolina; Willie Hamilton of the New York *Amsterdam News;* Milton Kramer of Empress Music, Inc.; Mr. Seaman of the National Biscuit Company; Doug Pomeroy; Pug Horton; Ronald Francis.

Finally, a very special thanks to Jack Gee, Jr., whose recollections of his mother gave this book an added dimension; to Maud Smith Faggins, who so graciously put up with my many questions; to Ruby Walker Smith, without whose cooperation there would be no book; to Dr. Hugh Smith, for contributing his memory of the circumstances surrounding Bessie Smith's death; to Larry Hiller, who burned the midnight oil in Columbia's studios continuing our work on the Bessie Smith reissue series while much of my time was absorbed by work on this book; and to my editors Renni Browne and Mary Solberg, who encouraged as they put up with missed deadlines and some deplorable passages of manuscript, finally whipping me and *Bessie* into shape.

# I

*No time to marry, no time to settle down;*
*I'm a young woman, and I ain't done runnin'*
*aroun'.*

"Young Woman's Blues"

On Monday, October 4, 1937, Philadelphia witnessed one of the most spectacular funerals in its history. Bessie Smith, a black superstar of the previous decade—a "has-been," fatally injured on a dark Mississippi road eight days earlier—was being given a send-off befitting the star she had never really ceased to be.

Two days earlier, on a cold Saturday morning, Bessie's brother Clarence, his wife Maud, and William Upshur, Jr., a prominent black funeral director, quietly awaited the arrival of Bessie's body at Philadelphia's Thirtieth Street station. They had been there at two-thirty that morning, but the train carrying Bessie and Richard didn't arrive until ten.

Richard Morgan and Bessie had shared each other's lives for the past six years; they had traveled thousands of miles together before making this last trip from Clarksdale, Mississippi. The four people now waiting for the pine box containing Bessie's remains to be lowered to the platform were silent. The railroad station setting was a painful reminder of good times shared by Richard, Maud, and Clarence on the road with Bessie. Maud still recalls the grief in Richard's eyes, and a small tear in the left shoulder of his dark suit—evidence of the tragic event that had brought them together that morning.

The Empress of the Blues lay in state at Upshur's funeral home on

Twenty-first and Christian Streets. No one came to see her on the first day. But when word of her death reached the black community,[1] the body had to be moved to the O. V. Catto Elks Lodge, which more readily accommodated the estimated ten thousand mourners who filed past her bier on Sunday, October 3.

What they saw told them little about the remarkable woman whose last performance was being played out. The expression of serenity on Bessie's face suggested nothing of the turbulence that had characterized her life. Her final costume was a long silk dress she was reported to have admired but been unable to afford. The newspapers said the gown was a farewell gift from her estranged husband, Jack Gee. "That should be turned around," suggested a family member thirty-five years later. "Maybe he was wearing a suit he never could afford, which Bessie bought for him." Actually, Bessie's life insurance paid for the gown.

Bessie's last moments of real glory and prosperity were eight years past, but thanks to the insurance policy, her exit was grand. The silvery metallic coffin trimmed with gold had cost close to five hundred dollars. It was lined with pink two-tone velvet, which, according to the black press, matched her "flesh-colored" gown and slippers.

The auditorium of the O. V. Catto Elks Lodge at Sixteenth and Fitzwater Streets had on happier occasions resounded with Bessie's powerful voice and the cheers of those who came to hear it. Now the hall was filled long before the Reverend Andrew J. Sullivan mounted the pulpit to intone the opening words of the funeral service.

Sobs competed with the ministerial voice that rose solemnly from behind a pyramid of forty floral arrangements. When Mrs. Emily Moten read a poem called "Oh, Life," there was a small commotion in the rear—two registered nurses on duty rushed to the aid of a lady who had fainted. Three other mourners, including Bessie's oldest sister, Viola, fainted before dancer (and sometimes female impersonator) Rubberlegs Williams, and a choir brought the service to a tearful conclusion with their rendition of "My Buddy," a pop song from 1922 when Bessie, living in that same Philadelphia neighborhood, had stood at the threshold of success.

Bessie and her husband had been separated for more than seven years, but Jack told reporters at the funeral that they had never lost

---

1. Late, because black newspapers were published weekly.

touch. During their marriage the Gees had known few moments of harmony. Their life together had been a continuous contest of physical and emotional strength, but Jack made every effort to give the impression that in Bessie's mind he had always been her man.

Leading a small group of close relatives[2] and friends—including Bessie's three sisters; her brother Clarence, and his wife Maud; Thomas J. Hill, a nephew—Jack moved slowly toward the open casket to view his wife's body for the last time. Some papers reported that he threw himself at Bessie's still form, that he wept, that forty-five minutes passed before the six young pallbearers could lift the casket onto their shoulders and bear it out into the street. "Jack didn't throw himself over no casket," recalls Maud, "but he was good for putting up a cry, he'd cry in two minutes, and I'd have to say 'Stop those crocodile tears, Jack,' because he was just putting on a show."

The crowd outside was now seven thousand strong, and policemen were having a hard time holding it back. To those who had known Bessie in better days, the sight was familiar, although this was undoubtedly the largest crowd she had ever attracted.

As the front door of the hall opened, mourners broke through the police lines and rushed forward for a final look. A woman and her child were knocked down and injured before calm was restored and the procession begun.

The professional pallbearers,[3] who had never known Bessie, walked a block down Sixteenth Street to the waiting hearse. At the head of the procession, flanked by the tight-packed mob of mourners and onlookers, a choir softly intoned "Rest in Peace."

It was 4:20 P.M. before the cortege of thirty-nine cars began to move; another half hour before the last car had passed in front of the Elks Lodge. The procession did not head straight for the cemetery. Instead, as if to give South Philadelphia a last look at the Empress, it crawled along Fitzwater Street to Eighteenth, turned left at Lombard and on to Twelfth Street, then moved south on Twelfth Street and crossed Kater into Bessie's old neighborhood. There men dressed in rags stopped and watched until the procession had passed out of sight.

2. Absent from the family gathering was Bessie and Jack's adopted son, Jack Gee, Jr.—driving down from New York, his father had not found room for him in the car.

3. James Harris, Jack Brady, Cecilus Remson, Louis Siceluff, William Battis, and Herbert Jenkins, who are said to have been making a bit of history themselves in that hired pallbearers had never before been used at a Philadelphia funeral.

The grand exit. Scene outside of the O. V. Catto Elks Home (Philadelphia) as the casket bearing Bessie Smith's remains is carried from the auditorium to a waiting hearse, October 4, 1937.

Today it would be unthinkable for a star of Bessie's magnitude to be buried without major show business personalities in attendance.[4] Several celebrities, including Ethel Waters, had promised to attend the funeral, but no major star showed up. Performers, promoters, and others in the entertainment field who later claimed Bessie as friend, idol, or inspiration were conspicuously absent. Although Claude Hopkins, Duke Ellington, Noble Sissle, Buck and Bubbles, Bill "Bojangles" Robinson, Ethel Waters, and the cast of the Cotton Club Revue sent telegrams, the industry of which Bessie had been

4. By extreme contrast, Louis Armstrong's funeral in 1971 was a disgraceful farce staged for the benefit of TV talk show celebrities with tickets, admitting the likes of Johnny Carson while Armstrong's real friends and colleagues—some of whom had barely managed the fare from New Orleans to New York—were refused entrance.

such a big part was represented only by a handful of local show people and a few chorines who had once worked with her. Richard Morgan, whom Bessie had truly loved during her last years, was there, but his presence went unnoticed as Jack Gee basked in the publicity.

At dusk Bessie's body was laid to rest in grave no. 3, range 12, lot 20, section C, of Mount Lawn Cemetery in nearby Sharon Hill, Pennsylvania. A hundred and fifty people watched as a smaller group of mourners formed a semicircle around a sunken, marble-finished burial vault.

A reporter dramatized the scene for Philadelphia *Tribune* readers:

> Two heavily veiled women wept steadily. In the strained silence, the breathing of the men was plainly audible. The clergyman cleared his throat softly, "I am the resurrection and the life . . ." The casket slid down into the grave. A woman screamed, and the broad shoulders of Jack Gee heaved and writhed as he buried his face in his hands. Hoarse sobs broke from his lips. "Bessie! Oh, Bessie . . ."
>
> "Earth to earth, ashes to ashes . . ." The minister closed his book. The mourners faltered forward to cast their flowers into the grave. Bessie Smith Gee, late "Queen of the Blues," was but a memory.

The airtight vault was guaranteed against corrosion or leakage for one hundred years. The funeral had cost approximately a thousand dollars, about half of what Bessie made in one of her better weeks.

The grave remained unmarked for thirty-three years.

At the time of Bessie's death, jazz documentation was in its infancy. In Robert Goffin's *Aux Frontières du Jazz,* published in 1932, and Hughes Panassie's *Le Jazz Hot,* published two years later, both writers plunged naïvely into their subject, led only by enthusiasm and curiosity. Their books inspired new writers, who began gradually to piece together the details of Afro-American music's development. In 1937 most of the jazz writers were focusing their attention on the activities of the big swing bands, while those writers who bothered at all with Bessie Smith dealt mostly with the controversy surrounding her death—a controversy that in retrospect seems largely of their own making.

These early jazz writers, all of them white, were tremendously enthusiastic about the music, but they showed little understanding of its social significance—and no understanding of its creators and their culture. Black artists were stereotyped in the same patronizing terms as the maids and handymen in Hollywood movies. Bessie's death, they seemed to say, was tragic not so much because a human life had been lost as because it meant she wouldn't be making any more records for blues fans to collect.

It was not until the mid-forties that writers began looking into the details of Bessie's life. Even then it was Bessie Smith the blues singer, not the woman, who interested them. The research was superficial, but a few memories were recorded before it was too late.

Most people remember Bessie as crude, tough, or ill-mannered; irresponsible; passionate, kind, or generous. She was all these things, but the most vivid memory that people who knew or heard her have is of her extraordinary power as a performer. Bessie had vocal abilities no one in her field could equal, and she had a gift for showmanship to match. She sang, she danced, she did comedy routines with a skill that evoked the envy of other performers. Tin Pan Alley tunesmiths created many of Bessie's songs, but she charged their lyrics with as much real joy and sorrow as she did the lyrics she herself wrote.

Throughout her life Bessie moved in a subculture that white America fostered but has only recently begun to understand. Her unique talent and her unflagging quest for a good time took her into a third world of segregated black entertainment where, in an atmosphere of make-believe, she stubbornly remained herself.

If she had a goal, no one knew just what it was, but those close to her agree that Bessie Smith yearned for acceptance rather than acclaim, and that she did not see the two as being the same. Without playing any show business games, she climbed as far up in her profession as a black artist of her time and genre could go. And when she tumbled from the pinnacle she landed without bitterness, gathered up the pieces, and began another climb.

Between the climb and the fall, Bessie had six glorious, eventful years, during which millions of followers clamored for her songs of love, misery, and joy.

Those few years of costly glory have been most frequently, if not accurately, chronicled. Less has been written about her last seven years, when she paid the price, and virtually nothing about her first twenty-five years, when she stood in the wings.

Bessie[5] Smith was born in Chattanooga, Tennessee, on a date that

5. Her given name—not Elizabeth, as has often been said.

will probably never be verified. Southern bureaucracy made little distinction between its black population and its dogs; such official records as a birth certificate were not always considered necessary. Black people often recorded such events themselves, in the family Bible, but such a book has not turned up from the Smith household. In later years Bessie was known to lower her age a bit, but April 15, 1894, is the birth date that appears on her 1923 application for a marriage license.

In the eighteen-nineties, less than thirty years after the Thirteenth Amendment had officially abolished slavery in the United States, most black Americans accepted poverty as a fact of life. Slavery in a different form was still very much a reality; as second-class citizens most black people continued to face a future of servitude.

Chattanooga, located on the Tennessee River 138 miles southeast of Nashville, was settled as a trading post in 1828 and grew with the coming of railroads in the mid-nineteenth century. By 1900 Bessie's hometown had become an important trade center with a population of thirty thousand, nearly half of it black. Unemployment was high; "abject poverty" would scarcely suffice to describe the economic status of the family into which Bessie was born.

William and Laura Smith lived in what Bessie herself described as "a little ramshackle cabin." They had seven children, one of whom, Son, died before Bessie's birth. Where there was little food and no medical attention, death was a frequent visitor. William Smith—a part-time Baptist preacher who ran a small mission—died shortly after Bessie's birth, and by the time she was eight or nine, her mother and another brother, Bud, had gone as well.

Viola, the oldest, raised the remaining brothers and sisters: Bessie, Tinnie, Lulu, Andrew, and Clarence. The last two soon became self-supporting, but the burden on Viola was not eased, for she herself and Tinnie—neither of whom was married—soon bore children of their own.

Being poor, uneducated, and black gave even less hope for the future seventy years ago than it does today. There were really only two things a black person could do: resign himself to a life of ill-paid manual or domestic labor or join a traveling show. The former was not always possible unless he moved to an area where jobs were available—but even the moving took money. The latter was possible only if he possessed some talent for entertaining. The traveling show was no idyll in those days; it offered an escape from servitude and at least the promise of better pay, but all it really guaranteed was a change of scenery, which in itself was often a sufficient lure.

Minstrel shows had flourished since the eighteen-sixties, and vaudeville had its beginnings in the eighteen-eighties. These traveling variety shows employed black performers even then, but not until the turn of the century did white impresarios begin to discover gold in black talent. When that happened, the doors of the rapidly growing entertainment industry opened wider to blacks, and the lines began forming.

Bessie entered the field during the period of transition that led an era of Victorian propriety into the madcap "modern age" of the nineteen-twenties. Her timing could hardly have been better.

Clarence, the oldest surviving male of the Smith family, joined a traveling show as a dancer and comedian. The show, owned by Moses Stokes, was playing in a Chattanooga storefront in 1912 when Clarence arranged an audition for Bessie. Bessie had been singing for nickels and dimes on Chattanooga's Ninth Street to the guitar accompaniment of her brother Andrew since she was about nine, but this was her first professional experience. Lonnie and Cora Fisher, who managed the Stokes troupe at the time, took her on principally as a dancer. The show's cast included Gertrude Rainey and Will, her husband of eight years, Gertrude McDonald, Son Riggins, Wiley Teasley, Len Collins, Isaac Bradford, and Abner Davis. No one knows how long Bessie stayed with that show, but a few months later she was appearing twenty miles away in Dalton, Georgia, with another troupe that also included the Raineys.

Gertrude "Ma" Rainey, born in Columbus, Georgia, on April 26, 1886, became famous as the Mother of the Blues throughout the South and Midwest well before nearly a hundred remarkable records assured her worldwide fame among critics and collectors, who hailed her as one of the greatest blues singers, second only to Bessie.

The tag "Mother of the Blues," though probably dreamed up by a record promoter, was an appropriate one. Jazz boasts many legendary figures in its early, unrecorded history, but the blues claim no predecessor to Ma Rainey. She appears to be the single or at least the earliest link between the male country blues artists who roamed the streets and back roads of the South and their female counterparts, the so-called "classic blues" singers.[6]

6. Who, in fact, were not classic in any explainable sense, nor strictly blues singers.

Legend has it that Ma Rainey literally kidnapped Bessie, that she and her husband forced the girl to tour with their show, teaching her in the process how to sing the blues. It's a colorful story, but almost certainly just a story. "I remember one time when we were in Augusta, Georgia," says Maud Smith. "Bessie and Ma Rainey sat down and had a good laugh about how people was making up stories of Ma taking Bessie from her home, and Ma's mother used to get the biggest laugh out of the kidnapping story whenever we visited her in Macon. Actually, Ma and Bessie got along fine, but Ma never taught Bessie how to sing. She was more like a mother to her." The Raineys didn't have their own show until after 1916, by which time Bessie had been on her own for several years.

Irvin C. Miller, a theatrical producer who became a major force in black entertainment during the nineteen-twenties, had two shows touring the South around 1912. Bessie was in the chorus of one of these shows. "She was a natural singer, even then," Miller recalls, "but we stressed beauty in the chorus line and Bessie did not meet my standards as far as looks were concerned. I told the manager to get rid of her, which he did." Mr. Miller's failure to see Bessie's physical beauty is explained by his well-known slogan, the theme of all his shows: "Glorifying the Brownskin Girl." To put it plainly, Bessie was too black.

Miller saw Bessie again in 1913 when she was performing on the stage of the "81" Theatre in Atlanta. So did veteran film actor Leigh Whipper, who, as manager of Newark's Orpheum Theatre, hired her twelve years later. "It was in the early part of the year," says Mr. Whipper, recalling his 1913 encounter. "She was just a teenager, and she obviously didn't know she was the artist she was. She didn't know how to dress—she just sang in her street clothes—but she was such a natural that she could wreck anybody's show. She only made ten dollars a week, but people would throw money on the stage, and the stage hands would pick up about three or four dollars for her after every performance, especially when she sang the 'Weary Blues.' That was her big number."[7]

Bessie spent a lot of time at the "81." Charles Bailey, owner of the theatre, told Jack Gee that Bessie was "practically raised" in the

---

7. "Weary Blues" was published in 1915, which suggests that Mr. Whipper's memory may be two years off, but it is also possible that Bessie sang a similar tune or that "Weary Blues" was around for two years prior to its publication.

theatre's back yard and that she spent her daytime hours there training girls for the chorus.

Thomas A. Dorsey, who as Georgia Tom later became a song-writer, piano accompanist for Ma Rainey, and a recording artist in his own right,[8] had a job selling soft drinks at the "81" in those days. "It was about 1913 or 1914," he recalls, "and Bessie was already a star in her own right, but she really got her start there at the '81'—I believe that's really where she made it—and I don't recall Ma Rainey ever having taken credit for helping her."

Just how long Bessie stayed with Bailey's theatre is not known. It was part of the Theatre Owner's Booking Association (T.O.B.A.), a major black vaudeville circuit which Bessie eventually began touring for, making the "81" her home base.

She also toured with Pete Werley's Florida Blossoms, a well-known troupe, and with the Silas Green show. An advertisement from the September 13, 1918, issue of *The Afro-American* shows that she was scheduled to open three days later at the Douglas Gilmor Theatre in Baltimore, Maryland. For that engagement she was teamed with Hazel Green.

While Bessie was appearing in Baltimore with Hazel Green, World War I was drawing to a close. The year before, America had entered the war, and a segregated army—including some two hundred thousand blacks—went to Europe under Woodrow Wilson's banner to "make the world safe for democracy." When the black troops returned home, many of them joined in a domestic war that rages still. Race riots were more widespread than indicated by the press of the day, and thousands of blacks rallied in Harlem under the red, black, and green banner of Marcus Garvey's back-to-Africa movement—a movement that gained support from white segregationists as well.

The black struggle for equality left most white Americans unconcerned. What did concern them was the Eighteenth Amendment, prohibiting the manufacture, sale, and consumption of alcoholic beverages. The new law went into effect January 17, 1920, and Prohibition became the hottest issue of the decade.

Although Bessie had long exhibited an immoderate taste for alcohol, Prohibition did not affect her directly. Like many Southerners, she had always preferred homemade liquor—"white lightning" as it was called—maintaining that "anything sealed" made her sick.

8. Mr. Dorsey co-founded and heads the National Gospel Singers Convention.

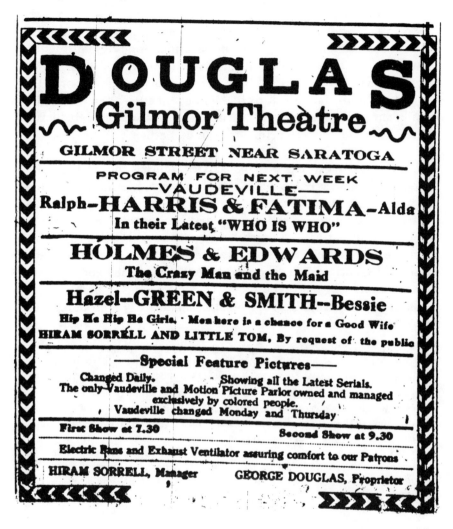

The earliest known advertisement for Bessie Smith. Baltimore *Afro-American,* September 13, 1918.

For most Americans, however, Prohibition offered a new challenge. No self-respecting collegian would be found without a hip flask, and the blaring horns and syncopated rhythms of jazz provided the perfect accompaniment for a generation of tradition-breakers.

White America was on a spending spree, and there was more to buy than ever before: automobiles, refrigerators, Victrolas, brightly colored bathtubs, radios—all to be had on something new called the installment plan. Luxury was becoming a reality for middle-class whites, but to most black people this state of affairs only emphasized their low status in society.

Information regarding Bessie's activities during the postwar prelude to the flapper era is scant, but it is clear that she was on the move (as far as Muskogee, Oklahoma, in May 1920, according to an item in the Chicago *Defender*), and that her career was heating up. At some point during those early years, she married Earl Love, about whom nothing is known except that he came from a prominent black Mississippi family and that he died before Bessie really had a chance to learn what being married was.

Singer May Wright, the wife of pianist James P. Johnson, recalled seeing her in Atlanta around 1920:

> I was playing at the "81" Theatre on Decatur Street in Atlanta, and Bessie Smith was at the "91" just down the street . . . the "91" was a smaller and rougher theatre, Bessie had her own show there, and I still fall out with laughter when I think about it, even today. You won't believe this, but Bessie was the smallest woman in that show. And you know how big *she* was. Well, that opening number was the funniest thing I ever saw. The curtain went up, and the floodlights came on, and there was the entire chorus dressed in close-fitting bloomers, bent over with their backs to the audience. The orchestra struck up "Liberty Belle," and there was that whole chorus shakin' every muscle in their bodies. I tell you I couldn't even keep a straight face when I was doing my own show after that.[9]

Often Bessie did not have her own show during this period. She appeared as a single with her own band at the Standard Theatre in Philadelphia during 1921, and—in the summer of 1922—she worked at the Paradise Gardens in Atlantic City, New Jersey, in a show directed by pianist/bandleader Charlie Johnson. Since the eighteen-seventies Atlantic City had been a popular resort for the well-to-do, who promenaded on its miles of boardwalk, amused themselves with

9. *Hear Me Talkin' to Ya*, by Nat Shapiro and Nat Hentoff (Rinehart and Company, 1955).

Bessie Smith awaits her cue—"She was just a teenager, and she obviously didn't know she was the artist she was." *Photo (ca. 1920) courtesy of Rudi Blesh.*

its coin-operated machines and mechanical rides, and met each other in the palm courts of its crystal palaces. When Bessie appeared there, Atlantic City was being invaded by the jet set of that era: flat-chested flappers and carousing collegians. "Hot" music was all the craze. The popular resort offered employment to many black musicians and entertainers, and the Paradise Gardens was one of the hottest spots in town.[10]

Bessie's appearance at the Paradise during the 1922 season is verified by a photograph showing her seated on the raised dance floor in the company of comedian Frankie "Half Pint" Jaxon, five young ladies, and the Johnson orchestra, but she may also have appeared there during the previous seasons. Jaxon, who is said to have started a nine-year summer residency as the club's entertainment director in 1918, was Bessie's close friend and admirer.

By 1922, Bessie had built up an enthusiastic following throughout the South and the Eastern seaboard. She had moved to Philadelphia; an embryonic record industry had made the startling discovery that black people, too, represented a source and market for their product; and the blues boom was gathering momentum. Destined to become its most potent force, Bessie, already a seasoned performer, awaited her cue.

10. So hot that Ed Smalls named his Smalls Paradise (on Seventh Avenue in Harlem) after it and engaged Charlie Johnson's orchestra as the house band, when the club opened in 1925. Basketball star Wilt Chamberlain purchased Smalls in the nineteen-sixties and continued to operate it.

# 2

*It's a long old road, but I know*
*I'm gonna find the end.*
"Long Old Road"

Bessie was now moving at a pretty fast clip down that long old road—at least the first, hard stretch of it. While she was working in the cabarets of Atlantic City and Philadelphia, things were happening in New York that would have a critical effect on her future.

The twenty-year-old record industry was discovering the commercial potential of the black talent that was packing people into cabarets and theatres throughout the country. Prior to 1920, record company decision-makers, assuming that only middle-class blacks could afford phonographs, had made no attempt to include in their repertoire material that might appeal to blacks. The recordings available ran to barbershop ballads, a studio orchestra grinding out a Rossini overture, Mme. Ernestine Schumann-Heink singing a Donizetti aria, or white vaudeville artists combining English music hall traditions with traces of sounds borrowed from as yet unrecorded black artists.

Black composers had for several years turned out hit tunes that caught the fancy of white America, but these tunes were always recorded by white artists. The first jazz records were made in January, 1917, when Columbia recorded the Original Dixieland Jazz Band, a white New Orleans group whose imitative hokum only faintly mirrored the real thing. The band scored a tremendous hit with its appearances in New York and London, and its second

33

recording, for the Victor Talking Machine Company, sold over a million copies and inspired many young musicians to take up jazz.

It was composer-pianist Perry Bradford whose persistence and faith in the blues brought about the first recordings of black music by black performers.

The blues, a distinctly Afro-American musical form, had been developed by generations of black people long before W. C. Handy, the so-called Father of the Blues, was born. In 1920 the blues was still very much a Southern phenomenon, and blacks born and reared in the urban centers of the North tended to regard it as something not meant for the ears of "better-class" people.

Perry Bradford, on the other hand, was from the South, where he had spent his early years traveling with minstrel shows. Steeped in the blues tradition, he was also a shrewd businessman who viewed the blues as a gem in the rough; give it a slight polish, he felt, and even Northerners would see its true beauty.

Bradford, aggressive and ambitious, began making the rounds of record companies in New York. Primarily interested in peddling his songs, he sought also to interest the companies in recording Mamie Smith, a black vaudeville singer from Ohio whom he represented. Turned down by the major companies, Victor[1] and Columbia, Bradford finally managed to talk Fred Hager, a director of the General Phonograph Corp., into recording two Bradford songs, "That Thing Called Love" and "You Can't Keep a Good Man Down," for the Okeh label. There was only one hitch: Hager wanted Sophie Tucker to sing them.

Fortunately Miss Tucker was under contract to another company. Bradford got his way, and Mamie Smith became the first black singer recorded in solo performance.[2]

Indistinguishable from white pop music fare of that period, "That Thing Called Love" did not make waves. But it did prove to skeptical record-company executives that a black singer was as marketable as a white one. The sales figures were sufficiently impressive to warrant a second Mamie Smith session six months later. This time Bradford was even more persuasive. He talked Hager into letting him provide a black band to accompany Mamie singing his "Harlem Blues," a song

1. On January 10, Victor had gone so far as to record a test with Mamie Smith singing "That Thing Called Love," but it was rejected.
2. Black comedian Bert Williams had previously recorded some humorous monologues for Columbia, using a small chorus.

Mamie Smith, the first black artist to record a solo vocal performance. Her "Crazy Blues" started the blues recording boom. *1925 photo courtesy of Frank Driggs.*

she was currently featuring in the show *Maid of Harlem*. Hager, not wanting to make his source too obvious, insisted that the song title be changed to "Crazy Blues." The general attitude toward "coloreds" was such that Hager's nervous approval actually represents a daring decision for the time: the result was sure to be a distinctly black sound, which dealers and the public might not welcome.

"Crazy Blues," cut on August 10, 1920, became the first vocal blues record. It was not a particularly interesting blues composition, nor was Mamie Smith really a blues singer. But the record struck a responsive chord, sold over a hundred thousand copies during the month of its release, and opened the eyes of the record industry to a totally new market. Before long several record companies dispatched talent scouts to black-populated parts of the country in search of women who sang the blues, and suddenly there appeared to be an abundance of such women. Most of them, as it turned out, were overnight converts from pop music who learned the form but lacked the feel of the blues idiom.

While Bradford was busy collecting his royalties and fighting lawsuits brought on by his having sold "Crazy Blues" to various publishers under different titles, his pioneer recording was giving birth to a new phenomenon, the "race" record. This term was henceforth applied to all recordings by black performers. The major companies—assuming incorrectly that such records would be of no interest to their white customers—began issuing special "race" catalogues. To avoid a mix-up, Victor even went so far as to have its engineers scratch the word "colored" in the recording wax.[3]

In the North, advertising of race records was restricted to the black press; and their distribution, to record outlets in black-populated areas. Thus, a white person—if he lived in the North—could conceivably live through the twenties without ever knowing that black music existed on records. White Southerners, on the other hand, became a part of the race market.

Bessie undoubtedly heard "Crazy Blues," and she may even have included it in her repertoire, for there was hardly a street in a black community where someone didn't own a copy of Mamie Smith's record.

Its success inspired other companies to enter the blues gold rush. New labels specializing in black music appeared. One of these, Black

3. The company changed the identification to "race" in the thirties.

Swan, was founded in 1921 by composer W. C. Handy and Harry Pace, Handy's partner in the music-publishing business. It was the first black-owned record company, a fact Handy and Pace played up in their advertising: "The Only Genuine Colored Record—Others Are Only Passing for Colored." Black pride notwithstanding, the company rejected the very black sound of Bessie Smith when she auditioned for Black Swan in 1921, while recording the "whiter" sound of Ethel Waters extensively.

Another label specializing in race music was Paramount,[4] a subdivision of the Wisconsin Chair Company. The company had decided to enter the record field because it manufactured phonograph cabinets but, thanks to blues artists like Alberta Hunter, Ida Cox, and the great Ma Rainey, it soon gave the full-time record companies some stiff competition. Paramount's recording activity, centered around Chicago, was too far away for Bessie to be considered, but that may have been fortunate, since Paramount's technical quality at the time could not have done her voice justice.

With all this interest in the blues, with the hopeful and the hopeless being hustled into recording studios, it seems strange that Bessie, who was already known as a blues singer with extraordinary drawing power, had to wait two years before making her recording debut.

If she did make records before 1923, none of them has been found. However, a few clues have turned up indicating that there might be some pre-Columbia Bessies collecting dust somewhere.

One such clue is an intriguing item buried in the entertainment pages of the February 12, 1921, issue of the Chicago *Defender,* under the heading NEW STAR :

> One of the greatest of all "blues" singers is Miss Bessie Smith, who is at present making records, with the aid of six jazz musicians, for the Emerson Record company. The first release will be made about Mar. 10. Bessie Smith is a native of Chattanooga, Tennessee.

The records referred to apparently were never released, and there is a good chance that they were never even recorded, but record collectors have not given up the search. Some believe they have found two Bessie sides issued under the name of Rosa Henderson.

Then, too, there is the odd reference to Columbia Records in a

---

4. Paramount also released a number of hillbilly and foreign language records.

Advertisement in the *Philadelphia Tribune,* May 14, 1921, two years
before Bessie began recording for Columbia.

May 14, 1921, advertisement for Bessie's appearance at the Standard Theatre in Philadelphia:

By the time this advertisement appeared in the Philadelphia *Tribune,* Columbia had entered the blues field with its own version of "Crazy Blues," sung by Mary Stafford, a singer who appeared with Bessie at the Paradise in Atlantic City. It is conceivable that Bessie auditioned for Columbia as early as 1921, and that the reference was an anticipatory one, but the earliest mention of Bessie in the company's files dates from February 1923.

According to pianist-composer Clarence Williams, Bessie auditioned for the Okeh label in January 1923, but after hearing her test record of "I Wish I Could Shimmy Like My Sister Kate," Fred Hager turned her down. Her voice, he said, was "too rough."

The Okeh audition is also referred to by veteran New Orleans musician Sidney Bechet[5] in his autobiography, *Treat It Gentle.* Bechet claimed to have arranged the session while he and Bessie were appearing in *How Come?,* a musical comedy then playing at the Dunbar Theatre in Philadelphia.[6] (He also claimed—with, one suspects, less accuracy—that he and Bessie traveled extensively with *How Come?* carrying on a love affair as they toured.)

At the time Bessie joined *How Come?* in January 1923, five of its twenty-three songs were blues, •and Bessie, appearing as herself, simply sang between acts. Her appearance with the show was cut short after a week, following a run-in with Eddie Hunter, the black comedian who had written the show.

The way Hunter recalls it, he had just come offstage and was rushing upstairs for a costume change. Bessie, her cue imminent, was heading down the narrow stairway. They bumped into each other and Bessie exploded. That Hunter was, in a sense, her employer, didn't intimidate her.

"What the fuck do you think you're doin'?" she yelled, and sent a barrage of curses echoing through the backstage area. Hunter tried to say something, but Bessie's voice grew louder and her language more

5. Bechet, then twenty-six, was to become one of black music's leading performers. A pioneer on the soprano saxophone, he inspired others, including John Coltrane, to take up the instrument. Bechet eventually settled in France, where he lived until his death in 1959.
6. *How Come?* opened at the Attucks Theatre, Norfolk, Virginia (since renamed the Booker T. Theatre), on January 15, 1923. It played between there, Washington, D.C., and Philadelphia for the next few weeks, but Bessie didn't join the show until January 29, 1923, when it played the Dunbar.

abusive at the sight of other members of the cast, who now stuck their heads out of dressing rooms to see what was going on.

Hunter, embarrassed by Bessie's lack of respect, and unable to get a word through to her, summoned the stage manager and instructed him, "Pay this woman off and let her out."

And so, on April 16, when a revised version of *How Come?* opened at the Apollo Theatre on New York's Forty-second Street, it still counted Bechet among its cast, but not Bessie. She had been replaced by Alberta Hunter, who, with some fifteen Paramount records to her credit, was far better known.

After thirty-two performances in New York, the show went on the road, playing in such cities as Cleveland, Cincinnati, and Chicago. Bechet wrote that Bessie was on that tour, but Miss Hunter remembers it otherwise.

As for Bechet's love affair with Bessie, it might have taken place earlier, although this seems unlikely. Bessie was promiscuous, but she had a strong preference for partners of dark complexion, and Bechet was extremely light. In any case, it is hard to believe that she would have involved herself with Bechet in 1923, for by then she had fallen in love with John Gee. Gee was a night watchman, an illiterate who had been turned down by the Philadelphia police department, but he often told people that he was a policeman.

Jack had seen Bessie perform in Atlantic City, but they did not meet until 1922, when Bessie was appearing in Philadelphia at Horan's cabaret. As they prepared to go to dinner on the night of their first date, a shooting incident occurred that nearly took Jack's life. A close relationship developed over the next five weeks as Bessie visited Jack daily at the hospital. It was to last through Bessie's "discovery," buildup, and at least part of her fame.

Bessie moved in with Jack soon after his release from the hospital. Writers who knew neither of them have been severe in their criticism of Jack—intimating that he was an opportunist. While it is true that opportunism has marked his actions since Bessie's death, and their relationship put Jack in the money for the first time in his life, it is also true that Jack's interest in Bessie preceded her "discovery."

Throughout the brief history of jazz—and, for that matter, modern show business—critics, agents, and recording executives have taken credit for the "discovery" of artists like Bessie. Artists, of course, are neither discovered nor rediscovered; they are simply

Frank Walker, who supervised all of Bessie's recording sessions from 1923 to 1931, was the only white man she trusted. *Photo courtesy of Sol Handwerger, MGM Records.*

Pianist Clarence Williams. He made more money on Bessie's records than she did.

recognized and given an opportunity to exhibit their talent. As a rule such opportunities are offered by people who see in an artist a means of making money and who are in a position to exploit talent. Bessie's artistry had matured through many hard years of performing before she achieved any measure of fame. By the time she made her first known recordings in 1923, she had, in a sense, already been discovered—by the thousands of people who paid to hear her sing throughout the South and in the Northeast. It was just a matter of time before someone recognized what she could do for him and gave her that sought-after "first big break."

Frank Walker, the man Columbia had put in charge of its "race" records, claimed to have heard Bessie sing in a "low-down dive" in Selma, Alabama, around 1917. She made such an impression on him, the story goes, that he sent his "race record judge," Clarence Williams, to the South in 1923 to get her: "I told Clarence about the Smith girl and said, 'This is what you've got to do. Go down there and find her and bring her back up here.'"

Williams—a pedestrian pianist who seemed to have made a close study of Tin Pan Alley's unscrupulous business habits—didn't have to go further than South Philadelphia. Besides, he had brought Bessie to New York for the Okeh audition a couple of weeks earlier, which prompts the question, Who told whom about Bessie Smith?

"When Mr. Walker came into Columbia," Williams told one interviewer, "he asked me to get that Bessie Smith I had been talking about. I said that those others had said that her voice was too rough. 'You just get her here,' he told me."

Perhaps the credit should go to Charlie Carson, the owner of a record shop at 518 South Street in Philadelphia. Jack Gee recalls that it was Carson who got in touch with Williams in February 1923 and persuaded him to take Bessie to Frank Walker. Williams took her, says Gee; there was a successful audition, and a deal was made.

Jack Gee bought Bessie a dress for her recording debut; he pawned his watchman's uniform and a pocket watch to get Bessie that dress, and she never forgot it. Fellow troupers recall that it became a standing joke between them a few months later, when Jack was sporting his two- and three-hundred-dollar suits.

From this point on, the story of Bessie Smith loses much of its vagueness and some of its mythical embroidery. People find it much easier to remember the famous, and Bessie was soon one of them.

During the first week of February 1923, Bessie and Jack went to New York, staying at his mother's house on 132nd Street between Fifth and Lenox Avenues. Below 132nd Street Harlem was still white, but from there on up it teemed with black people and dazzling night life. "The world's most glamorous atmosphere," young Duke Ellington said of black Harlem when he first saw it that same year. "Why, it's just like the Arabian Nights!" To Bessie, in 1923, Harlem probably evoked similar fantasies. Not content to stay at the Gee home, she went exploring.

The frenetic, pulsating beat that characterized much of Harlem's music at the time was in decided contrast with the slow, drawn-out blues sung by Bessie and her colleagues. "This is one reason she didn't go over too big with New York musicians," recalls Sam Wooding, whose band was featured at the Nest Club in 1923. "I remember her singing at the Nest one night, accompanied by my guitarist, John Mitchell, who liked her. She would sing something like 'Baby I love you, love you mo' and mo'.' I'd go to the bathroom, come back and catch the rest of the verse, 'I hope you never leave me, 'cause I don't wanna see you go.' She had dragged out each word so that I hadn't missed a thing."

After nights of visiting the hot spots of Harlem, and sometimes sitting in for a song or two, Bessie spent her days in the foyer of the Gee home, amid potted palms and Victorian furniture, preparing herself for the recording session that was to bring her lasting fame. With Clarence Williams at the old upright piano she learned some new songs and rehearsed them, including Williams' own "Gulf Coast Blues" and "Down Hearted Blues," a song written by pianist Lovie Austin and the new star of *How Come?*, Alberta Hunter.

Ruby Walker, Jack's niece, had met Bessie in Philadelphia, but this was the first time she had heard Bessie sing. Now Ruby stood in the living room and tried to sing along with her uncle's new girl friend. "I just stood there and watched her, and my whole life changed," she said years later. "Of course I didn't know it then, but that's what happened."

On February 15, Bessie went with Clarence Williams to the Columbia studio on Columbus Circle. According to Frank Walker, who would supervise all of Bessie's recordings for the next eight years, "She looked like anything *but* a singer, she looked about seventeen, tall and fat and scared to death—just awful!"

Bessie had auditioned before, but this was no test—it was the real thing. In 1923 recordings were still being made acoustically. Instead of a microphone, the performer faced the gaping hole of a large conical horn that protruded from a drapery-covered wall. Behind that wall, peering into the studio from a tiny window, was the engineer. There was no editing, no listening to a playback. You just kept on performing a number until it sounded right.

Maybe it was nerves, maybe equipment failure, maybe a little of both, but after nine takes of a tune called "'T'ain't Nobody's Business If I Do" and two of "Down Hearted Blues," the session was called off without an acceptable master having been made. Things went better the next day, when "Down Hearted Blues" was pronounced satisfactory after three takes. "Gulf Coast Blues" was also done in three, but another tune, "Keeps On a-Rainin'," was rejected five times.

Trying as the experience was, Bessie had recorded her first two releases. What is more, she had in one sense given the most important performance of her career.

The history of American show business offers many examples of whites exploiting black performers, but, even fifty years ago, not all exploiters were white. Among the most notorious black exploiters of the twenties were Perry Bradford and Clarence Williams, who often schemed together. Frequently acclaimed for their prolific output of songs, it turns out that they themselves did not write many of their "compositions," but that they either stole them or bought them for a few dollars from more creative people who lacked business acumen.

In the spring of 1923—while Bradford was serving out a jail sentence for subornation of perjury in a copyright suit, and Williams, acting as Bessie's manager, was getting her ready for a Southern tour—Jack began looking into his future wife's business affairs. He discovered that Bessie's contract was drawn up between her and Williams, and learned that Williams was pocketing half of her $125-per-selection fee. It was mid-April; Bessie had made four more recordings, and she should have received $750, which was more money than she or Jack had ever seen. Five dollars in the wrong hands would probably have prompted Jack to take action, but $375 spelled the doom of Clarence Williams' relationship with Bessie.

As the story goes, Jack stormed into Williams' midtown Manhattan office, with Bessie following after. Jack was a big, muscular man

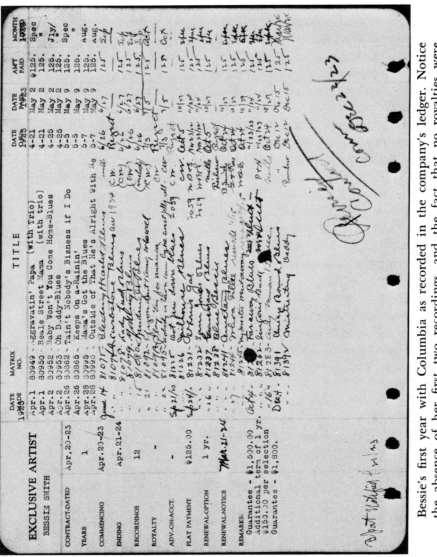

Bessie's first year with Columbia as recorded in the company's ledger. Notice the absence of her first two recordings, and the fact that no royalties were involved.

with persuasive-looking fists, and the sight of him sent Williams crawling underneath his desk.

"Come on out of there, you dirty no-good cheatin' bastard," yelled Jack, pounding on the desk.

Williams emerged slowly, shaking at the sight of two very big, very hot-tempered, very angry people. Before the two men knew what happened, Bessie jumped Williams and pounded him to the floor with her clenched fists. She kept pounding until she and Jack got what they were after—a release from all contractual obligations to Clarence Williams.

The next stop was Frank Walker's office. Walker, who apparently was unaware of Williams' private arrangements, offered Bessie an exclusive contract with Columbia. A one-year contract commencing April 20, 1923, it required her to record twelve selections, at $125 per usable side.[7] It guaranteed her $1500, and it contained a one-year renewal option for twelve sides at $150. Furthermore, since Clarence Williams had not yet received her fee for four sides made during the first week of April, Walker handed Bessie a check for five hundred dollars. This was more than they had bargained for. Walker, having struck out the royalty clause in the contract, had actually made a very good deal for Columbia, but neither Bessie nor Jack knew about such things as royalties—as far as they were concerned, *they* were the ones who made a good deal. Delighted with Walker's "generosity," Bessie appointed him her manager.

Alberta Hunter's recording of "Down Hearted Blues" had sold well when it was issued a year earlier. Other artists had recorded it since then, and the song was considered to have run its course by the time Bessie recorded it. To Columbia's surprise, Bessie's version soared to an impressive 780,000 copies in less than six months. As the copyright owner of "Gulf Coast Blues," which appeared on the other side of the record, Clarence Williams actually made more money on Bessie's first release than she did, and he continued to reap a financial harvest from Bessie's fame by seeing to it that she recorded many of his songs.

As "Down Hearted Blues" hit the market and Bessie prepared for her tour, Jack took care of a slight formality: on June 7 he and Bessie visited the clerk of the Orphan's Court of Philadelphia County

---

7. No payment was made for rejected recordings. Some of these were subsequently released—in the forties and fifties—without any payment to Bessie's estate.

Jack and Bessie as newlyweds, June, 1923—the smiles were still genuine. *Photo from Negro Press.*

and applied for a marriage license. Immediately afterward they went to the home of the Reverend C. A. Tindley[8] on Christian Street, where they were pronounced man and wife.

In the meantime Bessie had earned another five hundred dollars under her new Columbia contract. It was enough money to give her and Jack a honeymoon, if there had been time for such a luxury, but—with the first records going strong—the wedding was followed by another recording trip to New York.

Between June 14 and 22, Bessie recorded seven songs, exceeding the annual total required by her contract—a sure sign that Columbia valued her as an artist. She was now being accompanied by Fletcher Henderson, who had come to New York three years earlier to do his postgraduate research in chemistry, but had been forced by circumstances to enter the music field instead. Bessie soon developed a good working relationship with Henderson, who was only two months younger than Clarence Williams. Henderson's gentle personality eminently suited Bessie's needs to play the dominant role. Soft-spoken and amiable, he let Bessie call the shots. He was also a better pianist than Williams, but his real forte was arranging. Like Bessie, Fletcher Henderson stood on the brink of success. He soon became a leader in the big-band field, creating the sounds that would eventually make many view Bessie Smith as an anachronism.

Shortly after her recording sessions with Henderson, Bessie began her Southern tour. With pianist Irvin Johns as her new musical director, she opened at her old stomping grounds, the "81" in Atlanta, on Monday, June 25—a triumphant return that set the tone for the rest of the tour. The first show went so well that radio station WSB broadcast the entire performance the following night. Radio was something very new and its limited audience was mostly white, but Bessie soon became a veteran broadcaster. Although records were never aired, live performances helped to boost their sales. Bessie was always introduced as "the famous Columbia recording artist Bessie Smith."

Bessie's show was hardly as elaborate as those she would soon be presenting. In fact, hers was just the headline act of what was essentially a vaudeville show. As the star, she was presented last, preceded by a handful of performers, most of whom had been

8. Reverend Tindley was a prolific composer of gospel songs, his most famous being "I'll Overcome Some Day," which, with slightly changed lyrics, became "We Shall Overcome."

No longer wearing street clothes, Bessie dons a simple wig and lace dress for a 1923 publicity shot. *Photo by Edward Elcha, courtesy of Frank Driggs.*

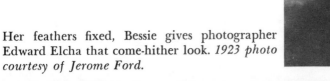

Her feathers fixed, Bessie gives photographer Edward Elcha that come-hither look. *1923 photo courtesy of Jerome Ford.*

engaged locally. Bessie's act consisted of a few simple dance steps, her arms, head, and wide hips moving suggestively to the music, and her songs.

She had no fancy costumes: usually she wore just a plain dress with beaded fringes, a Spanish shawl loosely draped around her shoulders, a string of pearls, a skullcap with beads and pearls sewn into it, and a wig with shiny black hair running down to her shoulders. Her one prop was a backdrop with the silhouette of magnolia trees set against an orange sky and a bright full moon. Such trimmings, however plain, faded the moment she raised the most powerful, soulful voice her audiences had ever heard.

Bessie's other magic ingredient was her ability to get an audience to identify with her songs: while the pop singers of the day were busy building a "Stairway to Paradise" or making love "'Neath the South Seas Moon," Bessie sang of mean mistreaters and two-timing husbands with tragicomic optimism, offered advice to the dejected, and made it quite clear that she herself was not immune to such problems. Occasionally she borrowed a song from Tin Pan Alley,[9] but only if its lyrics—which she often altered to suit her needs—bore similar messages.

Although Bessie must have known that hers was a very special talent, she occasionally showed signs of insecurity. For example while competition from non-blues-singing performers did not seem to bother her, she would not tolerate having another blues singer share the bill with her. Charles Anderson, a yodeler from Birmingham who received second billing to Bessie at the "81," came close to matching her popularity, but the two got along fine, and Bessie even helped Anderson obtain further bookings on her tour.

By June 1923, when Bessie's first record was released, she had recorded nine more sides under the new Columbia agreement. The label had in the meantime signed up another black singer, a twenty-nine-year-old woman from Spartanburg, South Carolina, named Clara Smith. Clara, an attractive woman of small build, had spent more than ten years on small Southern vaudeville circuits. She was not related to Bessie and she never represented a real threat to Bessie's popularity, but she did become Columbia's second most important female blues singer. Columbia's publicity people had already promoted Bessie as "Queen of the Blues," so Clara became "Queen of

9. In 1923 Bessie recorded two such songs from that period, "Aggravatin' Papa" and "My Sweetie Went Away."

the Moaners." A good relationship developed between the two singers, who occasionally pretended to be sisters.

As Columbia prepared to launch the career of Clara Smith, Bessie was closing in Atlanta with a special midnight performance for whites only.[10] Then her troupe moved on to the Frolic Theatre in Birmingham, Alabama, breaking all previous attendance records. Billy Chambers' review was carried by most of the black press:

> Streets blocked, hundreds and hundreds and hundreds were unable to gain entrance to this performance. . . . Bessie Smith with Irvin Johns at the piano before their own special drop opened full stage with "Nobody's Bizness if I Do," with the "Gulf Coast Blues" following, which received heavy applause, leaving the house in a riot.

Chambers, however, did not condone the commercial exploitation that went on between acts:

> "Buzzing" Harris [one of the performers] announced the "Gulf Coast Blues" for sale and went down into the audience to sell copies. This, we think, is nonprofessional at this or any other performance, as the lady's reputation should sell the songs at every music house in the city.

Everywhere they went it was the same story. People had heard Bessie's records and now they wanted to hear her in person. Five of the records were now on the market, and her reputation had grown beyond all expectations. Only one thing was missing from Bessie's happiness: since her marriage she had spent very little time with her new husband.

That situation was not remedied until August, when her tour took her back to Atlanta and she found Jack waiting at the train station. His job had kept him from making the tour with her, but Frank Walker had told him of her triumphs. Besides the money she was paid for the records, Bessie was now making $350 a week for personal appearances. Under the circumstances, it made little sense for Jack to continue in an ill-paid job, and he decided to quit.

If Jack had entertained any doubts about his wife's moneymaking potential, they were wiped away by what he saw at the theatre in Atlanta: three lines of people fighting to get in for the next performance as ten policemen tried to keep things under control.

From Atlanta Bessie went back to the Frolic Theatre in Birmingham, the Bijou in Nashville, and the Beale Street Palace in Memphis,

---

10. The custom of having special performances for whites had originated at the Lyric Theatre in New Orleans, but the practice soon became widespread.

where she did another broadcast. The Chicago *Defender* corre-spondent in Atlanta wrote a typical review:

> The spirit of the Old South came up from Beale Street at 11 o'clock last night to give the world a concert of Negro folk songs that will be remembered by WMC as long as a midnight frolic is broadcast from the roof of the Commercial Appeal. Bessie Smith, known from coast to coast as a singer of blues that are really blue, gave the air some currents that it will not forget as long as a cloud is left in the sky, and Memphis has its Beale Street. . . .
>
> The star of the frolic greeted the atmosphere with "'T'ain't Nobody's Business but My Own," which she gave with unction and a rich Negro accent. Accompanied by Irvin Johns, her pianist, she followed with "Beale Street Mama." Singers have come and gone with that number, but it remained for Bessie to sing it before its possibilities were fathomed.
>
> Perhaps the greatest hit Bessie registered last night for WMC was "Outside of That He's All Right with Me." She repeated the number upon the request of a large number, who telephoned to the studio and wired from the Memphis territory. . . . While the orchestra built up an excellent background for the entertainment, Bessie carried the evening with her "blues."

In those infant days of radio there was no such thing as a black station. Bessie and company were broadcasting over WMC, which was owned and operated by the Memphis *Commercial Appeal* and whose audience consisted for the most part of white Southerners.[11] The *Defender's* "Atlanta correspondent" was probably a white reporter working for the *Commercial Appeal*. It was only in the South that Bessie had a substantial following of whites, but their enthusiasm was reserved for her artistry.

Because she was who she was, Bessie was treated with unfailing courtesy by many establishments in the South, but what she received was good treatment "for a black person." "Bessie knew this, of course," a performer who traveled with her said, "but she went along with the game—unless somebody gave her trouble. Then, it didn't make any difference whether they were white, black, Southern, or Northern, she'd give them a tongue-beating or she'd beat up on them with her fists."

Bessie seemed to take her sudden fame in stride. The money was now beginning to come in, and as it did, she remembered the family she had left behind in Chattanooga. They had always shared what-

---

11. The average price of a radio set was $135.

ever she had, even in days when it didn't amount to much; now she could make life considerably easier for them.

Jack had not yet met the family, but the two of them stopped in Chattanooga on the way back to New York around the middle of September. While they were staying at Viola's house, Bessie received the offer of a ten-week contract at $350 a week from Sam Reevin, an officer of the T.O.B.A. and owner of Chattanooga's Liberty Theatre. Acting on Jack's advice, she turned the offer down.

Contrary to most accounts, Jack was never Bessie's manager, although he often indicated a desire to assume that role. Unable to travel with the troupe, Frank Walker managed only Bessie's recording affairs. Business on the road was handled by her brother Clarence, who also performed as comedian, and her nephew T. J. Hill, known to everyone as Teejay. Money decisions could not be left to Bessie, nor did she have time for or interest in such matters. Jack engaged in verbal negotiations with Sam Reevin during their visit to Chattanooga only because neither Clarence nor Teejay was around. Realizing that his wife had become hot property, he justifiably regarded all offers with suspicion and sought a higher price for her services. "Jack couldn't even manage himself," says Maud Smith. "He would always have signs saying 'Jack Gee presents Bessie Smith,' and he would call himself a manager, but he couldn't even sell a ticket. He could count money, and he could ask for money, but that's about it."

The Gees now had an apartment at 1236 Webster Street in Philadelphia. It was a place to stay between working engagements, but those who visited there recall that it lacked the atmosphere of a home. "There was nothing special about it," recalls Ruby Walker, "no fancy furniture or anything like that, just big easy chairs, a sofa, and lamps and tables with pictures and statues and things—Bessie never went in for no fancy stuff around the house, even when she made all that money, because she just wasn't there that much." Home or no home, Bessie seemed happy during those early months of her marriage—Jack was attentive, and her career was proceeding at an encouraging pace.

Arriving in Philadelphia, the Gees found telegraphed offers, followed by five and six more each day, but there was hardly time to consider them before they had to go to New York for more rehearsals and recording sessions. New York was livelier than ever. Jazz music, which had now caught the fancy of the whole country, was becoming the subject of controversy. Many papers carried a warning

Bessie never tangoed, but the Charleston was right up her alley. *1924 photo courtesy of Frank Driggs.*

from Dr. Elliot Rawlings, a "noted physician" whose research showed that "jazz music intoxicates like whisky and releases stronger animal passions." Needless to say, the warning was not heeded, and Dr. Rawlings soon saw a veritable epidemic of the Charleston, a dance introduced by Cecil Mack and Johnny Johnston in the revue *Runnin' Wild*.[12]

The contribution of black people to the life of white America in the twenties was—as it is today—particularly strong in the entertainment field. The dances, music, and humor of black people became a source of fame and money for white imitators. Their racist, satirical embellishments fostered a stereotype that so distorted the white man's image of black people that blacks themselves had to match that image in order to be "believable." Although most black entertainers recognized the "influence" of their culture as outright theft, the best they could do was to get as much out of it for themselves as possible. Bessie's share of the harvest was only a fraction of what it should have been, but even so, she did better than most black performers.

While Bessie and Irvin Johns were rehearsing in the foyer of the house on 132nd Street, Jack was on the phone in the living room, responding to an offer from Sherman H. Dudley, another T.O.B.A. officer. This time the offer was $1100 for a week's engagement at Dudley's Koppin Theatre in Detroit. Jack held out until Dudley agreed to $1500. The cast of Bessie's show—she was expected to present something far more impressive than a revue—had to be paid out of that, but in those unionless days salaries were far from impressive, and the star still got to keep most of the money.

That's the way it would have been, too, if Jack had had anything to say about it. But Bessie had different ideas. She lay awake at night, talking about her family and all the plans she had for them. She had already sent Jack to Western Union many times to wire money to Chattanooga, but the southward flow of money was just beginning.

Between September 21 and October 16, Bessie had seven record-

12. Pianist James P. Johnson wrote the music for *Runnin' Wild*, including the famous "Charleston," which was inspired by dances he saw patrons of the Jungle Casino (on West Sixty-fourth Street) do. The Jungle Casino was frequented by blacks from Charleston, South Carolina, whose variations on cotillion steps became the famous dance of the same name.

ing dates during which she made forty-nine takes, resulting in the release of five records. Of these sessions, the one that took place October 4 is of special interest because it yielded two duets with Clara Smith, whose fame was now spreading.

Bessie's willingness to record with Clara, sharing equal billing, has puzzled some scholars, who find it hard to square with stories of her intolerance toward other blues singers. It is true that Bessie did not appreciate competition, but another singer, even a blues singer, could not possibly pose a threat on a recording, which captured only the voice. Bessie could conceivably have been upstaged by Clara Smith's physical appearance, but any voice competition with Clara was decidedly lopsided.

One of the few singers who might have made Bessie uneasy was Ethel Waters, who, although her style was vastly different, possessed enormous talent, with personality to match. In her autobiography, *His Eye Is on the Sparrow*, Miss Waters recalls an incident at the "91" Theatre in Atlanta prior to 1920:

> Bessie was in a pretty good position to dictate to the managers. She had me put on my act for her and said I was a long goody. But she also told the men who ran No. 91 that she didn't want anyone else on the bill to sing the blues.
>
> I agreed to this, I could depend a lot on my shaking, though I never shimmied vulgarly and only to express myself. And when I went on I sang "I Want to Be Somebody's Baby Doll So I Can Get My Lovin' All the Time." But before I could finish this number the people out front started howling, "Blues! Blues! Come on, Stringbean, we want your blues!"
>
> Before the second show the manager went to Bessie's dressing room and told her he was going to revoke the order forbidding me to sing any blues. He said he couldn't have another such rumpus. There was quite a stormy discussion about this, and you could hear Bessie yelling things about "these Northern bitches." Now nobody could have taken the place of Bessie Smith. People everywhere loved her shouting with all their hearts and were loyal to her. But they wanted me too.
>
> When I closed my engagement in the theatre Miss Bessie called me to her. "Come here, long goody," she said. "You ain't so bad. It's only that I never dreamed that anyone would be able to do this to me in my own territory and with my own people. And you damn well know you can't sing worth a fuck."

There was no animosity between Bessie and Clara Smith at the time of their joint recording, but both singers surely knew that they were on an equal footing only so far as the billing itself was concerned. "Far Away Blues" and "I'm Going Back to My Used to

Be" show that Bessie had nothing to worry about. Her own performance is not quite up to her usual standards on these sides, but her rich voice resounds around Clara's thin one.

Although Clara and Bessie never performed together in public, they came close to it on October 21, when a "blues night" was held at the New Star Casino, a large dance hall at 107th Street and Third Avenue. Sponsored by a group of black songwriters and supported by various record and piano-roll companies who had reserved seats for their staff and friends, it promised to be a memorable affair. Two "well-known recording orchestras" were scheduled to accompany such singers as Mamie Smith, Sara Martin, Edna Hicks, Eva Taylor (Mrs. Clarence Williams), Clara, and Bessie.

The affair had been set up by Clarence Williams and Perry Bradford primarily to make money for themselves, and Bessie, hearing that Williams was involved, at first refused to go. Frank Walker finally talked her into attending.

"I don't know *what* happened," said one observer forty-eight years later, "but Bessie never sang that night. The place was full of people—everybody was there—and, all of a sudden, there was this great big commotion near the band, and I saw Bessie throw a chair at somebody who was mashing his way through the crowd, trying to get away from her. Then I saw them drag her out of there, cussing and carrying on. It took three strong men to get her out of there—she was a powerful woman and she could cuss worse than a sailor."

Bessie was also scheduled to perform at the California Rambler's Inn that week, but there is no evidence that she even showed up.

On October 29, her opening at the Koppin in Detroit caused a near-riot. With $1500 invested in her appearance, Sherman Dudley was going to make sure his theatre was packed for every performance, and Bessie's engagement was the most heavily promoted in Detroit's history. Dudley could probably have spared himself the effort. The city's automobile industry had attracted thousands of black workers from the South, and in 1923 it would have been difficult to find a black person who had not heard of the Queen of the Blues.

At the Globe Theatre in Cleveland, the story was the same. Higher-than-usual prices notwithstanding, there weren't enough seats in the theatre to hold her new fans. It was a long show, with Bessie headlining eight acts, and the pit band, (Doc) Cheatham's Jazz Syncopators, scheduled in between. Seeing the crowd outside, the

Globe's management pulled an old trick: they cut the show down and increased the number of performances per day. This meant more work for Bessie and her gang, but it enabled the theatre owner to meet her new price and also make a handsome profit.

The relationship between black stars—relatively new phenomena in the entertainment world—and their followers was quite different from that between white stars and their fans. The Valentinos, Swansons, and Negris were courted by heads of state and embraced by high society, which immediately set them apart from ordinary people; their vast income and worldwide fame gained them access to circles whose doors normally were closed to people of their more humble, real-life background.

Black entertainers continued to face closed doors; Josephine Baker and Ethel Waters were to be warmly welcomed in European high society, but—regardless of their income or the magnitude of their artistic talent—neither Warren Harding nor Calvin Coolidge ever sent them an invitation. Black people had their differences, of course, but there existed among them a certain feeling of togetherness that made it impossible for a black artist to rise to a superhuman level in the eyes of his own people. Blacks regarded Bessie Smith and her colleagues with due respect, but they knew that the Bakers, Waterses, and Smiths did not get invitations from the White House because they—like their fans—were black.

Not only was Bessie's reputation as a performer firmly established, but the black community also knew a great deal about her private personality. There were no fan magazines, nor would glorified write-ups of her comings and goings have been effective. Bessie's life-style demanded that she be in close contact with her community; she craved surroundings with access to the real emotions of real people, and no written word could match the verbal communication that black people had mastered in the days of slavery. Stories circulated throughout these communities within communities with the swiftness of small-town gossip, and spread from Atlanta's Fourth Ward to Chicago's South Side to Harlem by way of touring entertainers and Pullman porters—what you heard, no matter how it had been embellished, was more believable than what you read.

It was common knowledge that Bessie was a soft touch for a handout. For instance, it didn't take long for the story to reach Harlem from Cleveland that, despite her extraordinarily busy schedule at the Globe, Bessie found time to help a fellow performer.

Hearing that Buster Porter, a man she had worked with, was in a Cleveland hospital and unable to pay his doctor bills, she grabbed a cab during one of her breaks, went to the hospital, and gave the sick entertainer fifty dollars.

Bessie dispensed her money freely, bailing friends out of jail, responding to an unfortunate stranger's outstretched hand, buying luxuries for herself, her friends, and her family. The more she made, the more she doled out. Only when it came to paying her performers and crew did Bessie show restraint, but she was always willing to give a little extra change to an employee in need.

People also knew that Bessie had a fiery temper; that she would engage man or woman, regardless of size, in physical combat at the drop of the wrong word; that she had periods when she drank up a storm; that she carried an impressive quantity of corn liquor in her purse during these periods; that some of her people's servile behavior toward whites filled her with disgust.

Bessie did what she wanted to do, often evoking the envy of those who either couldn't or didn't dare to follow her example; the "dicty" black social set found her lack of grace and tact abhorrent, but she won the respect of those who had no social ambitions to protect. When Bessie drank and carried on with the man in the street, she was just one of the gang, but most people addressed her as "Miss Bessie."

On November 17, Bessie canceled two Nashville dates,[13] supposedly because of a death in the family and her own subsequent illness. But there is no corroboration for either the death or the illness; they were probably cover-ups for a drinking spree. In these early years of her success, Bessie was already a binge drinker, and it was beginning to affect her working schedule. Excessive drinking had become virtually a family tradition, as Jack realized when he found out how much of the money Bessie sent home went to buy liquor.

On December 4 the Gees were back in New York, where Bessie recorded her last two sides of the year, "Chicago-bound Blues" and "Mistreatin' Daddy." Her first year of recording had been prolific, resulting in twenty-nine satisfactory sides. In 1923 few singers could match that total. Counting all the takes that had not been used, Bessie had by now waxed close to 140 performances in the studio. Now able to face the forbidding-looking horn without apprehension,

13. At the Bijou Theatre and the Ryman Auditorium.

she sounded more self-assured on records, more like the Bessie Smith who sent theatre audiences into a religious frenzy.

Columbia had been in bad financial shape when Bessie first recorded for them. In February 1922, the company had applied for receivership, selling out to a British holding company[14] two months before Bessie's first session. In October 1923, Judge Learned Hand appointed two receivers for the American Columbia company, and it was then that Frank Walker initiated the label's official "race" series (the "Fourteen-Thousand" series)—launched, not surprisingly, with a Bessie Smith disc.

The oft-told story that Bessie saved Columbia Records from bankruptcy is an overstatement, unfair to such Columbia artists as Eddie Cantor, Ted Lewis, comedian Bert Williams (who died eight days after Bessie's recording debut), and the outrageously racist but popular comedy team known as the Two Black Crows,[15] whose records also sold extremely well. Nevertheless Bessie was Columbia's hottest artist at the time, and her contribution to the company's welfare was invaluable.

Nearing the end of an exhausting year, Bessie seemed tireless, though friends noticed subtle signs of fatigue and marveled at her ability to keep going. Four years had passed since her appearance in Baltimore as half of the team of Green & Smith. When she returned to Baltimore on December 17, circumstances were strikingly different: the manager of the Douglass Theatre later reported that her week's engagement there had been the most successful in the theatre's history.

With all that money coming in, Bessie's life-style hardly changed. She now had to spend more money on costumes and props, and hire more people to keep her touring companies running, but—except for the fact that her gifts were now more expensive—the only noticeable change was in her clothes. "Bessie liked to dress well," says Ruby Walker, "and she liked for her men to dress well, so she'd buy expensive suits for Jack and she got herself some fur coats and jewelry—real diamonds. At home she was still the same old Bessie, slopping around in her slippers, her hair flying all over the place, and cooking up a lot of greasy food."

If Bessie and Jack had wanted to enjoy their new prosperity, they

14. The Constructive Finance Company, Ltd.
15. Predecessors of Amos 'n' Andy, the Two Black Crows (Moran and Mack) were actually Irish.

Framed by a horse hair wig and ostrich plumes, Bessie, her career soaring, is ready for her closeup. *1924 photo by Edward Elcha, courtesy of Frank Driggs.*

would hardly have found the time; she now had more offers for well-paying engagements than she could possibly accept.

On December 22, 1923, four months before her first contract with Columbia was to expire, the company—overwhelmed by the success of her records—signed Bessie to a new and better contract. Again, she was to record a minimum of twelve sides, but she was to receive $200 per side rather than the $150 called for in the option. Bessie was guaranteed $2400 for the year, but it was clear that, even with the royalty clause struck from her new contract, she would make much more.[16]

Bessie concluded her week at the Douglass on the following day, and opened Christmas Eve at the Dunbar in Philadelphia—the same theatre she had been fired from earlier in the year. Now she was the boss, heading a cast of sixty performers for a two-week run of John T. Gibson's musical comedy extravaganza *Tunes and Topics*. When she found the time to rehearse for this show is hard to imagine, but Bessie's name alone was a big drawing card at this point, and she may simply have incorporated her own regular songs and routines into Gibson's show. Most of these shows lacked a theme, anyway—often the major change consisted of a new title.

As 1924 began, Bessie could have looked back on a wildly eventful year—except that it was not in her nature to look back when things were going well. Everything of interest to her lay ahead.

So far, she and Jack were enjoying a happy relationship. Their lives had taken a new turn, all the more dramatic because their marriage coincided with Bessie's sudden rise to fame. The glamour and wealth that suddenly surrounded Jack was a far cry from his lonesome nights as a "door shaker." To Bessie, the glamour had of course long since become routine, but wealth, even relative wealth, was new to her—and she seemed to derive a great deal of pleasure from having a husband to share it with.

Her love for Jack, her desire to make him happy, and the prospect of soon being able to move her family to Philadelphia, gave Bessie the energy to maintain a schedule that few could have endured as long as she did. It must have been obvious to Jack that his wife was literally wearing herself out to satisfy the appetites of others, but—busy savoring the fruits of her labors—he made no attempt to slow Bessie down.

16. Bessie's previous contract had brought her more than double the $1500 guaranteed her.

# 3

*From now on, small change I refuse;*
*Mama's got them one and two blues.*
"One and Two Blues"

In 1924, as Bessie's work schedule grew tighter, she began to feel the one and two blues: money solved old worries, but it brought new ones. The more she made, the less time she had to spend with Jack. In fact, she had very little time for anything but work. That these were the one- and two-thousand-dollar-a-week blues lessened the pain somewhat, but Bessie was driving herself too hard. She would have been content with less money and more leisure, but Jack Gee and Frank Walker wanted to cash in while the going was good.

Having closed at Philadelphia's Dunbar Theatre on January 6, Bessie was back in the recording studio two days later. She sounded tired. In "Frosty Mornin' Blues" and "Easy Come, Easy Go"[1] she is so spiritless that some blues scholars have suggested the voice belongs to another singer; it seems unusually high-pitched, and she is unable to sustain a note. Only the phrasing can convince the listener that the voice is Bessie's. In the same session "Blue Bessie (The Bluest Gal in Tennessee)," a song she had attempted to record earlier, was rejected once again.

The next two days' sessions produced slightly better results. Fletcher Henderson had started recording with Bessie the previous

1. Bessie's accompaniment for these two sides was provided by pianist Jimmy Jones and guitarist Harry Reser, who gained some notoriety as a member of the famous Cliquoe Club Eskimos, and was the first white musician to accompany Bessie.

summer. Now he brought with him to the studio outstanding musicians from his band, which became the source of Bessie's most memorable accompaniments.

Don Redman, later famous as an arranger and bandleader, was on hand January 9 for "Haunted House Blues" and "Eavesdropper's Blues," but his clarinet playing was marred by novelty effects and Bessie's own performance again seemed listless.

On January 10 she recorded "Rampart Street Blues" and "Lawdy, Lawdy Blues," accompanied by an unidentified group labeled as "her jazz band." Both songs had been written and previously recorded[2] by Ida Cox, Paramount's second biggest star. Bessie's versions were never released.

Bessie and Ida met four days later, when Bessie followed her into the Bijou Theatre in Nashville. "I had seen Bessie before, in Atlanta," recalled Miss Cox, "but this was the first time I actually spoke to her. She was as sweet as she could be—she told me she had recorded some of my songs, and she paid me a compliment on them. I heard later that she never said anything nice about other blues singers, so it just thrills me when I think about it."

When Bessie talked about other performers she rarely mentioned their work—an understandable omission since she rarely caught other people's acts unless it was an impromptu, after-hours performance or they happened to appear on a bill with her. Even then, she seldom found time to stand in the wings and watch. Her nonworking hours were spent with Jack or in search of fun—and going to a show was not her idea of fun.

If Bessie sounded tired these days, it was not apparent to her theatre audiences. *Billboard* magazine described her show at the Bijou as "drawing heavier than on previous appearances," and noted that she had done two "special shows" at Nashville's all-white Orpheum Theatre on January 15 and 16.

White Southerners, of course, had taken to Bessie long before their Northern counterparts. Her performances for whites were "special" only because the audience was Caucasian; she did not alter her material in any way to suit their taste. Certainly she would not have wanted to, and in any case there was no need for such tailoring.

Wherever Bessie appeared in the South, her songs and humor registered as well with whites as they did with her own people. Her

2. Ida Cox's records were titled *Blues for Rampart Street* and *Ida Cox's Lawdy, Lawdy Blues* on the original Paramount issue.

shows were considered pure entertainment, and she never touched directly on racial issues—although there were veiled implications here and there. Love, sex, and misery, the main themes of her songs, were universal, as were the hokum and hilarity of the acts that surrounded her. White Southerners, who had grown up hearing the blues, naturally felt more at home with it than black Northerners.

What remained a tradition in the South had by 1924 become a fading novelty in the North. In New York, the blues craze had passed its peak. W. C. Handy's Black Swan label, which after its first year, 1921, could boast receipts totaling $104,628, had been forced to sell out to Paramount. The *New York Clipper* sounded a death knell:

"RACE" SONGS ON THE WANE
Discs Not Selling—
Passing Craze Back to Normalcy

The "swan song" of "race" phonograph discs seems to have been sung. Only two of the larger companies, Columbia and Okeh, are going after their "race" catalogs with anything approaching the energy spent last year. . . .

Such news did not upset Bessie or her colleagues, for as the popularity of the blues waned in New York, it grew elsewhere. Many of the classic blues singers, including Ma Rainey, never appeared in New York anyway; and those who did continued to attract huge crowds—mostly recent immigrants from the South—with their appearances in Harlem.

During the first week of February, Bessie was back at the Beale Avenue Palace Theatre in Memphis. Again she did a broadcast over station WMC, owned by the white *Commercial Appeal*. "Bessie has a voice that will never be mistaken for another's," wrote that paper's reviewer. "She is in a class by herself in the field of 'blues.' "

Bessie ended her engagement at the Palace with another performance for whites only. Not all black shows were called upon for such command performances, which were much sought after because there was more money involved: the price of tickets went up, and so did the performers' fees, although not proportionately. Black performers, however, knew that white Southern audiences accepted them only as long as they conformed to a certain image. Ethel Waters would never have made it before a white Southern audience singing "Supper Time" or "Harlem on My Mind," but Steppin Fetchit, rolling his eyes and saying "Yawsuh," was fully in keeping with the image of blacks as simpleminded, obsequious Toms. In Bessie's case, Southern whites liked her comedy, her wild costumes, the enormous ostrich-plume headgear and glittering costume jewelry, her suggestive movements; above all, they liked her songs.

A review filed by the Pittsburgh *Courier*'s Atlanta correspondent following Bessie's whites-only show at the "81" on Friday, February 13, 1924, indicates that they were equally fond of her records:

> The program was greatly enjoyed by the white people who filled the house after the regular performance. According to the management, practically all seats in the house were taken for this special performance as early as Thursday morning. Miss Smith is a great favorite in Atlanta. Few white homes here are without her records. . . . A prominent white music dealer told a reporter of the *Preston News* that Bessie Smith's records actually outsell everything else in the catalog.

Much as white Southerners seemed to love Bessie, she still had to be on a record or on the radio to get into their homes. She could hardly get into their theatres. The two performances at Nashville's Orpheum represent the only known occasions of Bessie's appearing in a white theatre in the South. Even in the North she was relegated to bookings in predominantly black theatres, not because she was black, but because her presentation and the music she represented was not considered sophisticated enough for Northern white audiences. "Bessie wasn't fooled by those Southern crackers smiling at her," says Ruby. "She wasn't scared of any of those white people down there. Not Bessie—she would tell anybody to kiss her ass. Nobody messed with Bessie, black or white, it didn't make no difference."

There were several attempts to form black theatre circuits, but none could compete with the T.O.B.A., or Toby Time, as it was popularly called. The Theater Owners' Booking Association was the largest, most prestigious, and longest surviving of such organizations, but its operation was substandard. Founded around 1911, it was managed by an interracial group of theatre owners. Performers, unhappy with contracts that demanded a heavy work schedule and provided light recompense, said the initials really stood for Tough On Black Asses.

Headliners like Bessie could not complain of meager fees, though they could and did complain about the facilities in most of the theatres in the chain. They themselves were to blame for the nonstar-

## 1. Bessie Smith
—hear her—the Empress of Blues Singers—at her best.

## 2. Columbia Record
—"Careless Love" Blues—that popular
old-time tune, coupled with "He's Gone"
Blues. Two splendid selections un-
equalled for tone quality and clearness.
A record you'll want.

One of Bessie's elaborate pieces of headgear—a cross between a
football helmet and a tassled lamp shade. *From a 1924 Columbia
advertisement.*

ring artists' low fees, since they paid their own people out of what
they received. Bessie was known for receiving a lot and paying a
little.

The Roosevelt Theatre in Cincinnati was one of the few T.O.B.A.
houses that offered decent facilities. Newly built, it boasted ten
large, well-lighted dressing rooms, each with a sink, running water,
electric call bells, and mirrors: real luxury. Bessie opened there on
February 25, 1924. She now had a variety of highly imaginative
costumes: her favorite was a white and blue satin dress with a
moderate hoop skirt, adorned with strands of pearls and imitation

rubies. With it she wore headgear that looked like a cross between a football helmet and a tasseled lamp shade. The costume was in sharp contrast to the often brutal reality of her songs.

On this, her second visit to Cincinnati since her prestardom days, fellow performer Gang Jines—who also happened to be the *Defender's* Cincinnati correspondent—proclaimed her unspoiled by success:

> Bessie Smith has always been a headliner, even when the salaries were absolutely nothing. Of course, her recording has made her prestige rise higher, but glad to say, she is the same Bessie, wearing the same size shoes, where a few have let prosperity almost kill their drawing power, and without a doubt, regardless of other reports, Bessie Smith is "Queen of the Blues," and some more, and is positively the biggest attraction of her kind on the T.O.B.A. The act carries special settings and is attractive and immaculate. Twenty minutes in full ovation and bows.

From Cincinnati, Bessie and her company proceeded to Detroit for a return engagement at the Koppin. She and Jack had not had much time to themselves, and on an impulse of Bessie's they got off the train at Springfield, where Bessie bought Jack a car—a beauty, a 1924 Nash. Bessie paid cash for the car, and Jack drove the rest of the way to Detroit.

Bessie had already broken all attendance records at the Koppin, so the best she could do on this visit was to match that record. Even bigger crowds awaited her in Pittsburgh, her next stop, where advance publicity hailed her as "the most popular singer ever to appear in the city." On her opening night, March 17, scores of policemen were called to the front of the Lincoln Theatre, where they experienced a scene that became familiar over the next two weeks. The Pittsburgh *Courier* described it vividly:

> Early in the evening, crowds started to gather, and by 7 o'clock in the evening the street car traffic was blocked. Thousands of people were turned away and those who did attend stormed the theater. . . . Hundreds of letters, both out-of-town and local, have poured into the theater asking the management to hold Bessie Smith another week. . . .

Originally booked for only one week, Bessie had to stay another week in Pittsburgh, at the neighboring Star Theatre, postponing her Philadelphia opening scheduled for the following Monday. Although the management cut down each show and scheduled extra ones,

Bessie's two-week visit was still not long enough to accommodate her Pittsburgh fans. On Friday night, March 28, the city's largest "race" record dealer sponsored a half hour of Bessie over radio station WCAE.[3]

When Bessie and Jack arrived in Philadelphia four days later, they found that Frank Walker had booked studio time for Bessie throughout the first week of April. Inspired perhaps by the reception given John Snow's violin accompaniments on the tour, Irvin Johns had summoned Robert Robbins, a New York violinist, to accompany her.

The result was interesting. The three jazz violin virtuosi—Stuff Smith, Eddie South, and Joe Venuti—were still relatively unknown, although the fiddle was hardly new to jazz. It was often used in the early New Orleans jazz and ragtime bands, and, of course, in black and white country music. Robbins, whose style was close to that of the Southern country fiddlers, gave Bessie's recordings a folk flavor unlike anything heard on her previous records.

The series of recording sessions produced two tunes written by Bessie, "Sorrowful Blues" and "Rocking Chair Blues," and two written by Ma Rainey—the only Ma Rainey songs Bessie ever recorded. Ma's own original versions of "Boweavil Blues" and "Moonshine Blues"[4] featured a four- or five-piece accompanying band, including violin; Bessie is heard with piano only. Ma Rainey and Bessie approach the same material in ways sufficiently different to cast further doubt on their alleged teacher-pupil relationship. It would be hard, though, to say which singer produced better results.

Bessie was a good if not wholly original composer of lyrics. A personal experience or a story often gave her an idea for a new blues. She would make up the words, memorize them, and have someone else, usually her pianist, write the music. The music for "Rocking Chair Blues" and "Sorrowful Blues" was by Irvin Johns.

Columbia Records' publicity release described "Sorrowful Blues" as "despairing"; actually it is quite humorous, right from the unusual vocal opening, a sort of scat, which sounds as if Bessie is mocking Robbins' violin but is actually something she borrowed from Gertrude Saunders:

3. Bessie was accompanied by Irvin Johns and John V. Snow, a violinist who was traveling with her show.
4. Ma Rainey recorded her two songs in December 1923 and did new versions of them four years later.

*Twee twee twah twah twah,*
*Twee twah twah twah twah twee.*

*If you catch me stealin', I don't mean no harm,*
*If you catch me stealin', I don't mean no harm;*
*It's a mark in my family and it must be carried on.*

*I got nineteen men and I want one mo',*
*I got nineteen men and I want one mo';*
*If I get that one more, I'll let that nineteen go.*

*I'm goin' to tell you, daddy, like the Chinaman*
    *told the Jew,*
*I'm goin' to tell you, daddy, like the Chinaman*
    *told the Jew,*
*If you don't like-a me, me sure don't like-a you.*

*It's hard to love another woman's man,*
*It's hard to love another woman's man;*
*You can't git him when you want him, you*
    *got to catch him when you can.*

*Have you ever seen peaches grow on sweet*
    *potato vine,*
*Have you ever seen peaches grow on sweet*
    *potato vine;*
*Yes, step in my backyard and take a peep*
    *at mine.*

Someone once observed that there is no such thing as an original blues lyric—an overstatement of a truth. Lines were "borrowed" all the time in the heyday of blues. The blues ladies drew their material from commercial sources, but the roots of that material lay in the music of their nomadic, male counterparts—folk music that grew like a snowball and melted in myriad directions with a fair amount trickling into Tin Pan Alley.

In her "Sorrowful Blues" Bessie borrowed more than twees and twahs. Two verses are almost identical to ones sung by Ida Cox on her "Chicago Monkey Man Blues," recorded for Paramount a month or so earlier. Bessie could not possibly have heard Ida's recording before making her own; either singer could have heard the other perform it in person, but the most likely explanation is that the verses were borrowed from another source.

Sobbing sambos and juvenile text characterize a Columbia advertisement from 1924.

Having weathered the storms of two decades, Ruby Walker, Bessie's niece and companion, poses for an early forties' publicity shot. *Photo courtesy of Dan Morgenstern.*

Ida's lyrics recall the racism of that period's hillbilly records, which were often sprinkled with such words as "coon" and "nigger."

By 1924 race records were heavily advertised in the black press, which accepted such ads, however insulting they were to black people.

Record companies often depicted black people as sobbing or grinning Sambos, and the copy, typified by the following Columbia publicity release, befits the illustration:

> Bessie Smith certainly turned loose a red hot one when she made No. 14025-D. The title is "Ticket Agent, Ease Your Window Down." Here is a gazook who is about to hand his lady an arm full of adios. She knows that if he is refused the purchase of a ticket he will have to stick around a bit and she figures, with the past in mind, that if that happens, she will be able to "square" things for a real reconciliation. So she hies to the ticket man, and if you ever heard a plea that came from the bottom of an apprehensive heart you have a very slight idea of how the "gal" put her stuff over. It's a bear.

Throughout the month of April, Bessie and Jack stayed with Jack's mother on 132nd Street. Ruby Walker had been fascinated by her new aunt ever since she had heard Bessie rehearse for those first recordings, and Aunt Bessie the Star was even more fascinating. Though almost twenty years separated them, Bessie and Ruby found in each other a certain fulfillment: Bessie was Ruby's key to a show business career, and an inspiration; Ruby was someone Bessie could confide in, the kind of companion she needed on road tours.

Bessie was excited, if apprehensive, about her next tour. The first stop was Chicago, the blues center of the North, and Bessie had not appeared there before. She was scheduled to perform as a single but, when Ruby begged to accompany her on the tour, she decided she would teach her to dance and let her perform during costume changes. There would be plenty of these—Bessie had bought new costumes and headgear, elaborate getups that weighed as much as fifty pounds, and she was anxious to show them off.

Bessie was an excellent dancer, and it didn't take her long to teach Ruby a few routines. What she didn't know was that Ruby had been practicing for months, waiting for just such an opportunity.

Tony Langston, the Chicago *Defender*'s entertainment editor, was there for the opening at the Avenue Theatre on May 5:

> Bessie Smith, "Empress of Blues Singers," opened her first Chicago engage-

ment at the Avenue on Monday night to a capacity audience. So much has been said of Bessie that Chicagoans were looking for something far above the average in her line, and that's just what the famous artist handed them. Her routine of songs are new and well selected and she put each and every one of them over with the well-known "Bang." In fact, Bessie tied up her own show and it is a safe prediction that she has earned a standing welcome with "Blues" fans. She is aided at the piano by Irving [sic] Johns and a bit of speedy dancing between the changing of several gorgeous gowns is done by Ruby Walker.

Bessie shared the bill with a variety of acts that in Langston's description reads like a vintage Ed Sullivan show:

The curtain raiser is the act of Rastus and Jones, a mixed team working under cork, who have a more than ordinary offering. They are followed by Margaret Scott, a prima donna, who has been with us for some time but who never fails to "get hers" along the vocal line. Then comes the rightly named "Three Baby Vamps," whose dancing abilities have been developed by Hazel Thompson Davis to such an extent that the youngsters actually stopped the show. Robinson and Mack were fourth and on their "The Bootlegger" offering coupled with several nifty songs and a bit of dancing, went over in great shape. They preceded Jolly Saunders, one of the greatest of all comedy jugglers, and the Baby Ali Co., a singing and dancing trio of fine caliber. Tim[5] and Gerty Moore, in new songs and dialogue, led up to the big noise [Bessie], and proved by their popularity that they have not grown too old for high-speed competition. It is some bill.

By 1924 Chicago had become a melting pot for jazz and blues artists who brought their disparate styles to the city from different parts of the South and Midwest. Chicago was to Ma Rainey, Ida Cox, Alberta Hunter, and numerous other blues singers what New York was to Bessie: the city in which they recorded and from which they embarked on tours. But to Bessie it was foreign territory, and she worked hard to win over audiences she knew had their own local blues idols to applaud.

She could have spared herself any anxiety; thousands of Chicagoans agreed with Tony Langston: Bessie was no longer the Queen of the Blues—she was the Empress.

Chicago's night life rivaled Harlem's. It, too, was controlled by gangsters and racketeers who ran the cabarets and speakeasies that

5. Tim Moore later became nationally known as Kingfish in the TV version of the *Amos 'n' Andy* series.

employed some of the country's finest jazz musicians and singers. The music, though, had a slightly different sound; the Southern influence was stronger, there was a heavy emphasis on blues, and the style was more akin to the jazz traditions of New Orleans.

At the time of Bessie's first visit, South Side Chicago's biggest musical attraction was King Oliver's Creole Jazz Band, which was appearing nightly at the Lincoln Gardens Cafe. Musicians traveled miles to hear this great New Orleans band, whose main attraction was Oliver's second cornetist, twenty-three-year-old Louis Armstrong. Among Armstrong's many accomplishments must be considered the inspiration he gave to such younger musicians as Muggsy Spanier, Frank Teschmacher, Jimmy McPartland, and Bud Freeman, white kids who absorbed what they heard and later turned it into a style of their own, the Chicago style.

Some of these white musicians, members of the so-called Austin High School Gang, have recalled hearing Bessie sing in a cabaret. They claim to have seen the legendary cornetist Bix Beiderbecke throw a week's pay at her feet, but it is unlikely that she found time for such a performance on this particular trip.

Bessie did find time to look up an old friend, Richard Morgan, whom she had known in Birmingham, Alabama, during the years that preceded her fame.

Morgan now lived in Chicago, where he had become the South Side's most prominent bootlegger. Although he was not himself a musician, one might say that he was a patron of the arts. A man who shared Bessie's penchant for earthiness and a good time, night rarely turned to day without Morgan's having a party in one of his many houses on the South Side. The music, always in ample supply, was provided by guests from just about every bandstand and stage in town. It was, for instance, not unusual to find Ma Rainey there, singing to the accompaniment of pianist Jelly Roll Morton, or Louis Armstrong cutting through the smoke-filled air in royal musical battle with violinist Eddie South, while the rest of Jimmy Wade's Syncopators—who were almost nightly guests—joined in.

Nor was it unusual to see Richard Morgan's teenage nephew, himself destined for fame, sitting in a corner, taking it all in. "My uncle bought me everything," Lionel Hampton recalls. "Silk shirts, the finest clothes, my first marimba, my first set of drums—it had a light in it. Yeah, my uncle was a real cool dude, and he used to take me everyplace with him—he furnished whiskey and bathtub gin for almost all the dives on the South Side. He was crazy about piano players, but all the musicians used to love to come to his place because they could meet all the chicks there, and my uncle would give them all the whiskey they could drink, and all the chitterlins they could eat. I used to dream of joining Ma Rainey's band because she treated her musicians so wonderfully, and she always bought them an instrument, but my uncle always said that Bessie was the greatest singer—he was always very fond of her."

The late Lil Armstrong was presumably referring to Morgan's place in a 1969 interview with the author: "There was some big-time bootlegger on the South Side who always had these parties going. Louis took me there a couple of times and everybody got up and played. The music was always very loud, but one time Bessie Smith got up to sing, and the man who ran the place wouldn't let her start until everybody stopped laughing, talking, and carrying on. He didn't do that for us, but I guess maybe he was afraid of Bessie; she had a reputation for having a bad temper."

During her stay in Chicago, Bessie also found time for some shopping. As she and Ruby walked down a crowded South Side shopping street, they could hear record dealers playing Bessie's "Sorrowful Blues" and Ida Cox's "Chicago Monkey Man Blues." Bessie did not seem to notice. She almost never bought a record and seemed inattentive whenever her recordings were played in her presence.

Thousands of Chicagoans had seen her picture in the *Defender*, many had seen her at the Avenue the day before, and still others remembered her from appearances in the South. She could hardly walk a block without someone recognizing and stopping her. She would respond graciously enough, would even hand out money to a stranger if she thought he needed it, but her first purchase that day was a pair of dark glasses.

In spite of all the musical activity in Chicago night spots at the time, Bessie remained true to form; she left Chicago having heard only the informal sessions at Richard Morgan's house, and the backstage echoes of the acts that preceded her on the bill at the Avenue.

From Chicago Bessie went to Indianapolis, but there her tour was cut short. Scheduled to open at the Lyric in New Orleans the second week of June, she never showed up. The papers reported that she had been "called back to New York," but gave no details. Actually Bessie was just plain tired.

A year of almost constant work had passed since the release of her first record. She'd made more money that year than she'd made in all the others put together, and generous offers were still pouring in. At this stage she could afford to take a vacation without risking her career; but Bessie's idea of a vacation was not to stop working, just to do less strenuous work. Touring took a lot out of a performer—especially Bessie, for whom it involved heavy drinking and sleepless nights.

Bessie was now partying whenever Jack was not around. She knew every drinking joint from New Orleans to Detroit, and only Jack's presence could keep her away from them when she toured. "She was afraid of Jack," Ruby recalls, "because he'd beat her up so. If he was around she didn't allow you to talk to her about nothing except maybe the show—she didn't want to be bothered, she'd go into her room, afraid you might whisper something and Jack would think she was planning something terrible."

Jack, of course, had good reason to be suspicious. Not only was Bessie drinking excessively, but her remarkably uninhibited sexual appetites were indulged regularly as well. After a year of married life, he began to hear rumors, but they were for the most part still rumors. Jack could be certain only of his wife's weakness for alcohol and gift-giving. He did not, for instance, know about her feelings for Agie Pitts, a handsome young dancer from Detroit who was now part of her show, and, in a sense, her life.

"Some way or another Bessie fell for that boy," Ruby recalls, "and he *was* a boy compared to her." Ruby found out just how much Agie meant to her aunt one night when Bessie caught Ruby and Agie together in one of the dressing rooms at the Indianapolis theatre. They weren't doing anything eyebrow-raising—just some youthful fooling around and laughing. Suddenly the door flew open, and there stood Bessie.

"Everything I like, you like," she said, "and I'm going to break you out of the habit of trying to be Bessie Smith—I'm gonna let you *know* you ain't Bessie Smith." With that, she jumped Ruby and beat her up. Agie fled the room at once, and when Ruby finally managed to wrestle herself out of Bessie's grip, her screams had attracted the police. "I kept on hollerin' even when I saw the cops coming, I was that mad. They asked what had happened and I said, 'That woman beat me,' I acted like I didn't know Bessie. They took Bessie, me, and Agie in, and put us all in jail. Bessie was drunk, I was half drunk, and they locked Agie up because we were fighting over him. I wasn't fighting, it was Bessie, she was so jealous."

Someone paid their fine and got them out the next day. "I beat you up this time in this town," Bessie said, "and you'd better get ready to be beat up in the next town if you don't stop messin' aroun' with *my* men." She meant it, but as usual Bessie and Ruby quickly got over their differences.

When she returned from Indianapolis, Bessie went to Philadelphia for a few days with Jack before going to New York for more recording sessions. Feeling guilty, perhaps, she bought Jack a diamond ring that cost over two thousand dollars. Whenever he was the recipient, Jack made no move to discourage Bessie's wild spending. "So that's how crazy two young people with money was who never had anything," he later recalled in a *down beat* story. "We never, neither of us, really knew the value of money."

Between July 22 and August 8, 1924, Bessie did five recording sessions with Fletcher Henderson. Her voice had matured further; it had become richer and deeper, and she was in top form on "Lou'siana Low Down Blues" and "Mountain Top Blues," singing against Don Redman's painfully unimaginative alto saxophone. She was even better in the following day's takes, in which Henderson's piano was augmented by the trombone of Charlie Green.

Charlie Green, a young musician from Omaha, had just joined the Henderson band when he teamed up with Bessie on July 23. They recorded "Work House Blues" and "House Rent Blues," beginning a long and fruitful collaboration. Bessie had made close to fifty recordings at this point, but her backing had been pedestrian at best. Green gave her more than mere accompaniment; his horn commented on her lyrics and played to every subtlety in her phrasing.

While Bessie was busy rehearsing new songs and recordings, Frank Walker was planning her immediate future. The T.O.B.A. booked her for another season: a twenty-week nonconsecutive tour, allowing her to break for recording sessions in New York and trips to her Philadelphia home. She would no longer have to drive herself as hard as she had during her first year of fame.

The terms of the T.O.B.A. contract were the most generous in that organization's thirteen-year history. T.O.B.A. shows over the past months had drawn some criticism, and a September 9 publicity release noted that Bessie had been signed "to improve the quality of the circuit"—a peculiar statement, considering what a familiar figure she was by now on the T.O.B.A. trail.

She had kept to a relatively light schedule during the summer of 1924; now, well rested, she was ready to go again. She had become the highest-paid black performer in the country, and no one challenged her right to the title Empress of the Blues.

On September 24 she began a four-day engagement as an "extra attraction" and headliner at the Lafayette Theatre on 132nd Street, and the following morning she recorded again. According to *Billboard*, she suffered from a severe cold, which "prevented her from doing her usual stuff" that week, but the recordings themselves reveal no such handicap. This time Fletcher Henderson brought with him—in addition to Charlie Green—Joe Smith, a young cornet player from Ohio, who occasionally recorded with the Henderson band and eventually became a regular member.

Smith, who had played for Ethel Waters and Mamie Smith, was an experienced blues accompanist. Bessie rarely showed enthusiasm for other performers' work, but after listening a few minutes to Joe Smith she walked over to Frank Walker and pronounced Smith her favorite cornet player. "You got the best boys here today," she added, pointing to Smith and Green.

They recorded "The Bye Bye Blues" and "Weeping Willow Blues," with outstanding results. Bessie's admiration for Green and Smith shows excellent judgment, which makes it all the more regrettable that Columbia did not allow her to choose her own accompanists. Bessie was not even given a free hand in selecting her recording repertoire; still, her material usually outclassed her accompaniment.

Now she was getting better pianists as well as horn men. Irvin Johns had been an improvement over Clarence Williams and Fletcher Henderson, and her new accompanist, Fred Longshaw, was excellent. Longshaw first worked with Bessie during the four-day engagement at the Lafayette, then embarked on a tour with her the following week.

When they got to Birmingham, Bessie picked up some local musicians, giving Longshaw a seven-piece band to lead for the rest of the tour. The group included trumpeter Shelton Hemphill, who was later to record with her in New York, and saxophonist Teddy Hill,

Fred Longshaw's pick-up band, which accompanied Bessie in late 1924. Its members are (l. to r.) Murray Harper, Teddy Hill, Longshaw, Carl Bunch, Alec Nabors, Joe Britton, Shelton Hemphill. *Photo courtesy of Frank Driggs.*

whose band in the thirties included Dizzy Gillespie and who as manager of Minton's Playhouse during the early forties would play midwife to that radical departure from jazz traditions known as bop.

From Birmingham the tour took Bessie to Kansas City and Chicago, where she opened on October 27, this time at the T.O.B.A.'s Grand Theatre. Again Tony Langston offered his *Defender* readers a glowing review:

> Bessie Smith, the famous blues singer and Columbia record star, is the "piece de resistance" on an excellent show at the Grand this week. Bessie, whose reputation is world wide, had them howling long before her first number was half finished. Bessie, to say the least, is a bundle of personality and when we use the word bundle we are not casting disparagement at Bessie's generous shape. It takes personality to send over "blues" material. In a proper rendition of blues, art is a secondary consideration. Bessie has a routine which fits her like the well-known glove. There are four numbers offered and all of them made the bullseye. Following Bessie's first song, "Work House Blues," her pianist, Fred Longshaw, turned loose a thrilling solo that had everybody in the place pantomiming. Fred is there like a duck on the ivories and is in direct contrast to some of the freight carried by "blues queens" we have been pestered with from time to time. Bessie essayed a bit of monologue preceding her second song, and this writer is of the opinion that Bessie and the world at large would get along just as well without it. . . . A "sold out" sign showed for all three performances on Monday night, which indicates that the Grand patrons want what Bessie carries.

Bessie's next stop was the Howard Theatre in Washington for Thanksgiving week. Again she was an "added attraction," this time sharing top billing with the touring company of *Shuffle Along,* Broadway's first truly successful black musical.

A football game had attracted twenty-eight thousand visitors to Washington for the holiday weekend, and there was a near-riot in the streets outside the Howard. "It was almost disastrous," reported a *Journal and Guide* correspondent. "The 'Shuffle Along' gang attracted many of the sports enthusiasts, but if Miss Smith had appeared alone, it would hardly have made things easier for the police. The race never had a more popular star."

Returning to Philadelphia, Bessie had little more than a week's rest before going to New York for more recordings. Her tour had been successful but relatively uneventful, since Jack traveled with her all the way and squelched any opportunity for carousing. Married life still seemed to be agreeing with Bessie, but Jack obviously was not fulfilling all her needs. Ruby recalls that Bessie could sometimes go for weeks without touching liquor, "but when she went on one of those benders, she would stay on for weeks without letting up. When her and Jack were on good terms, you couldn't pay her to touch a drop, but when they had their fights she really carried on—she would drink like mad. You see, Jack was so conservative that you couldn't ball with him. He was so strict and he wasn't in Bessie's life at all—he was all right for her when she felt like being quiet, and no drinking, just a wife, a homebody. But when it came to a good time, and she got those spells and wanted to go off, Jack wasn't the one for her. That's why she always had to go and mess with the young people, those who were of her breed, those who could keep up with her.

"She was a strong woman with a beautiful strong constitution, and she loved a good time. She was strictly show business: sitting around was all right for a month or so, but that's as far as she could go without going out and clowning. She would go out, stay two or three weeks, ball, and then be ready to keep quiet for a month or so. Then Jack would come in handy, but Jack couldn't see it that way, that's why every time you looked he was knocking her down, or catching her going out of a place or coming into a place."

In the first week of December, Bessie was back at the recording studio for a session that produced "Sing Sing Prison Blues," a Porter Grainger tune, and five unusable selections, including "Sinful Blues," on which Bessie not only sings but plays a comb and tissue-paper kazoo. Rejected at first, Bessie's kazoo performance—her only one on record—was recaptured the following week when she successfully rerecorded the five selections. On December 13 she made her last record of 1924, her own "Dying Gambler's Blues,"[6] with superb backing by Charlie Green.

It had been a year of fairly hard work, yet Bessie had allowed herself more leisure that year than during the previous, hectic one. In terms of her popularity and income, 1924 had been her most successful, but not her happiest, year. Something was happening in her relationship with Jack; more and more they sought separate paths. There were still moments when they were happy being together, but material rewards could no longer ensure Jack's undivided attention, and Bessie was beginning to experience periods of loneliness.

6. Jack Gee is credited as the composer of "Dying Gambler's Blues," but Bessie is said to have actually written it. She occasionally had him listed as the composer of her songs, presumably as a gesture of generosity.

# 4

*I've got the world in a jug;*
*The stopper's in my hand.*
"Down Hearted Blues"

When Bessie sang those words on her first recording date in 1923, the outlook for her future was bright if still uncertain; but by 1925 she could rightly feel that she had "arrived." She had enjoyed a year and a half of prominence and prosperity; she had earned billing as "the Greatest and Highest Salaried Race Star in the World"; she was supporting her family in a fashion she had never thought possible; she was married, and she was still running around.

On January 14 Bessie entered the Columbia studio at Columbus Circle for the first and most memorable of three collaborations with Louis Armstrong.

Armstrong, twenty-four years old and fresh from King Oliver's Creole Jazz Band in Chicago, had come to New York some three months earlier to join the Fletcher Henderson orchestra. Although his reputation among musicians was already established, he was still relatively unknown to the public. His imaginative playing, dexterous technique, and full-bodied tone, which brought new life to the Henderson band at the Roseland ballroom, was soon to bring him worldwide fame.

Armstrong had previously recorded accompaniments for blues singers including Alberta Hunter and Clara Smith, but it was not until the first session with Bessie that he found his match—a more perfect team can hardly be imagined. Fred Longshaw was there as well, but Armstrong's cornet so perfectly complemented Bessie's voice that the result sounds more like a series of duets with harmonium accompaniment. For Bessie and Louis this was just another recording session; but for critics and scholars, January 14, 1925, would stand as a memorable date in jazz history.[1]

They started the session with W. C. Handy's "St. Louis Blues." It has since become the most widely recorded of all blues, but many consider the Armstrong-Smith version definitive. With Longshaw's harmonium lending a delightful country church air to the proceedings, the two voices blend so effectively that one might mistake this effort for the fruit of a long and happy association.

The rest of the session went equally well, "Reckless Blues," "Cold in Hand Blues," "Sobbin' Hearted Blues," and "You've Been a Good Ole Wagon"—song after song became a classic of the genre.

The year 1925 was off to a fine start.

In February, as her latest records were being readied for release, Bessie embarked on another theatre tour. There was something special about this one; the itinerary included a week at the Liberty Theatre in Chattanooga. Bessie had not performed in her hometown since her days with the Moses Stokes company. Her return as a star performer was an event, and tickets were sold out far in advance. Bessie was probably more excited than anybody else about her homecoming.

The Liberty Theatre was packed for all performances on opening day, and Bessie drew crowds backstage, too. People who remembered her as a child—or thought they did—came to her dressing room all day long to say hello. Of the dozens of invitations she received, Bessie accepted one from an old family friend who invited her and her friends to a pigs'-feet party following the last show on opening night.

It had been a particularly strenuous day, but the enthusiastic reception had put Bessie in a partying mood. So far she had remained sober despite Jack's absence, but it was time to have some fun. She went straight from the theatre to the party, taking Ruby and three other girls from the show with her.

---

1. The session was historic in more ways than one, for it marked the last time Bessie recorded acoustically. A technical revolution was about to replace the old horn with the microphone. Soon all recordings would be made electronically, and people would marvel at the "lifelike" quality thus achieved.

The house where the party was being held was in a fairly isolated part of town. An old house, it had been built in days when nobody thought of streets, and ignored when somebody did. The new concrete sidewalk was over a block away, and the only approach to the house was over bare ground, now muddy because of a downpour earlier in the evening.

The girls stepped along gingerly behind Bessie, trying hard to avoid splashing mud on their party dresses. The party was well under way, its lights and noise piloting the guest of honor and her entourage through the moonless night until they reached the sagging wooden front porch. Inside, the heavy-handed down-home playing of a local blues pianist competed bravely with the din of the cheerful crowd. "The funk is flyin'," said Bessie approvingly as she opened the front door and smelled the heavy odor of food, liquor, smoke, and perspiration.

The girls still following close behind her, she made her way through the tightly packed crowd, moving in the general direction of the kitchen. She stopped occasionally to greet a well-wisher or friend, but it was plain that she was hungry for food, not admiration or carousing.

The group withdrew to a corner of the kitchen, where the girls looked on as Bessie raided the steaming pots of pigs' feet, collard greens, black-eyed peas, and scallions. She sat down at the large kitchen table and started eating, washing the food down with gulps of homemade liquor.

She seemed oblivious to her surroundings and did not appear to notice the man who suddenly entered from the front room. He had been dancing—perspiration stained the shiny dark-blue suit that hung loosely on his huge frame—and he reeked of liquor. After standing for a minute inside the kitchen door surveying the scene, he spotted the girls, and grinned, drawing attention to the gold caps on his surviving teeth.

"C'mon, baby, let's dance." His tone of voice made it sound more like an order. As the girls retreated farther into their corner he approached, bent on grabbing at least one of them.

At this point Bessie shifted her attention from her plate to the man. Rising slowly, she struck a characteristic hands-on-hips pose and defiantly spit a small bone in his direction.

"We don't want to be bothered," she said, "so you just get back in there and let them alone."

"Who in the hell are *you?*"

Bessie's calm was deceptive. "Did that fucker say something to me?" she asked softly. Before anyone could respond to her question, she had jumped the intruder and hit him on the head with her two clenched fists. As stunned by surprise as by the blow itself, he fell to the floor.

Not waiting for a reaction, Bessie turned back to the table, sat down, and resumed eating. "This here sure is some delicious food, uhm, uhm, uhm," she said, as her victim got back on his feet and stumbled discreetly out of the kitchen.

When Bessie and the girls finally left the house three hours later, they had all but forgotten the unpleasant incident. Trudging through the mud to get back to the sidewalk, the girls giggled loudly as Bessie mimicked some of the guests they had just left.

They had reached the sidewalk and walked half a block when, without the slightest warning, the kitchen intruder stepped out of the darkness and thrust a long knife into Bessie's side.

It all happened very quickly. There was no exchange of words, just a slight groan from Bessie and the footsteps of the man running away. Bessie, holding her hand to the bleeding wound in her side, went in immediate pursuit, chasing him for three blocks before she finally sank to her knees in anguish. When the girls caught up with her, she turned to Ruby: "Baby, take this thing out of me."

Ruby tried, but she was too squeamish. When one of the other girls pulled the knife out, the blood spurted for several feet.

There had apparently been other witnesses to the stabbing, for the police and ambulance soon arrived. Bessie was taken to a hospital and the doctor suggested she stay there for a couple of days, but Bessie was not easily confined. She was determined to go on with her show and she raised so much hell that the hospital let her go a few hours later. The stabbing took place at about four o'clock in the morning; at two the following afternoon, Bessie was on stage at the Liberty Theatre for her scheduled matinee.

That is how Ruby Walker remembers the incident. A different story appeared under the heading BESSIE SMITH STABBED in the March 7, 1925, edition of the Chicago *Defender:*

Chattanooga, Tenn.—Bessie Smith, popular Columbia record artist, was stabbed by a man said to be Buck Hodge, in what is believed to have been an attempt at robbery. Miss Smith was brought to Chattanooga from

Chicago to sing at the Liberty Theatre. The robbery was brought on by her display of costly diamonds and gems. Nothing serious resulted, although she was rushed to Erlanger hospital for treatment.

Ruby also recalls hearing about an aftermath, which none of the papers reported: "They said some of the boys in the pool room got a hold of this man after he got out of jail, and that they beat him to death. I can believe it. This was Bessie's hometown—they loved her there."

After completing the week at the Liberty Theatre, Bessie and her show moved on to Memphis and Nashville, where they played the Bijou Theatre.

One of the show's routines had Bessie dressed as a Southern mammy, complete with bandanna, a red dress with white polka dots, and an exaggerated posterior, which was actually a pillow. The routine started with the girls doing a very straight Russian dance for about three minutes before Bessie made her entrance. Wearing the mammy getup and wielding a whiskbroom, Bessie proceeded to sweep the stage, occasionally giving the girls—who continued their dance—a look of annoyance, but otherwise ignoring them. When she found them in her way, Bessie tried to sweep them off, and eventually succeeded. The big laugh that climaxed the routine came as Bessie picked up her skirts, chased after Ruby, and hit her with the broom.

One afternoon at the Bijou, Bessie had a bit too much to drink. Staggering onto the stage, she managed to go through her usual sweeping routine, but when it came time to hit Ruby with the broom, the pillow slipped and Bessie's artificial behind dropped to the floor. The audience went into convulsions, but no one laughed harder than Ruby. Professional that she was, Bessie made the best out of a potentially embarrassing situation. Aiming her words at the audience, she shook her broom at Ruby and said, "I'm gonna buy you a damn ticket and let you sit up front, bitch, 'cause you're my best customer."

Most Southern theatres employed female ushers, and Bessie had caught Agie Pitts flirting with one of the Bijou's girls just before she went onstage. She managed to contain her jealousy until the show was over, but she had hardly taken her last bow before she started looking for Agie. When someone said he had gone back to the hotel, she grabbed Ruby by the arm. "C'mon, Ruby," she ordered, "don't worry about your costume, you're gonna help me find that no-good bastard." And out into the street they went, an obese, angry mammy stomping up the street with a frail Russian dancer tagging behind.

They were nearly a block away when they saw Agie and the girl about to enter the hotel arm in arm. Bessie made her presence known with a familiar insult. "You motherless bastard," she shouted, waving her fist in the air. Then she turned to Ruby: "If you can't keep up with me, you'd better get out of my way," she said, running as fast as her mammy costume would allow her.

Agie took off at the same time, leaving the startled usherette frozen in her steps. Bessie didn't stop when she reached the girl: she just threw her fist out, knocked the girl to the ground, and kept running in Agie's direction. He had in the meantime disappeared down some steps, and Bessie rushed down after him. Moments later she emerged, tearing up the steps at an even faster clip than before. It turned out to be the basement of a funeral parlor, and running into a room full of caskets Bessie had promptly given up her pursuit.

Bessie and Agie had made up by the following week when they reached Macon, Georgia, and, for a while at least, there was peace. Bessie had a special interest in Macon: a five-year-old boy whose mother, a niece of Margaret Warren (one of Bessie's chorus girls), had promised Bessie that she would let her adopt the boy should she ever need to give him up. Every time Bessie toured through Macon, she would spend time with "Snooks," as she called him, and shower him with affection.

For unknown reasons, Bessie had reduced the show to six people: herself, a pianist, Ruby, Agie, and his two male dancing partners. With this small troupe she began making her way north to New York.

They were appearing somewhere in Kentucky when Bessie and Agie had their next disagreement, a heated argument that developed into a physical fight. Ruby and the two dancers got into the act, too, holding Bessie back after she had knocked Agie to the floor. But they couldn't hold her for long, and she pried herself loose and stomped angrily into her dressing room, slamming the door behind her. "If you mess with me," she shouted through the closed door, "I'll leave the whole damn bunch of you."

It was Bessie against her youthful gang. They stepped into their dressing room, adjoining Bessie's, shut the door, and proceeded to plan their strategy. A thin wall separated the two rooms, and they could hear Bessie moving things around, mumbling to herself. When she occasionally raised her voice, she said, "That did it, *that* did it." Then they heard her door open, and Agie stuck his head out into the hall. "She's leavin' us, she's packed her stuff," he said. "I'd better go and get her back here." With that he left, running out the stage door, but he never returned—Bessie took him with her to New York, leaving the others stranded and penniless.

Ruby's mother eventually rescued her. With the money she sent, Ruby and the two dancers went to Atlanta, where a few nights of work earned them train fare to New York. What happened to Bessie's pianist is anybody's guess. "It was nothing for Bessie just to get up and leave if something made her mad enough, and then she didn't care what happened to anybody. But she always felt sorry for people who had been left by someone else and she used to often help a whole bunch of other people get home. She took a bunch of Ida Cox's girls out of Dallas once—she was funny that way."

Bessie had probably dismissed the whole incident from her mind by the time she arrived back in New York. There were other things to think about. Columbia had added Ethel Waters to its roster of black singers. Bessie and Ethel had, of course, worked on the same bill in the South, and they had spent a summer together at Horan's in Philadelphia before wide recognition came to either of them. Ethel hadn't made as many recordings as Bessie, but she had cut her first sides as early as 1921, and she was beginning to catch the fancy of white Northern audiences, delivering highly suggestive songs with charming innocence.

Born in Chester, Pennsylvania, a suburb of Philadelphia, Ethel lacked Bessie's natural earthiness: her songs were more literate, her diction always perfect, and her humor never too ethnic for whites to understand. Offstage, however, the disparity was less noticeable—in fact, Ethel Waters' life-style was quite similar to Bessie's. At least in the beginning Columbia obviously valued Bessie higher; they gave Ethel a three-month contract to do four sides at only one hundred dollars each. But the contract was renewed for a year, during which her recording of "Dinah" catapulted Ethel Waters to fame and gave Bessie good reason to be bitter. In the spring of 1925, however, Bessie had no more reason to feel threatened by Ethel Waters than by Clara Smith.

More important to her was something new she was about to try: recording with a microphone. Four of her acoustical recordings with Louis Armstrong had been released, and sales looked very promising. Frank Walker was anxious to record her again, particularly since Columbia was converting to the electrical method, which allowed greater flexibility and produced an infinitely superior sound. A larger backup band could now be used without drowning out the singer's voice. Walker arranged Bessie's next recording session for May 5, 1925.

The new technique was still in the experimental stage. Maggie Jones,[2] Columbia's first race artist to test the system, recorded only an hour or so before Bessie's session. The old system of waxlike discs, which had to be metal-plated and processed at the factory before a playback could be heard, was still being employed, so the results were still not in. The band that accompanied Miss Jones was also to back up Bessie. It was a choice group consisting of musicians from the Fletcher Henderson band, including Henderson himself, Buster Bailey, Coleman Hawkins, and Joe Smith.

Bessie had never recorded with so many musicians and engineers. She had previously been accompanied by a trio at most, along with one engineer.[3] Since the new system was being tested, Columbia's own engineers were assisted by their colleagues from Western Electric.

The Western Electric system was one of several being developed at the time, and Columbia, hoping to get a head start on the competition,[4] was eager to cooperate. One of Western's engineers felt that the Columbia studio was too large for the carbon microphone, and that a proper sound could only be achieved if its acoustics were altered. He had a theory to meet the problem, and it was put to the test that afternoon: a conical tent made of monk's cloth, large enough to cover Bessie, her six musicians, Frank Walker, the engineers, and the recording equipment, was suspended by a wire from the ceiling.

Kicking off the session with "Cake Walking Babies," a lively tune

2. A popular stage personality, Miss Jones was also well known as Fae Barnes.
3. Usually a Mr. Emerson.
4. Ma Rainey's label, Paramount, soon began using the imprint "Electrically Recorded" on its labels. Its engineers did employ some form of electrical system, but the quality was so inferior to those of the bigger companies that some said all Paramount did was turn on an electric bulb in the studio.

Alberta Hunter had recorded for the Gennett label[5] some months earlier, Bessie managed to sound extraordinarily vibrant despite the claustrophobic atmosphere beneath the tent.

Bessie's exuberance and Joe Smith's magnificent cornet break in the middle of the instrumental passage more than made up for a slightly rough ensemble. But Bessie's version of the song was never given the chance to compete with Miss Hunter's; it was not issued until 1940, when former Columbia executive George Avakian discovered the original metal master in the company's vault. It is not clear why it was rejected; one not very plausible theory has it that "Cake Walking Babies," as a Sophie Tucker-type vaudeville song, represented too radical a departure for Bessie, and the 1925 race market simply was not ready for it.

Next they recorded the more conventional "Yellow Dog Blues," by W. C. Handy. Again Bessie's voice was exuberant. She had a little trouble with the lyrics, mixing up words here and there as she often did, but her delivery was as fine as it had ever been, and the session would probably have yielded additional sides had it not come to an unexpected end: two minutes after the group finished the second take of "Yellow Dog Blues," the tent collapsed. "I'm telling you," said Walker, "it was the wildest scramble you ever saw."

As the musicians, the engineers, Frank Walker, and Bessie tried to get out from under the huge blanket, the Empress contributed her favorite expression: "I ain't never *heard* of such shit!"

Neither had her tentmates. The session ended, and, with it, the tent theory.

A week and a half later another session took place. On May 14, Fletcher Henderson brought with him only trombonist Charlie Green, and the session resulted in two very similar takes of "Soft Pedal Blues," both of which were eventually released. Written by Bessie and featuring her in an appropriately rowdy mood, "Soft Pedal Blues" is about a woman who runs a "buffet flat," but its lyrics only hint at the goings on in such establishments. Preceding a cowboy yell that must have knocked the engineer out of his seat, she sings "I'm drunk and full of booze" with great conviction—she

---

5. Still under contract to Paramount, Miss Hunter recorded under the pseudonym Josephine Beatty, which was actually the name of her younger sister.

was probably sober, for Walker would otherwise have called the session off.

Presumably she was still sober the next day when she recorded four more selections,[6] but that periodic restlessness was setting in again. She had left the house on 132nd Street early in the morning of May 15 to go to the studio, but she didn't show up for dinner that evening, and the family saw no sign of her for the next two or three days.

Bessie had pulled such disappearing acts before, so Jack was more angry than worried. All the same, he was getting ready to notify the police when a man telephoned the Gee home and asked to speak to Ruby.

When Ruby got to the phone, she found Bessie on the other end of the line. It seemed that she had spent the days of her absence in a Harlem hotel room with one of Fletcher Henderson's musicians, and now she was afraid to come home. She asked Ruby to hurry over to the hotel, give her a report on Jack's mood, and help her get out of her predicament as gracefully as possible.

Ruby rushed to the hotel, doing some speedy maneuvering with detours designed to confuse Jack, who was suspicious enough to follow her.

Ruby and Bessie, old hands at putting one over on Jack, decided it would be best to pretend that there had been some kind of accident and that the hotel, unable to identify Bessie, had simply cared for her until she regained consciousness.

To add drama and credibility to this somewhat farfetched story, Bessie threw herself down the stairs of the hotel. Ruby, not having been let in on this unexpected finishing touch to their plan, rushed down the stairs after her. "I saw you did that on purpose," she began, but Bessie quickly hushed her up.

"Shut up, baby," she whispered from her awkward position on the lobby floor. "I'm supposed to be real hurt," whereupon she let out an agonizing groan for the benefit of the approaching manager.

6. Of these, only "Dixie Flyer Blues" was released. The rejection of a recording was not always due to failure on the part of the performer. Improper storage conditions could dull the waxlike substance which formed the cutting disc; occasionally the lathe, powered by pulleys rather than a motor, ran at a slower speed than was desired. This usually occurred in extremely cold weather—the grease on the pulley would stiffen, causing a record cut under such conditions to play at a higher pitch than intended. Because such technical problems were not always detectable until the master had been processed and a test pressing played, the studios always made several takes of each song regardless of how flawless the first one might sound.

A frightened hotel owner was summoned. Bessie, after assuring him that she was in a good position to sue, offered to settle: she was prepared to forget the whole matter if he agreed to corroborate the story she and Ruby had made up. It worked—Jack pretended, at least, to accept the story.

For the next eight days Bessie stayed at home, "recuperating" and rehearsing for more records—a two-day session with Fletcher Henderson, Charlie Green, and Louis Armstrong. The resulting four sides, "Nashville Women's Blues," "Careless Love Blues," "J. C. Holmes's Blues," and "I Ain't Goin' to Play Second Fiddle," represent further artistic triumphs for Bessie, but Armstrong—perhaps somewhat inhibited by the presence of another horn—played a less dominant role this time around.

Bessie's between-tours rest period had been anything but a rest; now it was already time to prepare for the summer tent shows. Renting a rehearsal room in Lafayette Hall, next to the theatre at Seventh Avenue and 132nd Street, she began putting together *Harlem Frolics*. The Lafayette Theatre had just been purchased by Frank Schiffman, who later took over the 125th Street Apollo, and he was having it completely renovated. His first show, a musical extravaganza of sorts, had been booked for the entire summer, and would feature Clara Smith.

The two Columbia stars, rehearsing in adjoining buildings, frequently looked in on each other. They even sang together once or twice.

Comedian Dinah Scott was directing this show for Bessie. It was a fairly small production with a chorus of seven girls, a singing and dancing trio led by Agie Pitts, a tap dancer who also did some fancy juggling, and a trio of comedians consisting of Scott himself, James T. Wilson, and Bessie's brother Clarence, who acted as the straight man and now also looked after the troupe's business affairs. The music was provided by a seven-piece band conducted by James E. Jones.

Rehearsals had gone well, despite a last-minute change necessitated by the abrupt walkout of one of the acts, the team of Tolliver and Harris. Bessie had tried to settle a wage dispute by throwing a piano stool at Mr. Tolliver. When she wound up for an encore, Mr. Tolliver took his partner by the hand and left, exhibiting some fancy footwork as they went through the door.

By the end of June 1925, Bessie's *Harlem Frolics* was ready to hit the road south. For the first time, she would be traveling in her own personal railroad car.

In years past, Bessie had covered thousands of miles, barnstorming under the most primitive circumstances, but her tent shows were now elaborate, well-organized affairs, with an advance man traveling ahead of the company to secure the proper licenses, select an appropriate site, and herald the show's arrival. Her new show car, custom-made by the Southern Iron and Equipment Company in Atlanta, lent the finishing touch to Bessie's touring show; the magnificent bright-yellow car with its green lettering became familiar—you knew when the Empress was in town.

Maud Smith had just joined Bessie's show when the car was first delivered. "I'll never forget it. It was Clarence's idea to buy the car, and it was delivered to us in a small town near Atlanta on a sunny Monday. Everybody was so excited, and we laughed and carried on as we walked through the car and examined every corner. And what a difference it made—some of the towns we hit didn't have hotels for us so we used to have to spread out, one staying here, another one there. Now we could just live on the train."

Seventy-eight feet long, the car was large enough to carry the entire show. It had seven staterooms—each one comfortably sleeping four—kitchen, bathroom with hot and cold running water, and a lower level accommodating as many as thirty-five people. A corridor, long enough to transport the tent's big center pole, ran the length of the car. A room in the rear housed the canvas, along with cases of soft drinks, Crackerjacks, peanuts, and other items sold by Bessie's crew doubling as vendors. It also served as sleeping quarters for the prop boys—sometimes called canvas boys—young men who were picked up en route and hired to erect the tent and perform whatever manual labor was required. These young men were told to keep to themselves if they valued their jobs. Their liking for the girls and their aversion to soap and water displeased Bessie, and to "protect" the girls in the show, she went out of her way to discourage fraternization.

The late Lonnie Johnson, who toured with Bessie in 1929, recalled an incident involving one of the prop boys.

Bessie had noticed the young man making eyes at one of her girls in the show, but she conveniently suppressed her anger until payday. Johnson recalled Bessie slowly advancing on the youth as he stood in line, waiting to be paid five dollars or so due him for a week of hard work:

She walks up to him, smiling and looking real friendly. So he starts smiling, too, thinkin' she's gonna say something nice, but he should have known better, Bessie never said anything nice to those boys. This one never knew what hit him; Bessie just stood there, looking at him and smiling, and then, *wham*, she punched him in the face and knocked him several feet away from the line. "You lowly bastards ain't messin' aroun' with *my* girls," she said—and then she told her nephew, Teejay, not to pay him. She left that poor kid there, somewhere in South Carolina, without any money.[7]

Bessie could certainly be as hard-hearted as she was generous. The prop boy's punishment was unquestionably too severe, prompted perhaps by her conflicting emotions toward the chorus girls. Her girls were always very young, most of them in their teens, and, no doubt, Bessie had some maternal feelings for them. But she was jealous of them, too—doubly jealous—because Bessie loved women as well as men.

Working on the road for Bessie didn't make anyone rich—the chorus girls and dancing boys received fifteen dollars a week spending money; Bessie provided transportation and room and board—but there was a certain amount of prestige to be gained from it. Many novices became seasoned performers—in more ways than one—after a relatively short period in the Empress's training camp.

Bessie's overhead was considerably reduced when she acquired the railroad car. The quarters were relatively cramped, and waking up in the middle of the night as the car jerked from being hitched to an outgoing train took some getting used to, but most of the performers preferred this arrangement to hotel living. Food was prepared in the car's galley, often by Bessie herself, and the musicians might be drafted to peel potatoes. The meals most often consisted of stew, pigs' feet, or other Southern specialties, and supplies were always ample. If the weather permitted, they ate picnic-style somewhere near the dead track where the car was stationed.

Although the close quarters could on occasion produce friction, the general feeling was one of togetherness, from which only the prop boys were excluded. Their bunks were the least comfortable

7. There is a slight discrepancy in Johnson's story, since *Midnight Steppers,* the show he toured in with Bessie, did not appear in South Carolina, but his report checks out with similar stories told by those who witnessed Bessie's actions toward her prop boys.

and they were made to eat their meals a safe distance away from the rest of the troupe.

After dinner the band members would don their short red coats and march through town announcing the show. Playing such tunes as "St. Louis Blues," "Cake Walking Babies," or "There'll Be a Hot Time in the Old Town Tonight," they led a parade of lower-echelon troupers who waved placards advertising "A Hot Show Tonight" or "Bessie Smith and Her Gang Are Here." Hand-painted by members of the troupe, the signs often featured the names of entertainers who weren't even with the show, or such exotic imaginary acts as "Beula, the Ball of Fire." By the time Bessie's pied pipers returned to the tent, they were followed by a large entourage of eager customers and children.

Bessie's vendors would greet them all, offering soft drinks, Crackerjacks, hot dogs, and cheap novelty items like the very practical paper fans bought for a penny in New York and sold by the hundreds at ten cents apiece.

The huge round tent was divided into two segregated sections, of which each offered two kinds of seats: fifty cents admission was charged for the long strips of wooden seats in the back, and a more comfortable front seat with a back rest cost seventy-five cents. Only members of the family—usually Maud, Clarence, or Teejay—were entrusted with ticket sales. The railroad car carried a small safe to which the day's take was transported in a small trunk, poured out on a table, carefully counted, and put away. When Jack was with the show he always kept his loaded revolver on the table, just in case. After a few weeks of touring a considerable sum of money had accumulated in the safe.

Jack was always eager to count the money—he was good with figures—but he did not know how to make up a payroll. The payroll, of course, was relatively small, but Jack trusted no one, and if he happened to be with the show on a payday he always kept his gun handy. An expert crap shooter, he liked to engage members of the show in a game and win back some of their pay. From time to time members of the troupe would ask Bessie for a loan because they had lost their salaries to Jack. Even though she was usually known to be an easy touch, she never sympathized in such cases. "If you're dumb enough to let him take your money back," she would say, "he *should* take it back." She took this attitude only to discourage them from gambling with Jack, whose greed she neither shared nor approved of. She herself was no dilettante when it came to playing card games, and there were times when she indulged in a little game with her performers, but she was known to have refused money from someone who could ill afford to lose it.

Jack was exactly the opposite. His respect for money often kept him up for hours, separating nickels from dimes, quarters from halves. Bessie, though she disapproved, found his preoccupation with money a constant source of amusement and often entertained her friends by mimicking the wide-eyed Jack, crouching greedily over imaginary piles of change.

In mid-August Bessie abandoned her 1925 tent show to make recordings in New York. On August 19, she did "Nobody's Blues But Mine" and "I Ain't Got Nobody," with a trio including banjo player Elmer Snowden, whose band—the Washingtonians—had been taken over two years earlier by his pianist, Duke Ellington. The session had originally been scheduled for the day before, but Bessie showed up drunk and Frank Walker immediately sent everybody home. "She took it very nicely," Snowden recalls, "and said to us, 'I'm sorry, boys, but Mr. Walker is the boss and I'll sing twice as good tomorrow.' Then she walked out, arm in arm with Mr. Walker."

On September 1 Bessie returned to the studio for another duet session with Clara Smith. Columbia, presumably regarding duet singing as half a job, paid Bessie a fee of only one hundred dollars per side for this date. "Down Old Georgia Way" was rejected (the master is presumably lost); "My Man Blues" survived, and is infinitely superior to their previous joint effort. Bessie and Clara engage in a humorous dialogue—part of which is spoken—discover that their man is one and the same, and agree that they will have to "have him on the cooperation plan."

Those who heard Bessie in the years right after World War I, when she teamed up with Hazel Green and others, cite her duets with Clara—particularly "My Man Blues"—as a throwback to that period in her life. Clara's voice shows a fine development. On the earlier duets it had sounded thin compared to Bessie's; now it approached the power if not the richness of her famous collaborator.

After the session with Clara, Bessie prepared to return south. Her tent show had now wound up its tour in Atlanta—the depot there served as a winter storage for her new railroad car, paid for in full with income from its first tour. Atlanta became the traditional last

Two hundred dollars per usable side was the most Bessie ever received from Columbia Records. Notice the half payment for a duet with Clara Smith. *Page from a Columbia Records ledger.*

stop for the tent tours, around Labor Day, and the troupe made its way back to New York playing one- or two-week engagements in T.O.B.A. theatres.

"We always had a lot of fun in Atlanta," recalls Ruby, "because Bessie had so many friends there, and the people loved her so. That's where the garbage man sold liquor in the streets, he'd push this big can on wheels through the alley near the theatre, shouting 'Garbage man, garbage man,' and the people would run out there with their whiskey glasses and buy that bad liquor from his can. Bessie didn't buy from him—she had to have it by the half gallon, and she'd buy it from a man who lived under the viaduct, near the boardinghouse where we stayed. One time the police caught me getting some liquor for Bessie. I was runnin' with this half gallon, and to make it worse, it was after the twelve-o'clock curfew, so they put me in jail overnight—it was nothing for us to spend a night in jail."

Bessie's show was scheduled to open at the Frolic in Birmingham September 7, but Bessie went to Atlanta first because she had promised Charles Bailey, the white owner of the "81," that she would do a couple of performances for whites.

Bailey never allowed entertainers to enter the theatre through the front; he thought it improper for the audience to get a glimpse before showtime. In order to get to the stage entrance, you had to go through the yard that Bessie had rehearsed in as a young girl, now strewn with garbage and infested with rats. Rule or no rule, Bessie was not about to pick her way through such filth. She grabbed Ruby's arm and led her past the box office and into the theatre through the front door. Bailey caught up with them just as they entered the auditorium.

"It's me, goddammit," said Bessie as he approached, "and I ain't goin' no other way."

"Take it easy, Bessie," Bailey whispered. "If they see you before the show, they won't find you as interesting."

"I don't give a fuck," said Bessie, not bothering to lower her voice, "and if you don't like it, kiss my black ass and give me my drops." Then she strutted down the aisle, drawing stares from some astonished patrons. Bailey shrugged his shoulders and let her go—he knew Bessie meant what she said. "I knew he wasn't going to make a big thing out of it," recalls Ruby, "because when she got mad or drunk, it was nothing for Bessie to jump up and pull those curtains.

I've seen her pull those drops down—hanging on them. She'd pull them down anywhere if the theatre owner said the wrong thing."

While rehearsing in New York, Bessie had bought a new pair of dancing shoes for Ruby. The purchase infuriated a less favored chorine, who took the shoes that night and cut them into shreds of silk and leather. Ruby was unaware of what had happened, but Bessie caught the girl. After blasting the chorine with obscenities, Bessie looked as if she might attack the girl physically, but the girl beat her to it. Hurling a Coca-Cola bottle across the room, she barely missed her target.

"You close here, baby," Bessie screamed. "Get your stuff together, and don't let me see your damn face again."

"You ain't so much," was the angry retort.

"Never mind the damn argument, you get the fuck out of here."

The chorine was asking for trouble, "I ain't stayin', you better believe that," she said, "but I ain't leavin' either, until I get good and ready."

Bessie wasn't going to stand for more. The ensuing fight, which all but wrecked the hotel room, lasted until other members of the troupe managed to break it up.

Bleeding and disheveled, the chorine summoned the police and pressed charges against Bessie, who was taken to jail. Before they took her away, Bessie asked Agie to get an advance from Charles Bailey and give it to Ruby so that she could arrange for the bail.

Ruby heard about the melee the next morning. When she called Bailey he told her that he had given Agie the money—over a thousand dollars. Agie was nowhere to be found. Taking advantage of Ruby's condition—she had too much to drink—he had caught a cab for Birmingham, where he planned to board a Detroit-bound train. Bailey placed a call to the Birmingham police and had Agie stopped. Thus ended *that* romance.

On Sunday night, September 6, Ma Rainey's all-star review was closing at Birmingham's Frolic Theatre, with Bessie and her troupe—now minus two performers—due for a Labor Day opening the following afternoon. They were booked for two weeks, to be followed by another two weeks at the Frolic in nearby Bessemer. A streetcar ride separated the two theatres, so Bessie and her gang decided to stay at the same hotel for four weeks, commuting during the last two.

Arriving at the Birmingham hotel a day before their opening,

Bessie wanted to rest after the eventful stay in Atlanta, but as soon as she heard that Ma Rainey was in town, she asked Ruby to go with her to the Frolic. That suited Ruby fine. She'd been hearing about the legendary Mother of the Blues for years, but she had never met her or heard her sing. If Bessie bothered to catch her act, she had to be something special.

Ma's closing show was already in progress when they entered the packed theatre. Whistling Rufus—one of Ma's top performers, who later made it on his own—was finishing off his act with some fancy knee drops, accompanied by a lady pianist.

Bessie secured a seat for Ruby in a box close to the stage and disappeared through a small door as Rufus took a bow and his audience thundered approval.

As the ovation died down and Ma Rainey's five-piece Georgia Jazz Band began assembling in the pit, the restless audience fell silent. Suddenly someone in the balcony shouted "The Phaaantuhm," and a growing chorus of voices from all parts of the theatre joined in.

Lon Chaney's silent movie *The Phantom of the Opera* had recently received widespread publicity, and Ruby assumed the shouts to be a sign of its popularity.

"The phaaantuhm—the phaaantuhm." When the Georgia Jazz Band started playing, the shouts grew louder as the curtain rose to reveal a giant replica of a Victrola, bathed in a bluish hue on the otherwise darkened stage.

From inside this huge cabinet there rose a familiar, gravelly voice, its delivery of a mournful song undeterred by the commotion out front. When the enormous doors of the cabinet swung open, the audience chatter stopped and Ruby realized that Ma Rainey, not Lon Chaney, was the phantom of the Frolic.

Looking closer to fifty than to her real age of thirty-nine, Ma Rainey was no beauty by anyone's standards, but neither did she deserve the reputation for having—as black performers liked to put it—"the ugliest face in show business." ("Ma, there are two things I've never seen," vaudeville performer Billy Gunn once told her. "That's an ugly woman and a pretty monkey." "Bless you, darling," was Ma's reply.) With her thick straightened hair sticking out in all directions, gold caps on her huge teeth, a fan of ostrich plumes in her hand, and a long triple necklace of shiny gold coins reflecting the blue spotlight that danced on her sequined black dress, Ma was a sight to behold.

Gertrude "Ma" Rainey, 1924. The Phantom of the Frolic had inner beauty. *Photo courtesy of Frank Driggs.*

Ethel Waters, early 1920's. They called her "Sweet Mama Stringbean,"
but to Bessie she was "one of them Northern bitches." *Photo courtesy
of Frank Driggs.*

Her audience had been rude to her, but she took it with good humor; it was obvious that they loved her as much as they loved Bessie. In fact, Southern audiences sometimes preferred Ma's more earthy delivery, material, and accompaniment to Bessie's, and Ma rarely appeared in the North.

> . . . Now all the people wonder why I'm
> all alone;
> A sissy shook that thing, and took my
> man from home.

Her fans screamed. "Amens!" filled the air. Three songs left them whistling for more, but it was time for Danny Rainey, "The World's Greatest Juvenile Stepper," to go into his act. Danny was the Rainey's adopted son. (Those who knew Ma and Pa Rainey say that's the only way they could possibly have got a child; the idea of Ma Rainey in a mother's role sends them into hysterics.)

During Danny's performance, Bessie emerged from the wings and signaled Ruby to come backstage.

"There's a phantom—" Ruby began, but Bessie hushed her up. "Don't say that in front of Ma," she said. "She's a sweet lady, and I want you to meet her."

When Ma Rainey made her entrance shortly thereafter Mother and Empress locked in a warm embrace. Ma had some time left before her final appearance onstage, so she and Bessie sat down and talked for twenty minutes or so.

One of the things they laughed about was an incident that apparently had happened earlier that year. It seemed that Ma had found herself in an embarrassing tangle with the Chicago police. She and a group of young ladies had been drinking and were making so much noise that a neighbor summoned the police. Unfortunately for Ma and her girls, the law arrived just as the impromptu party got intimate. There was pandemonium as everyone madly scrambled for her clothes and ran out the back door. Ma, clutching someone else's dress, was the last to exit, but a nasty fall down a staircase foiled her escape. Accusing her of running an indecent party, the police threw her in jail, and Bessie bailed her out the following morning.

Ruby, having heard the two blues queens laugh and talk that evening, never believed stories about rivalry or bad feelings between Ma and Bessie.

Bessie didn't return to Philadelphia until October. She had worked hard during the past months and seemed ready to enjoy some home life with Jack. Certainly there were moments when she preferred the relatively quiet Philadelphia living. She stayed home and cooked for Jack, jumped over the fence in her housecoat to visit with neighbors, and enjoyed an occasional card game. This was the closest Bessie ever came to leading a normal married life, but even these periods, frequently interrupted by performances or recording dates, lasted only until she grew restless again.

Bessie had a fairly busy recording schedule for the rest of the year and, as usual, a number of new songs to learn. The first session was scheduled for November, when she would have another go at "I Wish I Could Shimmy Like My Sister Kate," the tune she had recorded at her abortive Okeh audition almost three years earlier. Also planned was a new version of an early hit, "Gulf Coast Blues," for which Clarence Williams had written new lyrics, and "Florida Bound Blues."

In mid-October she arrived at the house on 132nd Street to rehearse for the record dates. She never really liked New York, didn't like having to dress up every time she went out instead of running around in her housecoat and slippers the way she did in Philadelphia.

Clara Smith, who had spent the summer headlining the show at New York's newly renovated Lafayette Theatre, was still in town, and Columbia was about to release "My Man Blues," one of the sides Clara had recorded with Bessie the month before.

Writers have often alluded to the bad feeling between Bessie and Clara. Their tenures with Columbia coincided, their records were aimed at the same market, and they frequently used the same accompanists, though Frank Walker saw to it that they never duplicated each other's material. A certain professional rivalry must indeed have existed, but there is no evidence to support the stories that it was either personal or intense from the beginning.

Bessie certainly had no reason to feel threatened. Her records consistently outsold Clara's; Columbia paid her twice as much for recording and gave her preferential treatment on advertising and promotion. Any bitterness between the two stars would probably have originated with Clara, but surviving contemporaries say that the two were, at least on the surface, personal friends for a long time.

The friendship ended late that year at a party in New York. Bessie and Clara had been drinking, and a heated exchange over something, or someone, led to a fist fight. As might be expected, Bessie beat the daylights out of Clara. They never recorded together again, and so far as is known they never spoke to each other after that evening in 1925.

At about this time Leigh Whipper, as manager of Newark's Orpheum Theatre, offered Bessie a thousand dollars to play there all of Thanksgiving week. A few days after the deal had been made, Whipper attended a meeting called by Carl Van Vechten to plan what was later to become the James Weldon Johnson Memorial Collection of Negro Arts and Letters. When Whipper mentioned that Bessie would be appearing soon at the Orpheum, Van Vechten, a forty-five-year-old journalist who had a strong interest in black culture, asked if he might bring a party of ten people to the theatre on Thanksgiving night. He had collected Bessie's records for two years, and he had yet to hear her in person.

Whipper reserved a box for the ten-o'clock show, and Van Vechten filled it with prominent friends, including humorist Robert Benchley and Arthur Spingarn, an early supporter and later president of the N.A.A.C.P.

"I must say all of us enjoyed a mood of the highest anticipatory expectation," Van Vechten wrote years later. "It would be no exaggeration to assert that we felt as we might have felt before going to a Salzburg Festival to hear Lilli Lehmann sing Donna Anna in *Don Giovanni*."[8]

By 1947, when Van Vechten wrote his description of the 1925 event, black music was no longer regarded as a novelty. By then it had its own critics, and the wide-eyed wonderment of the twenties had changed to a more straightforward appraisal of the music and its performers. Van Vechten's account seems anachronistic, but it does give us a white intellectual's impression of Bessie at a time when few such people had recognized her talent:

> She was at this time the size of Fay Templeton in her Weber and Fields days, which means very large, and she wore a crimson satin robe, sweeping up from her trim ankles, and embroidered in multicolored sequins in designs. Her face was beautiful with the rich ripe beauty of southern darkness, a deep bronze, matching the bronze of her bare arms. Walking slowly to the footlights, to the accompaniment of the wailing, muted brasses, the monotonous African pounding of the drum, the dromedary glide of the pianist's fingers over the responsive keys, she began her

8. "Memories of Bessie Smith," *Jazz Records*, September 1947, p. 6.

strange, rhythmic rites in a voice full of shouting and moaning and praying and suffering, a wild, rough, Ethiopian voice, harsh and volcanic, but seductive and sensuous too, released between rouged lips and the whitest of teeth, the singer swaying slightly to the beat, as is the Negro custom:

"Yo' brag to women I was yo' fool, so den I got dose sobbin' hahted Blues." Celebrating her unfortunate love adventures, the Blues are the Negro's prayer to a cruel Cupid.

Now, inspired partly by the powerfully magnetic personality of this elemental conjure woman with her plangent African voice, quivering with passion and pain, sounding as if it had been developed at the sources of the Nile, the black and blue-black crowd, notable for the absence of mulattoes, burst into hysterical, semi-religious shrieks of sorrow and lamentation. Amens rent the air. Little nervous giggles, like the shattering of Venetian glass, shocked our nerves. When Bessie proclaimed, "It's true I loves you, but I won't take mistreatment any mo," a girl sitting beneath our box called "Dat's right! Say it, sister!"

After the curtain had fallen, Leigh Whipper guided us back stage where he introduced us to Bessie Smith and this proved to be exactly the same experience that meeting any great interpreter is likely to be: we paid our homages humbly and she accepted them with just the right amount of deference.

I believe I kissed her hand. I hope I did.

The Orpheum had made a good investment in Bessie. During her seven-day stay there she played to capacity audiences at each performance, despite the fact that ticket prices had been raised for the occasion: matinees were twenty-five cents in the balcony and fifty cents downstairs; evening prices were twice that.

Several times police had to be called to control the crowds outside the theatre. This sort of turnout, combined with her high record sales, hardly supported the contention of some that Bessie's type of blues was on the wane. Just two weeks before Bessie started packing them in at the Orpheum, the Chicago *Defender's* William Potter had taken a pessimistic look at the future of the blues ladies:

### THE BLUES SINGER

The profession is facing another climax. The day of the straight blues singer is passing. No doubt, there are many who will discount this statement, nevertheless, it is true and, being on the inside looking out, it is an easy matter to see how things are breaking. In the first place, as an attraction theatrically the blues singer has lost a hold. People will not go to the theater just to hear a blues singer. They have their radios and phonographs and they don't have to attend the theater to hear them. Salaries, according to direct reports, are cut. This proves that the straight blues singer generally is not an attraction within herself. They must feature some sort of novelty along with their regular line of work in order to even get

# 5

*I got a letter from my daddy, he bought*
*me a sweet piece of land;*
*I got a letter from my daddy, he bought*
*me a small piece of ground;*
*You can't blame me for leavin', Lawd,*
*I'm Florida bound.*
                    "Florida Bound Blues"

The Florida land boom reached its peak in the mid-twenties. A spectacular real estate venture, it sent thousands of American *nouveaux riches* to the Sunshine State in search of fun and fortune, rivaled the California gold rush of '49, and gave birth to that capital of gaucherie, Miami.

Black people were, of course, excluded from the Florida frolics, and Bessie's world was as far removed from the Addison Mizner architectural mish-mash that characterized the new resort as her "Florida Bound Blues" was from Jan Garber's rendition of "When the Moon Shines on Coral Gables." There was bitter humor in Bessie's tale, but a bit of parental advice contained in the last verse was a warning to any black who might seriously be Florida-bound:

*My papa told me, my mama told me, too;*
*Don't let them bell-bottom britches*
*make a fool out of you.*

As it turned out, the "bell-bottom britches"—the white elite who romped around Palm Beach and Coral Gables in yachting outfits—were making fools of themselves: the release of Bessie's record, in

February 1926, coincided with the public exposure of giant real estate frauds and a collapse of the new empire so devastating that it has been described as a dress rehearsal for the stock market crash of 1929.

The Florida land boom and the antics of the idle rich that went with it did not directly affect the lives of black people except those who found employment there as servants. But ghetto residents in Atlanta, Chicago, Detroit, and New York were kept well informed of such goings on through the verbal reports of Pullman porters.

White people were often the subjects of ghetto humor, which perceptively penetrated their veneer of self-importance: it was a case of Mammy's white child never growing up. In one sense, black people knew more about white people than white people knew about them.

Unlike most white show business stars, who could ill afford to have their real private life exposed to the public, Bessie did not have to observe the cautions of her white counterparts. The only person from whom she had to hide her indiscretions was Jack. As her career reached its zenith, she was having more and more sexual relationships outside her marriage, drinking more heavily, and partying whenever she got the chance. As far as she was concerned, Jack was still her man, but he rarely drank and he didn't approve of her extramarital activities—even the most innocent ones—so the gap that separated their life-styles continued to widen. No legal document, no marriage certificate, was going to change Bessie's way of living.

Jack wasn't around as much as he had been, and his absences—for which he did not always have a legitimate excuse—gave Bessie more opportunities for a good time. He had a way of showing up suddenly during her tours, so Bessie and Ruby were always alert. In fact, a series of explosive meetings between Jack and Bessie now kept the whole company on its toes. When Jack did show up, an argument or fight usually ensued, followed by a reconciliation and a brief period during which Bessie was on her best behavior.

This sort of cat-and-mouse game eventually affected everybody who traveled with Bessie, and it wasn't long before they were all afraid of Jack. "Jack was the fightingest man you've ever seen," recalls Ruby. "He'd walk into a room hittin'. Every time they had their fights he'd hit her so hard I'd think he was going to kill her, and I'd butt in and he'd slap me down like I wasn't even there—and I got tired of getting beat up on account of Bessie."

Bessie's popularity had leveled off now, without actually declining; she was still commanding higher salaries and selling more records[1] than her blues-singing contemporaries, although such singers as Ethel Waters and Josephine Baker were attracting wider attention: Miss Baker was thrilling Parisians in *La Revue Nègre,* and was about to open at the Folies-Bergère, while Miss Waters would soon entertain the Prince of Wales in London. Bessie was never to travel farther east than Long Island.

Bessie's male blues-singing counterparts were hardly a threat: their live performances were relegated to street corners, back roads, and traveling medicine shows, and they were virtually ignored by the press, who referred to blues only in the urban female terms Bessie represented. If there was any competition from the male country blues singers, it was in the field of recordings, but Bessie hardly felt it. Her records were still outselling even Ethel Waters', and Columbia continued to renew her contract each year.

What *was* affecting Bessie financially was her heavy drinking. Liquor could turn the hardworking performer who ran her shows with military discipline into a mean drunk who thought nothing of breaking a contract and leaving a troupe stranded penniless in some godforsaken town. As the novelty of fame wore off, this side of Bessie emerged more often.

Those close to Bessie during this period agree that marital problems provoked her heavy drinking and increasingly erratic behavior. The attentive Jack, who had accompanied her on the first tent tours, discouraged her appetite for alcohol, and taken a positive interest in her work, now spent most of his time pursuing other interests. He no longer sat in the audience, ready to fine those who got out of step. When he did show up it was usually because he needed money.

They say he did a lot of hunting—at least that was the excuse given for many of his absences—but Bessie probably sensed that she was not the only promiscuous member of the Gee family.

After two and a half years of marriage, the Gees were still childless, and perhaps Bessie was attempting to save what so briefly had been a happy relationship when she decided to add another member to her immediate family: Maggie's niece had long been ready to make good her promise to let Bessie have Snooks, and now Bessie, too, was ready.

1. Columbia pressed 27,675 copies of Bessie's "I've Been Mistreated and I Don't Like It," as opposed to 12,200 of a Clara Smith recording released at the same time, January 1926.

A few weeks later, in the spring of 1926, the six-year-old boy was brought aboard the railroad car in Macon, Georgia. "Bessie was very proud of Snooks," recalls Maud, who immediately assumed the unofficial role of governess. "He cried, screamed, and hollered that day when I gave him a needed bath, but Bessie was so thrilled that it sounded like music to her." Snooks was taken along for the rest of the tour, and once they returned to Philadelphia, Bessie and Jack legally adopted him and named him Jack, Jr. Now, more than ever, Bessie was determined to bring her family up from Chattanooga: someone had to take care of the boy while she and Jack were away.

Bessie knew perfectly well how Jack felt about moving her family to Philadelphia. She had often announced such plans, but so far without taking any positive steps. Now she had both the means and a legitimate excuse.

While she was preparing Jack for the move, she made him a gift of the finest car she could find, a very special 1926 Cadillac (the two-year-old Nash had been stolen some time earlier). As with the Nash, the new car was purchased on impulse: Bessie and Jack, waiting for a trolley to take them to the theatre, happened to be standing in front of the Scott and Smith showroom at Broad and Fairmount. Jack was admiring an eye-catching Cadillac convertible in the window.

"That's a beautiful car," she said. "Do you like it?"

Jack nodded. "Then I'll get it for you tomorrow," said Bessie.

The following day she went to the showroom, pointed to the car, and told the startled salesman, "I'll take that one." The salesman explained that this was a very special automobile, that it was intended as a showpiece, and that only two such cars had been made. Then he tried to talk her into looking at some of the other models, but Bessie's mind was made up.

"That's the car I came here for," she said, "and I ain't buyin' any of them others."

The salesman made a final attempt to discourage her: "Lady, if you want that car it will cost you five thousand dollars."

"I'll take it," she said, "and I'm going to pay cash for it." She dipped into her pocket and handed him the money.

Jack was not at all happy at the prospect of Bessie's moving her family up from Chattanooga, but the new car somehow lessened the pain. Bessie's next step was to rent two adjoining houses at 1143 and 1147 Kater Street near the Standard Theatre, one for the oldest

LEFT: Jack Gee, Jr. as he looked at the time of his mother's death. *Photo by Woodard, from the Afro-American.* RIGHT: Jack Gee, Jr., today. His father kept him a secret for thirty-three years. *Photo courtesy of Jack Gee, Jr.*

sister, Viola, her daughter Laura, and grandson Buster; the other for her sisters Lulu and Tinnie and Tinnie's two sons. Clarence Smith was, of course, already in the North, working as a comedian with her show and handling her business, and Andrew Smith preferred to remain in Chattanooga, where he was comfortably situated with a family of his own and a good job as turnkey in a local prison.

While Jack made two trips to Chattanooga to move her family, Bessie went to New York to record. She did four sides on March 5, accompanied by Clarence Williams. It was her first contact with Williams since their stormy meeting in his office in 1923, but Frank Walker had talked Bessie into letting bygones be bygones. Jack was less forgiving, and it would appear that in an effort to maintain peace in the family, Bessie tried to keep him from knowing about her working with Williams on her new records. She specifically requested that his name not be printed on the labels. Williams' playing is as pedestrian as ever on these sides, but Bessie is unusually exuberant on "What's the Matter Now?" and "I Want Ev'ry Bit of It," written by Williams, and she almost outdid herself on "Squeeze Me," a tune

Williams is said to have written in collaboration with Fats Waller. It's obvious who picked the repertoire for the session—Clarence Williams was up to his old tricks.

Another session took place March 18. With Fletcher Henderson at the piano and Buster Bailey on clarinet, she did "Jazzbo Brown from Memphis Town," a gusty novelty number about a "clarinet hound" who "don't play no fancy stuff like them Hoffmann Tales, but what he plays is good enough for the Prince of Wales," and "The Gin House Blues,"[2] which many like to think is autobiographical.

At this point in her life, Bessie's happiness easily outweighed her sorrows: her family was with her at last, and she had a son. Those who knew her could hardly imagine Bessie in a mother's role, but she took to it heart and soul. Nothing was too good for little Jack; Bessie was generous with gifts and affection, and she spoke of the child with tremendous pride. Even Jack seemed to be pleased with the new addition to the family, at least in the beginning.

Viola was given the job of caring for little Jack in Bessie's absence. She and the rest of the family were now well provided for; none of them worked—except, of course, Clarence and Teejay—and Bessie saw to it that they lacked nothing.

Stories of how Bessie and Jack "squandered" some sixteen thousand dollars during the early part of 1926 still circulate, suggesting that the two of them went on a spending spree.[3] The implication is usually that Jack mismanaged his wife's affairs, but his alleged control over Bessie's finances is grossly exaggerated. The fact is that—even in the twenties—a new Cadillac, the rental and furnishings of two houses, and moving seven people from Chattanooga to Philadelphia could easily consume such a sum.

Bessie decided to forgo her usual summer schedule in 1926 so she could spend some time with little Jack and get her family properly situated. Her sisters and their children soon began to take Bessie's generosity for granted, but if she realized this, she didn't seem to care.

Jack, on the other hand, was perfectly aware of the situation: neither Viola, Tinnie, nor Lulu had any intention of working. Bessie

2. Not to be confused with Nina Simone's recording of the same title, which is actually "Me and My Gin," another tune from Bessie Smith's recorded repertoire.
3. Some reports add that she purchased a house for total strangers or, at best, casual acquaintances.

had been the breadwinner of the family for many years. Clarence, who had always supported himself, was now also helping out, and the Smith sisters knew neither Bessie nor Clarence would let them down. They also knew how Jack felt about them—and their complacency annoyed him no end. Jack, obviously in an awkward position, tried repeatedly to tell Bessie that she was being taken advantage of and pointed out that much of her money was going to support her sisters' drinking habits. Bessie, fully aware of his strong prejudices, refused to listen.

Adding more fuel to Jack's jealousy was Bessie's new financial arrangement: "She sent all her money home to Viola," Maud remembers. "It was all deposited in the First National Bank, but in Viola's name. When Jack wanted money, he had to wire Bessie, and she would tell him to get it from Viola, so he would have to go to the bank with her and wait while she drew out whatever amount Bessie said Jack could have. As for Bessie herself, when she needed money on the road she always wired Frank Walker or Sam Reevin for an advance."

During mid-1926 Bessie slowed down her professional activities, but she didn't stop working altogether. The results of a May recording date with Fletcher Henderson and Joe Smith show that her artistry hadn't stopped developing. "Money Blues," "Baby Doll," "Hard Driving Papa," and "Lost Your Head Blues" are superb. They were also commercially successful, selling a total of fifty-three thousand copies within a few months of their release. This figure hardly compared with the sales of her first recordings, but the initial blues boom was long past, and the race record market had become even more competitive as electric recording techniques brought needed clarity to instrumental jazz.[4] In view of this and in comparison to other sales figures of the day, fifty-three thousand (in the race field) was easily equivalent to today's million sellers. In fact, Columbia records was now doing so well that it bought out Okeh, one of its major competitors in the race record field.

After an unusually quiet and sober summer in Philadelphia, it was time for Bessie to go back to work in earnest. Her expenditures over the past few months had far exceeded her income. Normally it would

4. Added competition came from the white comedy team of Charles Correll and Freeman Gosden, whose racist dialogues as "Sam 'n' Henry" now began to appear on the Victor label, with blacks accounting for an astonishing percentage of sales. Correll and Gosden later gained an even bigger following as radio's "Amos 'n' Andy."

have been time for a T.O.B.A. tour, but the circuit was being reorganized, so Bessie decided to hit the Southern tent trail. Even though the tent season was officially over, the weather was still warm enough for such a tour, and Bessie wanted to use her new railroad car again.

In New York Bessie assembled and rehearsed a troupe of entertainers, including comedian Dinah Scott, who would also function as stage manager; Dinah's wife, Gertrude; Clarence Smith; a chorus of young ladies, including Maud, whom Clarence had recently married; and a six-piece band under the direction of pianist Bill Woods.

In late October, after a month of successful touring with this company, Bessie returned to New York for another recording session. Ruby, who had stayed in New York this time, had often asked Bessie to take her to the studio. On October 25 she finally got her chance. While Bessie and Fletcher Henderson were running through "Honey Man Blues," Ruby made the mistake of suggesting to Frank Walker that he record her, too. She had been practicing Bessie's style and she felt she was ready to step out of the background.

Bessie, although she was singing, hadn't missed a thing. As soon as she heard Ruby talking to Walker she threw her sheet music in the air and started shouting: "You ain't gonna take *my* place, you little bitch." She vowed on the spot never to take Ruby to another recording session. She never did.

Bessie was too dependent on Ruby to stay angry at her for long. Before the day was over, Bessie had promised to take Ruby with her when she rejoined her tour, and the two women spent the remainder of the day and evening making the rounds of their favorite hangouts, armed with a six-hundred-dollar advance Bessie had received from Frank Walker that day. "We'd walk into a joint," recalls Ruby, "and Bessie would say 'Here's a hundred dollars. Set the house up and don't let nobody out and nobody in.' and she enjoyed getting everybody drunk with her. I would be running behind her saying 'Give me the change,' because people used to take advantage of her and keep the change."

Bessie tried to keep Jack from discovering several aspects of her private life, such as the wide range of her sexual tastes. Fortunately Jack could not read; otherwise he might have seen a short item in a black gossip paper called the *Interstate Tattler*. Its publisher, Floyd Snelson, made other people's business his business; very little escaped him or agents who tipped him off to the latest dirt from different parts of the country. "Look out for Snelson" was common advice in Harlem, and the enterprising publisher had more than one violent clash with an irate victim. His item on Bessie appeared in the paper's "Town Tattle" column on February 27, 1925, under the by-line "I. Telonyou":

> Gladys, if you don't keep away from B., G. is going to do a little convincing that he is her husband. Aren't you capable of finding some unexplored land "all alone."

Fortunately for Snelson, Bessie, who was said to be chummy with male impersonator Gladys Ferguson at that time, neither saw nor heard about the item.

It is not known at what stage in her life Bessie began to embrace her own sex. Some have assumed that Ma Rainey, who was similarly inclined, initiated her, but this theory is supported by no more evidence than the improbable story of Bessie's "kidnapping." But by late 1926, when Lillian Simpson entered her life, Bessie's sexual relationships included women.

Like many young girls, Lillian, who had been a schoolmate of Ruby's, romanticized show business life. At sixteen her head was filled with hazy pictures of life on the road; her heart was set on becoming, at the least, a chorine. Ruby's tales of her touring experience impressed Lillian and she persuaded Ruby to teach her a few dance steps. Ruby then arranged an impromptu audition before Bessie in the Gee living room on 132nd Street. The last thing the show needed was another chorus girl, but Lillian's mother had once been Bessie's wardrobe mistress, so Bessie finally gave in, and even started teaching the young girl some additional steps.

And so Bessie headed south with Ruby and Lillian, joining her *Harlem Frolics* company in Ozark, Alabama, on the first of November. They were playing the smaller communities—Eufaula, Alabama, and the little Georgia towns of Dawson, Americus, and Albany—but by the end of November it was time to pack up the tent and continue the tour on the reorganized T.O.B.A. theatre circuit.

Jack, who had stayed with the show while Bessie was in New York, left it when she returned. His departure was as dramatic as it was unexpected. Just before the troupe got ready to pull out of Ozark, a chorus girl told Bessie that while she was in New York, Jack had "messed around" with another chorus girl.

Without taking time to check out the story, Bessie jumped the girl, beat her up, and threw her off the railroad car, which was still parked on a dead track, waiting to be coupled to an outgoing train. The girl landed in the middle of an adjoining track. Suffering some physical pain as well as intense embarrassment, she screamed at the top of her lungs while Bessie, cursing, disappeared back into the car. Moments later, she returned with her arms full of the girl's personal effects and threw them out on the track. Then she stormed through the railroad car looking for Jack.

"Come out, you motherless bastard," she screamed, as the rest of the troupe huddled in fearful anticipation of the inevitable encounter to follow.

Bessie didn't find Jack on the car—he had gone into town for some last-minute business—but she found his gun, and when she came out of their stateroom, Jack was standing over the sobbing girl, trying to find out what had happened.

A shot rang out. Bessie stood on the rear platform of the car, gun in hand.

"You no good two-timing bastard," she shouted, waving the gun in the air. "I couldn't even go to New York and record without you fuckin' around with these damn chorus bitches. Well, I'm gonna make you remember me today."

Jack started toward her. "Put that gun down, Bessie." Another shot sent him racing down the track. Bessie jumped off the platform and went after him, emptying the gun. "I've never seen Jack run so fast," recalls Ruby. "Everybody was scared to death that Bessie would kill him this time, but I think she missed him on purpose." A couple of hours later the troupe left Ozark without Jack.

Bessie had been on good behavior for several months, and now she was ready for some fun. Jack's departure after the alleged indiscretion provided both the opportunity and the excuse.

The troupe spent Christmas of 1926 on the road somewhere in Tennessee, where Bessie threw a small party for her gang. She went out and got eggs, milk, and liquor for eggnog, but after the girls had beaten the eggs and added sugar and liquor, Bessie had second thoughts about the milk—it seemed a shame to dilute that good corn liquor any further. The resulting concoction left no one sober.

As the party showed signs of ending, Bessie approached Ruby, cocked her head in Lillian's direction, and said, "I *like* that gal."

Ruby assumed that she was referring to Lillian's dance routine, which had improved in the past month. "I'm glad you like her—she's doing good, ain't she?"

"No, I don't mean that," said her aunt. "I'll tell her myself, 'cause you don't know *nothin'*, child." Whereupon she walked over to Lillian, whispered something to her, and led her out of the room.

Ruby and Lillian shared a room, but when Ruby awoke the next day she saw that Lillian had not slept in her bed. No one in the troupe was shocked when Lillian and Bessie began sleeping together regularly. The one thing the members of the *Harlem Frolics* company were worried about was Jack's sudden, inevitable return.

Lillian herself seemed to adjust to her relationship with Bessie as quickly as she had adjusted to the other unorthodox aspects of her newly chosen profession. The day after her initiation, she confessed to Ruby what was going on, suggesting that Ruby didn't know what she was missing, and that she "try it" with Boula Lee, a chorus girl who was also the wife of the show's musical director, Bill Woods. Boula had made subtle passes at Ruby, but Bessie had warned her niece that she'd be sent home if she fooled around with any of the girls in the show.

Several days later, Bessie was on stage at the Frolic Theatre in Bessemer, Alabama, singing; the chorus was ready to go on. Ruby, first in line, stood in the wings not far from where Bessie was performing. Ruby had developed a boil under her left arm, and was holding her painful left arm in the air. Concentrating on her cue, she did not notice Dinah Scott sneaking up behind her. He grabbed her under the arms and Ruby let out a scream.

Bessie kept on singing, but she jerked her head in Ruby's direction and frowned: she never tolerated any noise from backstage during a performance. Helen, another chorine, ran forward with a tissue and put her arms around Ruby while she gently daubed at what was left of the boil.

Boula, looking on from the other side of the stage, misunderstood Helen's intentions. Shortly after the curtain came down, she stomped over to Ruby and asked her to step outside. "You ain't gonna mess around with them other bitches," she said, then lunged forward and scratched Ruby's face. Ruby fought back, and the two were deeply entangled when Bessie made a sudden appearance.

"I know Jack's gonna blame me for this," said Bessie, separating the two and knocking Boula clear across the small alley.

Jack was due to join the show that night, and when he showed up, Bessie was ready for him. Several members of the troupe were sitting in her room when Jack entered and looked around. "What y'all doin' up here drinkin'?"

"Nobody been drinkin' any liquor, nigger," said Bessie. "You're not in the police force, you're in show business, so don't come in here pushin' on people all the damn time."

During this exchange Ruby had been standing with her back to Jack. When Jack asked her to turn around, she explained—as her aunt had instructed her—that her face was scratched because she and some of the girls had fought over costumes. Bessie was adding a few details when Bill Woods, who had been standing quietly in the corner, blurted out, "It was one of them bulldykers who's after Ruby."

"What do you mean *one* of them?" Bessie shouted. "It was *your* wife!"

Jack grabbed Boula, carried her into the hall, threw her down the stairs, and ordered Woods to send her home. While Jack was out of the room, Bessie noticed the fear in Lillian's face. Turning to Ruby, she said, "Whatever you do, you better not tell on me and Lillian."

On January 10, 1927, Bessie's show began a week's engagement at the Booker Washington Theatre in St. Louis. Jack had left the troupe again, and Bessie and Lillian continued their affair. On their first day in St. Louis, Bessie entered the room shared by Ruby and Lillian. She walked up behind Lillian, leaned forward, and kissed her.

Embarrassed, Lillian looked at Ruby and jerked away. "Don't play around with me like that," she said.

Bessie grabbed her around the waist. "Is that how you feel?"

"Yes!" Lillian said. "That's *exactly* how I feel."

"The hell with you, bitch," said Bessie. "I got twelve women on this show and I can have one every night if I want it. Don't you feel so important, and don't you say another word to me while you're on this show, or I'll send you home bag and baggage."

For three days and nights Bessie ignored Lillian totally. On the fourth night Lillian did not show up at the theatre. The show went on without her, but as soon as the curtain fell Bessie started to worry. "She's just tryin' to pout," she told Ruby. Just then, Maud burst into the room. "I had left the theatre and gone into the hotel," she recalls. "When I passed Lillian's room, I saw an envelope sticking out from under the door. The door was locked, so I pulled the envelope out, opened it and saw that it was a suicide note. That's when I ran back to the theatre to get Bessie."

Without taking time to read the note, Bessie, with Ruby and Maud at her heels, ran next door to the hotel. When they reached Lillian's door, they smelled gas. Bessie tried to force the door, panicked, rushed downstairs, and got the proprietor. When he let them in, they found Lillian lying across the bed, unconscious. The proprietor had to break the windowpanes: Lillian had nailed the window shut. She was taken in an ambulance to the nearest hospital.

Bessie didn't sleep that night. The next morning she went to the hospital and got Lillian out. The episode apparently put an end to Lillian's inhibitions. "From that day on," says Ruby, "she didn't care where or when Bessie kissed her—she got real bold."

Bessie and company played the Roosevelt Theatre in Cincinnati during the week of January 17, and opened at the Grand in Chicago the following Monday. The *Defender*'s review was shorter than usual, but no less enthusiastic:

> Bessie Smith and her unit fairly took Chicago by storm last Monday night, Jan. 24, when the curtain descended on her fine show. The house was packed and a large crowd waited outside for the second show. You know one show a night will not accommodate the Chicago lovers of the empress of the blues. She is a real blues artist and an actor, too. She works all through the show, well showing her versatility. Bessie Smith is the largest box office draw the T.O.B.A. has today.

After the final show on opening night, Richard Morgan sent a car to bring Bessie and her party to one of his popular after-hours gatherings. As usual, the place was packed, and the noise level threatened to drown out the sound of the music. Pianist Cow Cow Davenport was accompanying a young lady with a weak voice who was trying to sing a blues song.

Suddenly a deep, rich voice commanded attention. "Hold *every*-thing," the Empress demanded, coming to the aid of a colleague. The two words had just enough musical embellishment so that no one was in doubt about who had spoken. "This young lady is singin', and I say we should listen."

As one might expect, everybody did.

During their stay in Chicago Lillian first tried to leave the show. She had lost her inhibitions but not her fear; Jack, she knew, would find out about her and Bessie sooner or later, and she wanted to get out while the getting was good. Bessie persuaded her to stay.

But when they opened at the Koppin Theatre in Detroit on February 5, Lillian decided to leave once and for all. This time Bessie expressed no anger, made no pleas.

The affair with Lillian had kept Bessie relatively sober, but on the night following Lillian's departure, she cut loose. Detroit was a fine town for that. On previous trips, Bessie had befriended a woman[5] who ran a buffet flat. Buffet flats—sometimes referred to as good-time flats—were small, privately owned establishments featuring all sorts of illegal activities: gambling and erotic shows, as well as sex acts of every conceivable kind. These buffet flats were usually owned by women, who ran them with admirable efficiency, catering to the occasional thrill-seeker as well as to regular clients whose personal tastes they knew intimately. Often the hostess also served as a bank. A customer with a sizable amount of cash could turn it over to her for safekeeping, drawing what he might need in the course of an evening.

Buffet flats had a reputation for being safe, and reports of violent incidents and thefts were rare. Originally set up for the benefit of Pullman porters[6] whose travels, contacts with the white world, gentlemanly manners, and good income gained them much respect in the black communities—these establishments served as models for the outwardly legitimate "high-class" night clubs where tuxedoed maître d's discreetly provided "important persons" with sexual liaisons that suited their tastes. Buffet flats were always located in private homes or apartments. Bootleg liquor was plentiful, and a different "show" was usually presented in each room. Patrons who were so inclined could participate by paying an additional fee.

Each time Bessie appeared at the Koppin, her proprietress friend would send one or two cars to the stage door to transport Bessie and her party—usually a coterie of girls who knew how to keep their mouths shut—to the notorious establishment. The night after Lillian left, Bessie took five girls, including Ruby, with her. As they walked out the stage door she delivered a familiar threat: "If any of you tell Jack about this, you'll never work in my shows again."

The house was packed with all kinds of people. Laughing pleasure-

---

5. Immortalized by Bessie in "Soft Pedal Blues."
6. The Pullman Porters Club in St. Louis is said to have started as a buffet flat.

seekers, drinks in hand, formed human chains as they wandered up and down the linoleum-covered staircase, stopping in the various rooms along the way to take a peek at the shows. "It was nothing but faggots and bulldykers, a real open house. Everything went on in that house—tongue baths, you name it. They called them buffet flats because buffet means everything, everything that was in the life. Bessie was well known in that place."

Bessie's pleasure-seeking that night was limited to watching and drinking. That was usually the extent of her activity in such places, for she could ill afford to have word get back to Jack.

Although the flat's most popular attraction that season seemed to be a young man who made expert love to another man, Bessie was most intrigued by an obese lady who performed an amazing trick with a lighted cigarette, then repeated it in the old-fashioned way with a Coca-Cola bottle. "She was real great, she could do all them things with her pussy—an educated pussy." Bessie, being a Southerner, was, of course, inordinately fond of Coca-Cola.

After two hours or so, she gathered her girls together and took them back to Kate's theatrical boardinghouse, where the troupe was staying.

They closed the following night, and after the final performance Bessie and her gang went straight to their rooms. Kate's was hardly the sort of place where one today would find an entertainer of Bessie's stature, but in the nineteen-twenties black people could not even stay at most third-rate hotels. Though this probably bothered Bessie in principle, she preferred a place where the atmosphere was informal and she could cook her own meals. There was no lobby at Kate's, just three floors with long, narrow corridors and rows of rooms.

As was their custom, especially on a closing night, they all changed into nightgowns and pajamas and paraded from room to room, drinking, eating some of Bessie's cooking, passing along the latest gossip.

On this night they all wound up in Bessie's room on the first floor. Marie, a young girl who did a ballet-tap dance number in the show, was wearing a pair of bright-red pajamas Bessie had bought her, and everybody laughed when she did a few comic steps in them. Bessie laughed loudest. "C'mon, Marie, show your stuff," she shouted.

Bessie's good mood was understandable: the week in Detroit had been a good one, the show had gone smoothly, the newspapers had given them all rave notices, there had been no unpleasant incidents, and everybody had had a very good time. "We were drinking, clowning, and having ourselves a ball in Bessie's room, and, as usual, I was the first one to pass out—I just couldn't keep up with that crowd," recalls Ruby. Someone carried her to her room, which adjoined Bessie's, and a couple of hours passed before she was awakened by shouts and running footsteps outside her door. She jumped out of bed, dashed to the door, and opened it.

The first thing Ruby saw was Marie tearing down the corridor. Bessie, right on her heels, almost knocked Ruby over as she pushed into her room and locked the door behind her. All hell was breaking loose: Jack had made one of his surprise appearances and caught Marie in a compromising situation with Bessie.

Bessie was terrified as only Jack could make her. "If Jack knocks, you don't know where I'm at," she said to Ruby. They huddled together as Jack's heavy footsteps passed down the corridor. "Come out here, I'm going to kill you tonight, you bitch," he shouted.

There were further threats and pacing until Kate stepped out of her room and pleaded for calm.

"I think I know where she is," they heard Jack say in a softer tone, "but when she comes back, you tell her I'm lookin' for her." His voice trailed off as he stepped down the wooden stairway that led to the street.

Bessie waited a few seconds, then got Ruby to open the door and check the lay of the land. The other members of the troupe were now standing in their doorways or at the top of the staircase, waiting for Bessie to make her next move. She told them to gather whatever they could carry of their belongings, and head for the train depot. They all obliged, quickly and quietly—everybody was scared of Jack, and that night he was angrier than they had ever seen him.

No one took the time to dress. Carrying armloads of clothes and other personal effects, the troupe made its way through the cold February night to Bessie's railroad car. At Bessie's instructions no lights were turned on, and the dark car was hitched to the next outgoing train. Fortunately Jack didn't find them; an hour later the Empress, still in her pajamas, quietly slipped out of Detroit with her entourage.

# 6

*There's two things got me puzzled, there's
two things I don't understand,
There's two things got me puzzled, there's
two things I don't understand;
That's a mannish-acting woman, and a
skipping, twistin' woman-acting man.*
                    "Foolish Man Blues"

Bessie knew, of course, what she was singing about when she recorded those words in 1927. Most urban blacks—whether they indulged or not—accepted homosexuality as a fact of life. Jack probably did, too, but not when it was so close to home. Not that he was
totally straitlaced—he did indulge in heterosexual promiscuity. He
may have suspected Bessie's sexual interest in women before the
incident with Marie, but that appears to have been his first actual
confrontation with his wife's bisexuality. Clearly it was more than he
was prepared to take.

Their getaway successful, Bessie and her company headed for
Columbus, Ohio, where they were scheduled to open at the Pythian
Theatre. Fortunately, most of the costumes and all the drops had
been put on the train right after the last show in Detroit, but many
of the troupe's personal effects had been left behind at Kate's in the
hasty exit. "That's how I lost the only fur coat I ever had," Ruby
recalls. "I had to leave it at Kate's—Bessie took us out of Detroit
almost naked."

Following the first evening performance at the Pythian, some
local admirers joined members of Bessie's troupe for a drink in her

dressing room. Bessie knew perfectly well that she hadn't heard the end of the Detroit incident; Jack was bound to catch up with her before long. She did not, however, expect him to appear as soon as he did. Any performer who had spent time with a Bessie Smith show was automatically on the alert for a sudden appearance of Jack, but this time he caught them all off guard. No one except Ruby even noticed him until he was halfway into the room. She had seen Jack head for Bessie's dressing room; unable to warn anybody, she did the next best thing: she ran in the opposite direction.

Jack charged into the crowded dressing room and knocked Bessie to the floor. "I'm not going to do any more to you now," he said, looking down at her, "but wait until the show is done tonight—you ain't a man, but you better be like one because we're gonna have it out." He would be waiting at the hotel, he said, and walked out.

Bessie wasn't ready to face Jack. "I'm in real trouble now," she told Ruby after clearing her room of performers and guests, "and I ain't about to mess with Jack as mad as he is. Fix my feathers, baby, and let's get this show over with and get out of town."

Bessie rushed everybody through the grand finale, made a quick change into street clothes, and took Ruby with her to the station, where they caught the next train for Cincinnati. Never one to worry about contractual obligations, Bessie was an old hand at walking out on her shows; somehow things always seemed to mend themselves. As always, someone else had to do the mending, and Clarence Smith was becoming an expert at calming down stranded performers and irate theatre owners.

When the two runaways reached Cincinnati, Bessie wired Frank Walker for some money, and she and Ruby spent a few days "relaxing" before traveling on to New York. "Did we have a ball! We went into every joint, and Bessie knew more joints. I don't know how that woman knew so many joints, but she could take you into more beat-up places. And we just did everything we were big enough to do, from one place to the other, and when we walked in, there was no telling when we'd walk out again—Bessie stayed drunk, and me right along with her."

Bessie's road company had been through a flood during this last tour, inspiring her to write her most famous blues. Maud recalls the event:

After we left Cincinnati, we came to this little town, which was flooded, so everybody had to step off the train into little rowboats that took us to where we were staying. It was an undertaker parlor next door to the theatre, and we were supposed to stay in some rooms they had upstairs there. So after we had put our bags down, Bessie looked around and said, "No, no, I can't stay *here* tonight." But there was a lot of other people there, and they were trying to get her to stay, so they started hollerin', "Miss Bessie, please sing the 'Back Water Blues,' please sing the 'Back Water Blues.' " Well, Bessie didn't know anything about any "Back Water Blues," but after we came back home to 1926 Christian Street where we were living, Bessie came in the kitchen one day, and she had a pencil and paper, and she started singing and writing. That's when she wrote the "Back Water Blues"—she got the title from those people down South.

On February 17, 1927, she recorded it with James P. Johnson:

*When it rains five days, and the sky turns dark as night,*
*When it rains five days, and the sky turns dark as night;*
*Then trouble's takin' place in the lowlands at night.*

*I woke up this mornin', can't even get out of my do',*
*I woke up this mornin', can't even get out of my do';*
*There's enough trouble to make a poor girl wonder where*
*    she wanna go.*

*Then they rowed a little boat about five miles 'cross*
*    the pond,*
*Then they rowed a little boat about five miles 'cross*
*    the pond;*
*I packed all my clothes, throwed them in, and they*
*    rowed me along.*

*Back Water Blues done caused me to pack my things and go,*
*Back Water Blues done caused me to pack my things and go;*
*'Cause my house fell down, and I can't live there no mo'.*

*Mmmmmmmm Mmmmmmmm, I can't move no more,*
*Mmmmmmmm Mmmmmmmm, I can't move no more;*
*There ain't no place for a poor old girl to go.*

That session, which also produced "Preachin' the Blues," another of Bessie's own compositions, was her first collaboration with James P. Johnson, unquestionably her finest piano accompanist. The acknowledged master of the complicated, highly rhythmic Harlem "stride" piano style, Johnson was a complementary voice, like Louis Armstrong had been two years earlier.

On this New York trip Bessie did not stay at the Gee home.

Instead she used an apartment near the Lafayette Theatre—one she rented in Ruby's name, ostensibly to carry on an affair with Fred Longshaw when he was her accompanist. Because Jack did not know about this apartment, she felt safe there.

Sooner or later, of course, she knew she would have to face Jack. She made a trip home to Philadelphia at the risk of running into him. This trip, she figured, might result in smoothing things over with Jack even though it involved an expenditure. The great amounts of money she spent on her family had caused many fights between her and Jack. If she could make her sister Viola self-supporting, perhaps there wouldn't be so many fights. So she bought Viola and her daughter Laura a restaurant at 1244 South Street in Philadelphia.

About the time Bessie bought Viola the restaurant, Jack had a nervous breakdown and went to Hot Springs, Arkansas. to recuperate. The timing was perfect. Now Bessie could go to Hot Springs and play the Good Samaritan. She visited him and showed genuine concern for his health. They made up, and she returned to New York with a promise that all would be well in the future. Soon after she got back, she wrote and recorded "Hot Springs Blues."

Jack suffered such "breakdowns" on more than one occasion, but it appears that they were merely a part of the game he played. "Jack never had no nervous breakdowns," insists Maud. "We were the ones who should have had nervous breakdowns. He wasn't sick. Bessie would do anything for him, so she'd give him all the money he wanted, and tell him to go and take a rest."

On March 2, Bessie was back in the New York studio for an unusual recording session with Fletcher Henderson and five members of his orchestra, including Joe Smith and Coleman Hawkins. What made it unusual was the repertoire of four popular songs: "After You've Gone," Irving Berlin's "Alexander's Ragtime Band," a 1926 Tin Pan Alley hit called "Muddy Water (a Mississippi Moan)," and "There'll Be a Hot Time in the Old Town Tonight," a rallying song from the Spanish-American War.

Blues purists—who, oddly enough, don't complain about Bessie's 1923 recordings of lesser-known pop fare—have bemoaned her "commercial" repertoire for this session, and critics have rationalized it as an attempt to regain lost ground. But Bessie's popularity was not threatened at the time, and her recordings reflected only a part of her actual repertoire. Her treatment of these songs offers delightful evidence of her talent for turning banal material into something special.

At the time these recordings were made, Bessie was headlining at the Lincoln Theatre on Lenox Avenue. The show, which boasted thirty "famous artists" in its advertisements, was called *Bessie Smith and Her Yellow Girl Revue*, but one suspects that she was not responsible for putting the show together: she had always expressed monumental disdain for light-complexioned women.

While at the Lincoln, Bessie was preparing for another tent tour. There was little rehearsal involved since her lineup was almost the same as it had been the previous year, and "new" routines often were mere variations on the old ones. Her brother Clarence and the husband-and-wife team of Gertie and Dinah Scott were the featured co-performers. Thomas Hill, an elderly tuba player, was the new musical director, replacing Bill Woods, who had left Bessie after the incident involving his wife, Boula. Bessie's nephew Teejay was still the troupe's secretary—and Jack, now "well enough" to resume his "managerial" role, was to join them in the South.

After a quick recording session with James P. Johnson on April 1,[1] Bessie headed for Atlanta to pick up the railroad car. Jack was already there, having spent a few days getting the car ready. A freshly painted sign on its side announced: "Jack Gee presents Bessie Smith and Her Harlem Frolics of 1927."

A minor incident occurred during the week they spent in Atlanta before moving on to North Carolina for the first stretch of the tour. A chorine named Elsie Ferbee got into a fight with one of the musicians, who pushed her down the steps of the hotel where they were staying. Though she was not seriously injured, it was bad enough so that she had to quit the show. Bessie fired the musician, paid Miss Ferbee's medical bills, and, in general, gave her more personal attention than the circumstances warranted.

Two weeks later, while Bessie's show was playing Asheville, North Carolina, a letter from Miss Ferbee appeared in the Pittsburgh *Courier,* her hometown newspaper. Annoyed at having been left behind in Atlanta, she accused her former boss of unfair treatment. Bessie's reply was prompt:

1. "Sweet Mistreater" and "Lock and Key."

Theatrical Department
Pittsburgh Courier
Pittsburgh, Pa.

Gentlemen:

In regards to the letter sent you by Elsie Ferbee, she or no one else can truthfully say that I did not do anything for her when she was ill, because I did. I paid her room rent and board and she was treated by one of the best specialists in Atlanta from Grady Hospital and her doctor bill was paid by me. I had her moved in where I was staying so I could be near her to see that she got the best attention. As for my mistreating anybody who is sick, I have given and helped more people in and out of the profession than I ever hope to be repaid for on earth, but I will get my reward later from the man higher up.

However, I wish Elsie success in what she undertakes to do.

Yours professionally,
BESSIE SMITH
Care the Bessie Smith Show

Bessie probably dictated the content of the letter, if not the wording, to T. J. Hill, who took care of most correspondence, and seized the opportunity to throw in a little plug for the show: a postscript described a successful tour and listed the complete itinerary for the rest of the month.

The letter's reference to a reward from "the man higher up" is a little hard to reconcile with Bessie's worldly life-style, but she was actually quite religious. "In every town that we would get in, if we got in on a Sunday morning early enough, we'd all go to church," says Maud. "Bessie could sing some of the most beautiful church hymns, and she often did that around the house."

Bessie did, after all, grow up in a religious household. All who heard her in person agree that her vocal delivery and coordinated movements evoked the fervor of a Southern Baptist prayer meeting. "She was real close to God, very religious," recalls drummer Zutty Singleton, who often accompanied Bessie at the Lyric Theatre in New Orleans. "She always mentioned the Lord's name. That's why her blues seemed almost like hymns."

"If you had any church background, like people who came from the South, as I did," said guitarist Danny Barker, "you would recognize a similarity between what she was doing and what those preachers and evangelists from there did, and how they moved people. Bessie did the same thing on stage. She, in a sense, was like people like Billy Graham are today. Bessie was in a class with those people. She could bring about mass hypnotism."

Actually, Bessie's double life, her mixing of debauchery with divinity, did not seem to cause her any great inner conflict.[2]

The smaller rural communities of North Carolina, starved for entertainment after the winter, had nothing to complain about during the 1927 tent season. Blazing the trail for Bessie were several other touring companies, including those of Clara Smith and Ma Rainey, with Ma showing off her new thirteen-thousand-dollar Mack bus and Koehler electric generator.

Ma's show, *Louisiana Blackbirds*, had played Asheville less than a month before Bessie's arrival there, but Bessie and her troupe were able to attract enough people to stay a whole week, sometimes filling the huge tent with over a hundred standees in addition to the 1500 ticketholders who had seats.

Working their way eastward across the state, Bessie and her entertainers stopped in Hickory, Statesville, Salisbury, High Point, Reidsville, and Greensboro during the month of May; went on to Burlington, Chapel Hill, Durham, Raleigh, Louisburg, Oxford, Henderson, and Franklin, Virginia, in June; and in July they headed south.

So far the tour had been uneventful. Bessie and Jack were enjoying a period of tranquillity following their fight over the Detroit incident. Keeping her promise, Bessie was staying off the bottle and concentrating on her work. Attendance had been excellent at each station along their way, and "Back Water Blues" was enjoying phenomenal sales, spurred no doubt by the fact that its release coincided with the worst flood disaster in the recorded history of the Mississippi River.[3] The record had also given Bessie's popularity an extra boost, which must have accounted in part for the tour's extraordinary success.

Although Southern rural whites were among Bessie's staunchest

2. The name of the game seemed to be repent before it's too late. "I truly believe Bessie was getting ready to turn," says Maud Smith. Bessie never made it, but some of her fun-loving colleagues, like Lizzie Miles and Ethel Waters, did, in fact, "turn" to a life of religion, and Ma Rainey spent her last years as an active member of the Friendship Baptist Church in Columbus, Georgia.

3. Floods inundated twenty thousand square miles, leaving seven hundred thousand persons homeless.

fans, there was of course still a segment of the population that resented the success of any black artist. The Ku Klux Klan, revived and reorganized in 1915, claimed its largest membership in the mid-twenties, when the Klan's effort to establish white supremacy took its most virulent form. Trading on the fears and suspicions of rural whites, the Klan became a law unto itself in many communities. Many law-enforcement officers were Klan members.

Having grown up and spent much of her life in Klan-infested territory, Bessie was well aware of the threat the Klan posed. The Klan, however pernicious, had become a fact of life in Southern society. But what could anyone—especially a black person—do against it?

Bessie must have known that many of the Southern followers who flocked to her tent, laughed at her jokes, and applauded her singing were Klansmen who had left their sheets at home. But like many Southern blacks, she ignored the Klan and assumed she'd receive no more malice than she gave.

Still, Bessie often found trouble whether she looked for it or not. In July 1927, in Concord, North Carolina, she was forced out of her complacency toward the Klan. It was a hot July night, and Bessie's electric generator was creating additional heat, making the packed tent almost unbearable, especially for the lively performers. Halfway through the show, one of the musicians was close to passing out. He left his seat and stepped outside.

As he walked around the huge tent, he heard soft voices and a grunting sound nearby. Following the sound, he came upon a half dozen hooded figures, the moonlight showing up their white robes. They were obviously getting ready to collapse Bessie's tent; they had already pulled up several stakes.

Unseen by the preoccupied Klansmen, the musician hurried back to the rear entrance of the tent. Bessie had just come off stage, and the audience was hollering for her to return. Before she could raise hell with the musician for not being inside with the rest of the band, he managed to blurt out what he'd seen.

"*Some* shit!" she said, and ordered the prop boys to follow her around the tent. When they were within a few feet of the Klansmen, the boys withdrew to a safe distance. Bessie had not told them why she wanted them, and one look at the white hoods was all the discouragement they needed.

Not Bessie. She ran toward the intruders, stopped within ten feet of them, placed one hand on her hip, and shook a clenched fist at the Klansmen. "What the fuck you think you're doin'?" she shouted above the sound of the band. "I'll get the whole damn tent out here if I have to. You just pick up them sheets and run!"

The Klansmen, apparently too surprised to move, just stood there and gawked. Bessie hurled obscenities at them until they finally turned and disappeared quietly into the darkness.

"I ain't never *heard* of such shit," said Bessie, and walked back to where her prop boys stood. "And as for you, you ain't nothin' but a bunch of sissies."

Then she went back into the tent as if she had just settled a routine matter.

There was trouble of a different kind the following night, when the show played Charlotte, North Carolina. Thomas Hill, Bessie's orchestra leader, had gone into town after the show and had got into a fight with two young men, who beat him up very badly.

The musicians were a close-knit group, and after hearing what happened to Hill, several of them set out to look for his assailants. In the meantime, Bessie's railroad car was ready to be hitched to the next southbound train. There was no set schedule on these tours; the troupe's movement depended entirely on the sometimes erratic schedule of the railroads. This meant that its members had to board the car as soon as the tent and other equipment were packed.

On this particular night Bessie's car was pulled out before Hill's colleagues returned from their mission. Bessie, unaware of the incident, did not notice their absence until the following day when they stopped at Sumter, North Carolina. She flew into a rage, threatening to fire Hill unless his musicians reached Sumter in time for the evening's show.

Fortunately for everybody concerned, they did show up that night, disheveled and scared. They had done the job—located the two men and given them such a severe beating that they believed they'd killed one of them.

Bessie was not supposed to know that part of the story, but she found out and came up with the appropriate threat: "If anybody comes lookin' for y'all, I'm gonna let 'em have you."

Throughout August and most of September, *Harlem Frolics* did one- and two-nighters in Georgia and Alabama. The tent tour had been Bessie's most successful to date, but it had been long and tiring. She skipped the traditional homebound theatre route and headed for Philadelphia, where she disbanded her troupe.

Things had not gone well in her absence. Inexperience and a general lack of interest had put Viola and Laura out of the restaurant business. Bessie paid their debts and continued supporting them. She also broke her four-month abstinence.

In late September she made four recordings with a new accompanist, Porter Grainger. They worked well together, and Frank Walker scheduled their first collaboration, "A Good Man Is Hard to Find" (originally introduced by Alberta Hunter) and "Mean Old Bedbug Blues" for "special release"—both were hit material, and Bessie's delivery was superb. "Good Man," in fact, became a standard, and "Bedbug's" humor and double-entendre made it an instant hit.

Bessie was now drinking heavily again. She opened at the Lafayette on October 17, but her trips to the nearby speakeasy were so frequent that it was said she often had to be propped up on stage. This may well be an exaggeration; Frank Schiffman, then the owner of the Lafayette, does not recall anything of the kind. He does remember that Bessie never missed a show. "She had love problems all the time, and they might have impaired some of her performances, but we could always count on Bessie to be there, and to put on a show—a good one."

The drinking could not, of course, be kept from Jack, who knew where to look when he couldn't find Bessie at the theatre between shows. To avoid Jack, Bessie made a special arrangement with the bartender: she would take her drinks in the one place Jack couldn't surprise her: the ladies' room. It worked until the day he caught her coming out and knocked her down in front of everybody. Bessie picked herself up and took off down Seventh Avenue, with Ruby following close behind.

They were almost a block ahead of Jack when Bessie stopped a cab and jumped in with Ruby. "Hurry up," Bessie told the driver. "That man back there just held up somebody and he's after us because he knows we seen him—hurry up, he's gonna kill us!"

Having escaped from her husband once again, Bessie sobered up—these unexpected encounters usually had that effect on her. And, as usual, a separation followed the incident.

This one was brief, but it had all happened too many times— Bessie was unable to summon the control for a period of sobriety and good behavior. And Jack was beginning to fall apart again.

Bessie stayed sober long enough to record two of her finest sides, "Dying by the Hour" and "Foolish Man Blues," on October 27. Her accompaniment included Ma Rainey's favorite cornetist, Tommy Ladnier, a first-rate blues player from Louisiana who was then a member of the Fletcher Henderson orchestra.

Four days later Bessie took her new *Harlem Frolics* into Gibson's Standard Theatre in Philadelphia. On her return home the news was not good. Jack had run up a considerable gambling debt, and he was having another "nervous breakdown." Bessie spent the month of November in Philadelphia, paid Jack's debt, and sent him to Hot Springs, Arkansas, again for recuperation before embarking on a brief theatre tour, starting at the Grand in Chicago on December 3.

Business at the Grand was good, not great. A "Free Marcus Garvey" movement was on, and political awareness was growing among urban blacks. Some saw this as the reason the T.O.B.A. and most black theatres registered 1927 as the most disastrous box office year to date while business along the tent trail was at its peak and the white legitimate theatre—with a record 268 Broadway openings—had never had a better year.

The truth was that urban black audiences had become more demanding—what knocked them for a loop in Concord, North Carolina, could fall flat in Chicago—and black vaudeville, a throwback to minstrel days, was becoming as outdated as the parlor piano and ankle-length skirts. Bessie herself had not lost her drawing power; as a singer she was certainly in a class by herself, and her appeal went far beyond that. We think of her as a singer because recordings reveal only her extraordinary voice; those who experienced her on the stage think of her as an actress, comedienne, dancer, and mime as well. And in all these guises she had no equal in her ability to communicate with an audience, to command its involvement in whatever she was doing, and to control and even shape its responses.

The week of December 12, she commanded packed houses in Indianapolis, and she was told that a thousand people were turned away during the *Harlem Frolics* appearance at the Lincoln in Kansas City. Jack rejoined her on the road in time for Christmas, and he and Bessie made their way to New York.

Five years had passed since she first faced Columbia's recording horn and turned it into a horn of plenty. If somebody hadn't told Bessie that 1927 had been a very bad year for her profession, she would never have known it.

# 7

*There ain't nothin' I can do, or nothin'*
*I can say, that folks don't criticize me.*
*But I'm goin' to do just as I want to anyway,*
*and don't care if they all despise me.*
"'T'ain't Nobody's Biz-ness If I Do"

In the early months of 1928, Harlem, still mourning the recent death of Florence Mills, heard Duke Ellington's posthumous tribute, "Black Beauty"; Lew Leslie's *Blackbirds of 1928* was about to make stars of Adelaide Hall and Bill "Bojangles" Robinson. Helen Morgan was introducing the "torch" song as she produced tears with her rendition of "Bill," a P. G. Wodehouse–Jerome Kern collaboration. And Bessie, making the rounds of Eastern theatres with her *Mississippi Days* show, evoked laughter with a blatantly pornographic, wildly humorous "Empty Bed Blues."

To millions of people, Bessie was now a superstar. She did wear ermine coats and diamond rings, but she still preferred eating pigs' feet and drinking bad liquor in a ghetto alley to sampling canapés and cocktails at the gatherings of a white society that now sought to embrace her.

It was a ninety-minute walk from the middle of Harlem to midtown Manhattan, but to the blacks who lived around 132nd Street in the late nineteen-twenties, most parts of the midtown area might as well have been the Côte d'Azur.

There was, however, an extraordinary flow of traffic in the opposite direction. Whites whose modern counterparts would feel ill at ease above Ninety-sixth Street swarmed uptown to the "colorful" ghetto and became tourists in their own city.

Harlem's celebrated night life had experienced a slump following World War I, but Prohibition had given it new scope and frenetic energy. Seemingly oblivious to the conditions all around them, black Harlemites catered to the white socialites and celebrities who were turning this foreign, fascinating community into a playground for the privileged.

Night after night the bejeweled and befurred flocked to black Harlem from their homes on Park Avenue or Riverside Drive to hear the great black entertainers at Smalls' Paradise, Connie's Inn, or the Cotton Club. There they were assured an elaborate show in an atmosphere that seemed congenial, even though some of these clubs appeared to have a whites-only policy. Actually, few black people could afford the high prices, and of those who could many did not want to subject themselves to the curious stares of white visitors. Some Harlem cabarets, like Leroy's at 135th Street and Fifth Avenue,[1] maintained a strict nonwhite policy, but the community's many after-hours spots had no racial barriers.

Shedding their inhibitions along with their furs—feeling adventuresome among the natives—whites would round off an evening in Harlem by slumming it in a variety of speakeasies or buffet flats bearing such names as Eunice's, Minnie's, or Mabel's, local Perle Mestas who assured their patrons anonymity and protection against the law.

Bessie was one native the visitors did not see. She had sampled Harlem's tourist spots in 1923 when she stood on the threshold of success, but she had no use for the make-believe paradise. In fact, she frequently expressed her disgust when "they" pulled up in their fancy limousines and cruised the teeming streets: the men in tuxedos, the women flaunting their Bergdorf-Goodman wraps.

She did not envy the women—she owned such trappings herself. But Bessie was a proud woman, and she knew perfectly well what white tourism in Harlem really meant to its residents.

Even some of the most perceptive white visitors to Harlem failed to sense the resentment behind the smiles that greeted them. They saw blacks as a happy-go-lucky people who laughed infectiously, showed an enviable lack of restraint, really understood how to have a good time. So the white elite came, laughed, sinned, and slipped back

---

1. It is said that only one white man, Al Jolson, was ever permitted to visit Leroy's during its thirteen years of operation (around 1910 to 1923).

into their Tiffany world before the first rays of dawn struck the ghetto.

Not all Harlemites pretended to welcome them. Class-conscious black social leaders who lived on Striver's Row or Sugar Hill, where Harlem's well-to-do could approximate the life-style of middle- and upper-middle-class whites, voiced their strong opposition to the influx—while they continued to identify themselves with the visiting whites.

In an article for the black *New York Age*, Archie Seale wrote:

> Our reactions toward these white people are not what the whites would expect them to be, because we find that the white people visiting Harlem are very courteous and very considerate, and all around democratic. . . . There are many of our social leaders who resent it from the standpoint that there isn't anything to be credited to the community through these visits because, as one of the leaders pointed out, when the whites visit Harlem for entertainment they do not come in contact with the better class of Negro residing in Harlem. They are seated by and with many undesirables of the community and these same undesirables leave the impression with the visitors that the type of people residing in the community of Harlem are really those whom they meet in these various places.

Carl Van Vechten—or "Carlo," as he was called by his friends— was one white man who shared the rather twisted concern of Harlem's social leaders. Since hearing and meeting Bessie at the Orpheum Theatre on Thanksgiving night in 1925, he had become assistant music editor for the *New York Times*. He had also deepened his already strong emotional and intellectual involvement with some of the era's aspiring black poets and writers. Van Vechten gained national prominence as a writer in 1926 when his controversial *Nigger Heaven* sparked the anger of blacks and whites alike. A novel about middle-class blacks in Harlem, its message, in retrospect, seems to have been that there were "good niggers," too.

Van Vechten typified the upper-class white liberal of his day. His attitude toward blacks can perhaps best be summed up with a paragraph from the author's notes, written for a 1950 paperback edition of *Nigger Heaven:*

> When I am asked how I happen to know so much about Negro character and Negro customs, I can answer proudly that many Negroes are my intimate friends. The Negro magazine *Ebony* once alluded to me as the white man who had more friends among colored people of distinction than

any other white person in America. With a high degree of accuracy, I can still boast that many Negroes are still my friends.

Certainly Van Vechten's writing, even in the nineteen-fifties, is characterized by a Great White Father tone that patronizes as it commends. But this "innocent" racism should not obscure his positive contributions. For his time, his attitude—regardless of what motivated it—represented a new liberating voice, and his support of black artists like Bessie must be seen in that context. At first his efforts benefited only a select few, but the Harlem Renaissance of the nineteen-twenties—which brought attention to the work of Langston Hughes, Claude McKay, and others, and behind which Van Vechten was an important force—was a landmark in the history of Afro-American culture.

In their spacious, lavishly decorated apartment on Manhattan's West Fifty-fifth Street, Van Vechten and his wife, the former Russian ballerina Fania Marinoff, presided over a remarkable salon. Their guest lists traditionally comprised some of the New York cultural community's foremost figures, including several representatives of black culture—an inclusion regarded as novel by the few people who recognized its existence—the radical chic of the nineteen-twenties.

Van Vechten loved the ghetto's pulsating music and strapping young men, and he maintained a Harlem apartment—decorated in black with silver stars on the ceiling and seductive red lights—for his notorious nocturnal gatherings. He collected records by black artists, particularly the female singers, and usually purchased two or more copies of each, always making sure that one was preserved in unplayed condition. In later years he donated these records to the James Weldon Johnson Memorial Collection of Negro Arts and Letters, which he founded in the Yale University Library.[2]

His favorite black singers were Ethel Waters, Clara Smith, and Bessie.

He had heard Bessie sing several times since the Orpheum performance, but she made the greatest impression on him during an April evening in 1928, when she played jester to his court of celebrities.

As Van Vechten remembers it, Bessie, surrounded by such notables as Marguerite d'Alvarez, George Gershwin, Constance Collier,

---

2. Van Vechten stipulated that each record was to be played only once a year. His Bessie Smith collection was still in excellent condition in 1970, when Columbia Records transferred it for use in their reissue project.

and Adele Astaire, walked into the crowded drawing room, requested a glass of gin, and, with one gulp

> downed a glass holding nearly a pint. Then, with a burning cigarette depending from one corner of her mouth, she got down to the Blues, really down to 'em, with Porter [Grainger] at the piano. I am quite certain that anybody who was present that night will never forget it. This was no actress; no imitator of woman's woes; there was no pretense. It was the real thing: a woman cutting her heart open with a knife until it was exposed for us all to see, so that we suffered as she suffered, exposed with a rhythmic ferocity, which could hardly be borne.[3]

Bessie's singing style was hardly of the dangling-cigarette variety—she didn't smoke, at least not tobacco. Even her reputation as a gin drinker seems based largely on Van Vechten's recollection and on occasional references to gin in her songs (not, however, in her own compositions).

Curiously enough, although he added to the story his own highly colored emotional reaction, Van Vechten omitted any reference to the real drama of Bessie's visit. He was right that "anybody who was present that night will never forget it." But other guests' recollections of that evening suggest that Bessie's musical performance was the least memorable part of her visit.

Bessie's latest show, *Mississippi Days*—billed as a "Musical Comedy Triumph" with a cast of forty-five "noted" performers—was playing the Lafayette Theatre. Porter Grainger, who had composed the music for that show and was Bessie's accompanist at the time, had promised to deliver her between shows so that she might entertain Van Vechten's guests. Van Vechten assured Grainger that he would see to it Bessie got back to the Lafayette in time for the evening's final performance.

Grainger was a shy, handsome young man whose refined mannerisms and sartorial elegance were often targets for Bessie's sarcasm. "C'mon down front, *now* you're with me," she'd say. Although he was a homosexual, Grainger so respected and feared Bessie that he even obliged when, on occasion, she commanded him to bed.

There were those who felt that Porter Grainger's neatly pressed suits, spats, and walking stick were his way of commanding attention in the prestigious world of the white man. To gain entry into that

---

3. *Jazz Record* magazine, September 1947.

world, a black person either had to imitate white standards with some degree of success or, like Bessie, be gifted with an extraordinary talent. In neither case would a black person be accepted as an equal.

Grainger, of course, offered Van Vechten more than his musical talent, but his competition was fierce, and Bessie served well as an apple for the teacher. "Carlo pampered people like Leontyne Price," said the late Fannie Hurst, many years later, "but he would never think of inviting a Negro elevator operator to his home."

Bessie sensed such attitudes, of course, which may be one reason she never made any effort to befriend white people. She pretended not to care when "dicty"[4] black people rejected her, but she could not fool some of her closest friends. With her income Bessie could easily have taken up residence in Merrick Park, Long Island, where successful black entertainers and other well-to-do black people had established a colony, but she could not relate to pretentious people or their values.

It was equally difficult for the Merrick Park crowd to relate to Bessie; her prominence as an artist precluded their total rejection of her, but to them she was unforgivably crude, and her perceptions—and lack of tact—made them uneasy. The main reason for their discomfort was, of course, that Bessie saw right through them.

"Sometimes Bessie liked to dress up in expensive fur coats that really looked like money," recalls Ruby, "but she never put on airs, not Bessie. She wasn't going to change for anyone, she just wanted people to like her for what she was—a real person. She pretended she didn't care how people felt about her, but she really felt left out sometimes—not by white people; she *really* didn't care how they felt—she just loved her own people, and she hated to see them trying to act so dicty and white."

Considering her attitude, it is surprising that Bessie agreed to appear at the Van Vechten party. It may, of course, have been a paid engagement, but she probably did it as a favor to Porter Grainger, to whom such social contacts were important.

Whatever the reason, she did go, and she went in style.

Wrapped in her white ermine coat, accompanied by Grainger and Ruby, she stepped into the chauffeur-driven limousine Van Vechten had provided.

4. Black colloquial term meaning "highbrow."

They were met at the door to Van Vechten's apartment by an assortment of white faces wearing perfumed smiles and stares that blended outer warmth with cautious curiosity. Some of the guests undoubtedly shared their host's genuine admiration for Bessie's artistry, but she could hardly have failed to realize that she was being regarded more as a novelty than as a human being or even a performer. In any case, she breezed past the welcoming party and into the room beyond. Trailing behind her, Ruby wore a mink coat which belonged to Bessie and was far too big for her. Bringing up the rear, Grainger graciously returned smiles for Bessie.

Ignoring a chorus of salutatory "Oh, Miss Smiths," Bessie, cold sober at this point, did not come to a halt until someone mentioned a drink. Van Vechten, radiating the pleasure of a celebrity hunter who has at last captured his prey of the moment, beamed. "How about a lovely, lovely dry martini?"

"Whaaat—a *dry martini?*" bellowed Bessie. "Ain't you got some whiskey, man? That'll be the only way I'll touch it. I don't know about no dry martinis, nor wet ones either."

"Of course," said Van Vechten. "I think we can conjure up something you like," he purred, and disappeared to fulfill the request.

Bessie looked at Ruby, who was still tripping over the enormous mink. "Take that *damned* thing off," she ordered, handing Ruby her own coat. Grainger, thoroughly embarrassed, had pretended not to hear Bessie's exchange with her host, or those last words to Ruby. Now he proceeded to blend, as best he could, into the genteel atmosphere of the drawing room. Ruby, carrying the two huge fur coats, stumbled over to the side of the room.

Soon Grainger and Bessie, drink in hand, were marched toward the piano. Mumbling something about her throat being dry, Bessie gulped her drink down and handed her empty glass to Van Vechten. Someone asked her what she was going to sing. "Don't you worry about it," she said. "My piano player knows."

Grainger smiled apologetically and went into the opening bars of "Work House Blues." The guests listened with rapt attention as Bessie's tale of hard times cut through the perfumed air, and novelty became art.

With her subtle, sensual movements and heaving bosom, Bessie mesmerized her audience. She sang six or seven numbers, each one followed by enthusiastic applause and usually preceded by her request for "another one of these." Each time she handed Van Vechten her empty glass, he refilled it eagerly. Only Ruby and Grainger knew what effect the refills were having on Bessie.

"This is it," announced Bessie as she went into her final number. She was feeling her liquor at this point, and her two companions were watching her closely, knowing it wouldn't take much to set her off.

As soon as the last number was finished, Grainger walked over to Ruby, momentarily shedding his genteel demeanor: "Let's get her out of here quick, before she shows her ass." Draping the ermine over her shoulders, they fell into position on either side of Bessie and began what they hoped would be a graceful exit.

All went well until an effusive woman stopped them a few steps from the front door. It was Bessie's hostess, Fania Marinoff Van Vechten.

"Miss Smith," she said, throwing her arms around Bessie's massive neck and pulling it forward, "you're *not* leaving without kissing me goodbye."

That was all Bessie needed.

"Get the fuck away from me," she roared, thrusting her arms forward and knocking the woman to the floor. "I ain't never heard of such shit!"

In the silence that followed, Bessie stood in the middle of the foyer, ready to take on the whole crowd.

Grainger was the first to move. Gently he took one of Bessie's arms and told Ruby to take the other. Followed by the horrified stares of the guests, the two of them escorted the Empress out the door and down the richly carpeted hall to the elevator. Van Vechten, having helped his indignant wife to her feet, followed close behind.

"It's all right, Miss Smith," he said softly, trailing behind the threesome in the hall. "You were magnificent tonight."

They had reached the elevator before Bessie realized that she was actually being led away. She threw her arms in the air, almost knocking Ruby and Grainger to the floor, and started shouting again—"What the fuck are y'all pullin' me all over the damn place for?"

When the elevator door opened she stopped shouting, raised her head high, marched past the startled operator, and sank to the floor in the corner of the car.

"I don't care if she dies," said Grainger as he sighed and straightened the tam on his head.

A liberal application of cold water by Ruby and Grainger enabled

Their fascination with black people never ceased. The Carl Van Vechtens at the 1955 wedding of Carmen de Lavallade and Geoffrey Holder. *Photo by Sol Mauribu, courtesy of Mr. and Mrs. Holder.*

Bessie to make it through the final show at the Lafayette after the Van Vechten party, but she was now primed for one of her drinking sprees. When she was in New York and drinking, Bessie could often be found in a speakeasy on 134th Street near the Lafayette. Percy Brown's was a meeting place for performers and show business hangers-on—people who didn't themselves perform but who seemed to know just about everybody who did.

Bessie took Ruby to Brown's a couple of days after the Van Vechten affair. They had just finished a matinee, and there was time to kill before the first evening show. Again Bessie wore her ermine—sprinkled liberally with Evening in Paris, her favorite perfume—and Ruby wore the mink. But this time, although Bessie was very much in a drinking mood, the more compatible atmosphere at Brown's inspired an incident of quite a different sort.

Bessie hadn't had a drink all day, but it didn't take many to get her going again. The story of the Van Vechten party was already making the rounds in the Harlem gossip mill. Accounts varied, but the punch line remained the same: Bessie's words to Mrs. Van Vechten as she threw her to the floor. The story became so famous that Bessie's name soon found its way into the Harlem vocabulary as a code word for "shit." Musicians and entertainers, in the presence of white people, understood such new expressions as "*some* Bessie Smith" and "I never *heard* of such Bessie Smith."

Bessie herself had a hand in spreading the story, and that afternoon at Brown's she was breaking up the crowd with her version, which emphasized her sending Porter Grainger into acute, embarrassed shock. Bessie was a good storyteller and an even better mimic. "How about a lovely, lovely dry martini?" she said, opening her eyes wide and rubbing the palms of her hands together. The crowd roared as the elegant tones of Van Vechten stopped and Bessie returned: "Shiiiit, you should have seen them ofays lookin' at me like I was some kind of singin' monkey!"

She was high and she was in a good mood. Having milked that story dry, she turned to her niece and said, "C'mon, Ruby, let's go have us some fun." Ruby, as usual, knew she had better tag along.

They stepped out into the bright, cool Harlem day and turned right on Seventh Avenue, heading back toward the Lafayette. Ruby, handicapped by the mink coat, had a hard time keeping up with Bessie. When they reached the small alley that adjoined the Lafayette, Bessie suddenly ducked into it, seated herself on a garbage can, ermine and all, and let out a laugh so hearty that passersby turned their heads to see what was going on.

Then, with her legs dangling, she began swaying back and forth, snapping her fingers as her arms, shoulders, neck undulated rhythmically. Having thus established a tempo, she turned to Ruby. "C'mon, Ruby, let's show 'em," she said, and filled up the alley with her song:

> Show 'em how they do it in Virginia,
> hey, hey;
> Virginia, do it for me. . . .

It was a song from the finale of her show. The alley became a stage as Bessie's powerful voice rose above the garbage and out into the street. Ruby caught the mood, and, her movements largely concealed inside the huge mink coat, started doing the "Virginia" dance routine.

The growing crowd joined in. "They came from everywhere, clapping their hands, dancing, and carrying on. The more people came, the louder Bessie sang. These were her people, and she was giving them something they weren't gonna forget in a hurry. And me, I was so busy doing my dance. that I didn't see Jack until it was too late."

Totally involved in her song, Bessie didn't see him either.

> If music was action, and action so grand;
> You'd be the leader of a whole—

There was a loud crash as Jack jumped out of the crowd, knocked Bessie off her garbage can, and reduced her to a heap of ermine amid the trash.

"You ain't nothin' but tramps, both of you," he shouted as the crowd began to disperse. Ruby wasn't going to wait to hear the rest of Jack's sermon: "When I saw Jack, Bessie was already in the trash, so I just wrapped that mink around me, ran down Seventh Avenue, and grabbed the first cab I could find—we were used to grabbin' cabs runnin' from Jack."

Nobody seems to know what Jack did or said after that, but it was weeks before Bessie touched a drink.

In May 1928, Bessie skipped her traditional tent tour and took her *Mississippi Days* company on the road for the T.O.B.A. The classic blues had long since passed its peak of popularity, but Bessie's following remained steadfast. While she was touring, Columbia released the classic two-part "Empty Bed Blues," a tour de force of blatant double-entendres, with Porter Grainger's piano and Charlie Green's wildly humorous trombone comments complementing Bessie's tongue-in-cheek delivery. The record was a big hit for Bessie, making her theatre tour all the more successful.

"You could hear that record all over the South Side," recalled pianist Lovie Austin, then musical director of Chicago's Monogram Theatre. "We couldn't book her for the Monogram because she wanted too much money, and the theatre wasn't big enough to hold half the people who wanted to hear her. I don't think Bessie had seen such crowds since she first started out making records."

The success of Bessie's *Mississippi Days* tour gave renewed hope to officers of the ailing T.O.B.A. circuit, prompting Sam Reevin to telegraph Jack requesting that he put together two shows for the coming season. Reevin, possibly misled by the "Jack Gee presents" prefix on virtually all of Bessie's road shows, obviously did not know how limited Jack's involvement in his wife's business actually was. Nevertheless, Jack seized the opportunity to become a producer.

Bessie returned to New York in July, planning to spend the remainder of the summer playing mother to little Jack, who had grown into a handsome boy of eight, with light complexion and long, curly hair. Bessie's usual prejudices against such features seemed to have vanished. Her working schedule for the summer was light, consisting of more recordings and rehearsals for a new show.

Jack claims Bessie knew of Reevin's request, but later events suggest that he told her a half-truth, avoiding mention of the second show. Piecing together bits of evidence and recollections, it appears that Jack got Bessie to give him three thousand dollars for the production of her new show, *Steamboat Days*.

Members of Bessie's family, and others who had close contact with her at the time, insist that Jack new nothing about stage production, but that he took full advantage of his wife's vulnerability.

Bessie had been seeing less and less of Jack. He rarely traveled with the show any more, and when he did, he often left abruptly after a fight with her. She had on several occasions announced their official separation, but since a reconciliation invariably followed, such proclamations were taken lightly.

As their fifth wedding anniversary passed, the most one could say for Mr. and Mrs. Jack Gee was that they were still married. Strong-willed and set in their ways, each seemed unable or unwilling to adjust to the other. They fought incessantly, tolerated each other's promiscuities to a certain extent, and spent most of their married life playing a nerve-wracking game of hide and seek.

Giving Jack the three thousand dollars, and involving him actively in her show, indicated an attempt on Bessie's part to save her marriage. In any case, *Steamboat Days* soon went into rehearsal, and tranquillity again reigned in the Gee household.

On August 23 Bessie recorded four sides with Grainger and two unspeakably bad dance-band musicians, who played various reed instruments. One can only marvel at the way she survives this substandard accompaniment of sobbing clarinets and dance-hall saxophones. "Yes Indeed He Do," "Devil's Gonna Git You," and "You Ought to Be Ashamed" are proof that the world's greatest blues singer could withstand some of the world's worst accompaniments.

The following day she recorded three outstanding sides: "Me and My Gin," "Please Help Me Get Him off My Mind," and "Poor Man's Blues." The latter is a poignant song of social protest, written by Bessie herself, and considered by some to be the finest record she ever made:

> *Mister rich man, rich man, open up*
> *your heart and mind,*
> *Mister rich man, rich man, open up*
> *your heart and mind;*
> *Give the poor man a chance, help*
> *stop these hard, hard times.*
>
> *While you're living in your mansion, you*
> *don't know what hard times mean,*
> *While you're living in your mansion, you*
> *don't know what hard times mean;*
> *Poor working man's wife is starving; your*
> *wife is living like a queen.*
>
> *Please listen to my pleadin', 'cause I*
> *can't stand these hard times long,*
> *Aw, listen to my pleadin', can't stand*
> *these hard times long;*

> *They'll make an honest man do things*
> *that you know is wrong.*
>
> *Now the war is over; poor man must live the*
> *same as you,*
> *Now the war is over; poor man must live the*
> *same as you;*
> *If it wasn't for the poor man, mister rich*
> *man, what would you do?*

The war had been over for ten years, of course, but Wilson's promise of democracy—if it ever included blacks—had not been fulfilled, and neither the Harding nor the Coolidge administration had made any progress in that direction. Bessie had no interest in politics, but it was plain that the postwar boom favored the white man. "Poor Man's Blues" was, in fact, "Black Man's Blues."

"Please Help Me Get Him off My Mind," another of her own compositions, is perhaps Bessie's most autobiographical song. It became increasingly relevant in the months to come:

> *I cried and worried, all night I laid*
> *and groaned,*
> *I cried and worried, all night I laid*
> *and groaned;*
> *I used to weigh two hundred, now I'm*
> *down to skin and bone.*
>
> *It's all about a man, who always kicks*
> *and dogs me aroun',*
> *It's all about a man, who always kicks*
> *and dogs me aroun';*
> *And when I try to kill him, that's when*
> *my love for him come down.*
>
> *I've come to see you, gypsy, beggin' on*
> *my bended knee,*
> *I've come to see you, gypsy, beggin' on*
> *my bended knee;*
> *That man put somethin' on me; oh, take*
> *it off of me please.*

The song reveals the inner conflict that plagued Bessie: her instinct to hold on to Jack despite all the odds against their happiness. "I think she wanted to break away from him," said a onetime Smith chorine, "but it seemed like every time they had a fight he'd find some way to sweet her up again. He knew she couldn't leave him—Bessie always wound up feeling kinda sorry for him—but Gertie changed that."

Gertie was Gertrude Saunders, Irvin C. Miller's most glorious "brownskin beauty," and she was about to solve Bessie's inner conflict.

After touring Washington, D.C., and Pittsburgh, Bessie's *Steamboat Days* gave 1929 a lively welcome at the Standard Theatre in Philadelphia. On January 14, the show opened at the Lincoln Theatre in Harlem, with comedian Sam Davis, father of Sammy Davis, Jr., added to the cast. "While we were at the Lincoln," recalls Louise Alexander, "something happened to make Bessie mad. She showed her anger by marching up and down in front of the theatre, dragging her mink coat on the sidewalk. I guess she was demonstrating her independence."

In the meantime, Jack kept busy fulfilling Sam Reevin's request for a second show. Rehearsals had already begun at the Knights of Pythias hall, and Jack had picked Gertrude Saunders to star.

Miss Saunders had scored several hits as the star of Irvin C. Miller's *Red Hot Mama* during the 1926 season, and had headlined in various editions of that show ever since, but her most successful shows had been *Liza* and *Shuffle Along*. Lured away from *Shuffle Along* with promises that came to nothing, Miss Saunders' career had been on the downgrade ever since. Florence Mills—the ultimate black beauty of the day—had replaced Miss Saunders in *Shuffle Along*, capturing a limelight that even her death, in November 1927, could not restore to Gertrude Saunders.

Just when Jack's relationship with Miss Saunders began is not known; perhaps she accounts for some of his hunting trips. Her personality and looks contrasted sharply with Bessie's: her complexion was light, her hair long and soft, her disposition gentle. She was also slim and quite a bit younger than Bessie—a typical "Miller beauty." The artistic gap that separated the two was equally wide: Gertrude Saunders relied more on her looks than on her voice, which had a Florence Foster Jenkins quality with a range that made her the Yma Sumac of her day.

Jack Gee's financing of Miss Saunders' show came out of Bessie's three thousand dollars. Surviving relatives insist that Bessie didn't know this, and Miss Saunders is not sure: "Jack could very well have put the money in my show without telling Bessie," she says. "Naturally he wouldn't tell me if it was her money, he'd want to act like a big shot."

After a short run in New York, Bessie's own show, *Steamboat Days*, hit the road again—Detroit's Koppin Theatre, the Globe in Cleveland, and, on March 11, a week at the Roosevelt in Cincinnati. There Bessie and some of her crowd went to a favorite speakeasy on the other side of the Kentucky border for a few drinks before the final show one evening. Bessie had walked over to greet some friends at a table when a young man engaged Ruby in conversation. On discovering that she was with Bessie, he pulled a copy of the *Amsterdam News* from under his arm, unfolded it, and showed her a story about Jack's success with the Gertrude Saunders show, which was then on tour in Columbus, Ohio.

More frightened than surprised, Ruby begged the young man not to let her aunt see the item. Intrigued by Ruby's insistence, he took back his paper, walked over to Bessie, and showed her the story.

Bessie looked at the item long enough to read it several times, and the expression of utter disbelief on her face changed the mood of those seated around the table. It was a surprisingly calm reaction—not at all what Ruby expected. Bessie rose slowly to her feet, turned to her show crowd, and said, "Let's go, it's time to get ready for the show."

She didn't say another word until she and Ruby were back in her dressing room. Then she broke down and cried—cried as Ruby had never seen her cry before. "Ruby, I'm hurtin'," she said. "I'm *hurtin'* and I'm not ashamed to show it. To think that Jack would feature another woman with *my* money!"

She stopped crying, dried her eyes, and got into her opening costume. "She said, 'Ruby, fix my feathers,' and then she went on stage as if nothing had happened, but she hardly did the show that night, she was so upset." When the final curtain came down, Bessie ignored the calls for encores, grabbed Ruby by the arm, and went out on the street—feathers and all—to look for a cab.

They rode all the way to Columbus, arriving there at two o'clock in the morning. It took Bessie half an hour to find the hotel where Jack was staying. Gertrude Saunders was registered there, too, but she had the good fortune to be out when Bessie arrived.

Bessie remained quiet during the long cab ride; she was sober now, and hurt feelings had turned to rage. Leaving Ruby outside in the hall, she entered the arena fighting. The ensuing holocaust left the hotel room a shambles—"there were pieces of furniture and feathers everywhere"—and when Bessie finally emerged she was bleeding. The game was over. Jack claims that he and Bessie eventually made up, but others insist that she never forgave him. One thing is certain: their married life ended in that Columbus hotel room.

Jack made his choice, abandoned Gertrude, and went back to the Wallace Theatre in Indianapolis with Bessie, but their relationship was beyond salvation; Bessie stayed drunk, and they fought continuously. Before her engagement at the Wallace was up, Bessie packed her things and walked out on the show. Jack tried to save the engagement by substituting Ruby for Bessie: "They padded me up and put me on stage. I went along with it only because Bessie wasn't there, she was very jealous at the time, and she didn't want anybody to sing that was halfway good. Someone must have told her about me singing in Indianapolis because she came back, and ran me off stage."

Bessie also ran Jack off. He moved on to Gertrude Saunders' show, stepping out of Bessie's life. Bessie finished her engagement in Indianapolis, making her way back to New York via St. Louis, Chicago, Pittsburgh, and Philadelphia. In Chicago she disbanded her show, and completed the tour with a reorganized group of Chicago entertainers.

Not everybody was surprised to hear of Jack's affair with Gertrude Saunders. "A lot of nights when we'd be on the train," recalls Maud, "I'd get off to go in the station and get sandwiches, or something like that, and I'd catch Jack and that woman in there, but I never told Bessie because then we'd never have reached our destination—Bessie would have killed both of them, so I just kept my mouth shut."

On April 22, Bessie took her new, hastily assembled *Harlem Frolics* to the Lincoln Theatre on West 135th Street. The *Amsterdam News* hailed it as her best show to date, and packed houses roared approval all week long. People close to Bessie recall that she took the breakup with Jack very hard, but she seemed determined to show him that she could do very well without him.

So far no voice had posed a threat to the Empress of the Blues. Now, however, there was a new voice in town: on the screen at the Lincoln, Alice White was starring in *Show Girl*—a moving picture that talked.

**8**

*It's raining and it's storming*
*on the sea,*
*It's raining, it's storming on*
*the sea;*
*I feel like somebody has ship-*
*wrecked poor me.*
"Shipwreck Blues"

May Day, 1929. Jack was gone. No matter how stormy Bessie's life with him had been, the relative calm that followed their separation was far more difficult to weather. Maud recalls this as having been a particularly difficult period for Bessie: "I'd find her in the state-room, crying. She would sit up in bed, unable to sleep, and she said she was lonesome." Bessie felt shipwrecked.

While her *Harlem Frolics* was still at the Lincoln, Bessie was asked by Maceo Pinkard to star in a Broadway show he was producing with an all-black cast. To most people a Broadway show represented the ultimate engagement, but to black performers it meant even more: a giant step into the prestigious world of white show business, a step that often led to Hollywood or Europe. As far as Bessie's career was concerned, Pinkard's offer was perfectly timed; her brand of blues had definitely lost its broad appeal, and the talking picture was beginning to strangle vaudeville.

*Pansy,* a musical story of college shenanigans, was to open at the Belmont Theatre on May 14, which left only two weeks for rehearsals. Pinkard, however successful as a songwriter,[1] was totally inexperi-

1. Pinkard's compositions include such standards as "Sweet Georgia Brown," "Sugar," and "Them There Eyes."

enced as a producer, and things were going badly. In spite of the short rehearsal time, Bessie accepted the offer. Her part was not demanding; all she really had to do was sing a couple of songs in the final act. She was the star only because she was the only "name" on the bill, and she was on the bill because Pinkard had little else to offer a Broadway audience.

Irvin C. Miller, who was still one of the most successful black producers, attended one of the rehearsals and recalls that nothing seemed to be working out. When Pinkard saw Miller standing in the wings, he hurried over for some professional advice. "The only way I can help you," said Miller, "is to knock you unconscious and drag you back to Harlem." As a veteran trouper, Bessie must have realized she was involved in a catastrophic production. Still, she stuck it out.

During rehearsals she found time for a recording session. More than three years had passed since she had worked with Clarence Williams. She had long since forgiven him, and now that Jack no longer had any say in the matter it was safe for Williams to accompany her again. With Williams and Eddie Lang, a white guitarist from Paul Whiteman's orchestra (he eventually became Bing Crosby's accompanist), Bessie recorded three of her most blatantly pornographic songs. "I'm Wild About That Thing," "You've Got to Give Me Some," and "Kitchen Man."

Bessie's recording of these songs has been interpreted as an attempt by her to bolster a fading popularity. But her recording repertoire was strictly in the hands of Frank Walker, who from his position in the recording field had an overview of changing musical tastes including the diminishing blues record sales.

"I'm Wild About That Thing" and "You've Got to Give Me Some" were written by Spencer Williams—a prolific composer with many hits to his credit[2]—but, oddly enough, they feature the same melody, and seem as uninspired as Bessie's singing. "Kitchen Man" fares better all around. It was written by Andy Razaf,[3] whose real name is Andreamenentania Paul Razafinkeriefo, nephew of Queen Ranavalona III of Madagascar.

Bessie's next session was altogether different, and far more rewarding. On May 15, accompanied by an excellent five-piece band,

2. Williams' hits included "Royal Garden Blues," "Basin Street Blues," "I Ain't Got Nobody," "Everybody Loves My Baby," and "I Found a New Baby."
3. Razaf's 1929 output alone included "Black and Blue," "Honeysuckle Rose," and "Ain't Misbehavin'," all written in collaboration with Fats Waller.

she cut the lusty "I Got What It Takes (But It Breaks My Heart to Give It Away)" and a song that would be associated with her for years: "Nobody Knows You When You're Down and Out."

*Once I lived the life of a millionaire,*
*Spending all my money, I didn't care;*
*I carried my friends out for a good time,*
*Buyin' bootleg liquor, champagne and wine.*

*When I began to fall so low,*
*I didn't have a friend, and no place to go;*
*So, if I ever get my hands on a dollar again,*
*I'm goin' to hold on to it 'til them eagles grin.*

*Nobody knows you when you're down and out,*
*In my pocket, not one penny, and my friends,*
    *I haven't got any;*
*But if I ever get on my feet again, then I'll meet*
    *my long lost friends;*
*It's mighty strange, without a doubt,*
*Nobody knows you when you're down and out.*

Bessie's interpretation was cynical and poignant. When she came in again after the instrumental chorus—a moving solo by trumpeter Ed Allen—she hummed half of her lines, expressing the feeling behind the song more effectively than any words do:

*Mmmmmmmmmmm when you're down and out,*
*Mmmmmmmmmmm not one penny,*
*And my friends, I haven't any.*

*Mmmmmmmmmmm never felt so low,*
*Nobody wants me aroun' their door,*
*Mmmmmmmmmmm without a doubt,*
*No man can use you when you're down and out,*
*I mean when you're down and out.*

Bessie had every reason to feel depressed on the day of that recording: *Pansy* had opened the night before, with most of the drama taking place backstage, and its reviews were devastating, if not to her, then to the vehicle for her Broadway debut.

Disheartening as rehearsals had been, the opening was even worse. As the racially mixed first-night audience, including the top New York critics, filed slowly into the theatre from West Forty-eighth

Street, what was left of the cast backstage were still awaiting delivery of their costumes. Six of the principal players, fed up with the whole thing, had already walked out.

Half an hour past curtain time, the costumes finally arrived. A series of frantic telephone calls had produced six substitute performers, who were, of course, thoroughly unfamiliar with the show. It is a wonder that Bessie—or, for that matter, anyone—stayed, and that the show went on at all. One reviewer wrote it was "as if the dancers were meeting each other for the first time on stage."

The reviews speak for themselves. Under the innocuous heading "To Be Read into the Records," Brooks Atkinson's *Times* review read:

> Purely for purposes of historical record let this bema quietly announce that the worst show of all time was good-naturedly produced at the Belmont last evening by a handful of colored entertainers. . . . Until the audience had succumbed to the fatal fascination that always surrounds the successive "new lows" of the theatre, hisses and boos came out of the darkness with a vehemence that optimistic newspaper men expected to see transformed into a Big Demonstration.
>
> By the time the second act staggered behind the footlights, however, those who still remained in the audience had decided to entertain themselves, and succeeded after a fashion. Presently the obese and wicked-orbed Bessie Smith was shouting in splitcord tones, that "If the blues don't get you" neither she nor the devil would know what to do. Since she was the only practiced performer in the company, and a good one, too, the audience thereupon howled "Bessie Smith" until the poor woman, with a moon-shaped face, was completely exhausted. Three times she came from behind the scenes to break the shock of complete defeat. . . . By this time "Pansy" is well on the way to forgiveness and limbo.

Under the heading "A 'Musical Novelty,' Bad Beyond Belief," Richard Lockridge of the *Sun* took aim:

> "Pansy" is not a show in any possible construction of that loosely applied word. . . . It is, with one momentary interlude of professionalism, the sort of thing that children of five might put on in somebody's barn with costumes borrowed from their elders. . . . Bessie Smith furnished the contrast by which the least initiated could perceive how far even from amateur standing were the others. She sang and danced with gusto. She did more—she performed. And those of the audience who had waited for her shook the little theatre with cheers. Those cheers kept her out until she was weary and laughingly protesting. But they could not, finally, stave off the rest.

Wilella Waldorf of the *Evening Post* insisted that the audience had come to hear Bessie and that their staying through the first act, in which she did not appear, was "a remarkable testimonial to her powers as an entertainer." Her description of Bessie's appearance adds a detail or two not found in the other reviews:

> Miss Smith, a rather weighty personage of great good humor, sang a song called "If the Blues Don't Get You" over and over and over to wild applause, likewise executing sundry dance steps at intervals by way of variety. Just as it looked as though she might be kept there all night, Miss Smith announced breathlessly that she was tired and that she was too fat for that sort of thing, anyhow, whereupon she was allowed to retire.

Only Arthur Pollock of the *Brooklyn Eagle* seemed unfamiliar with Bessie. "A stout colored lady named Bessie Smith," he wrote, "sang as if perhaps she had sung somewhere before."

On May 16, after three such memorable performances, *Pansy* met the fate Brooks Atkinson had predicted. Even its closing was a minor disaster.

Before opening at the Belmont, a few performances of *Pansy* had been given at the Lafayette, and Maceo Pinkard owed the cast some money. He had promised to pay it after the May 16 performance, and when he failed to show up that night, the cast nearly rioted. The apprehensive theatre management, who were also owed money, ordered the show's effects removed. Five days later Maceo Pinkard announced that a "considerably revised" version of *Pansy* would soon open. It did, somewhere in the Bronx, where it quickly gasped its final breath.

As far as Bessie was concerned, her Broadway debut had come and gone. She had been good, the show hadn't, and now she was through thinking about it. She did not get involved in *Pansy*'s ill-fated Bronx revival, for better things were brewing. While the rest of Pinkard's cast remained in what appears to have been well-deserved obscurity, Bessie embarked on a totally new venture.

Bessie had long been fascinated by movies. From backstage she had seen many of them over the years, viewing the reversed images on the screen in a hand-held mirror. The film industry had not been interested in her services, but now that pictures featured sound she was a natural.

Kenneth W. Adams and W. C. Handy had collaborated on a short

Bessie has just caught her boyfriend (Jimmy Mordecai) in a compromising situation with a rival (Isabel Washington Powell). From the 1929 film *St. Louis Blues. Photo courtesy of Rudi Blesh.*

The eyes that lured Jack away. Gertrude Saunders, Bessie's real-life rival, in a 1922 publicity shot. *Photo courtesy of Frank Driggs.*

scenario based on Handy's "St. Louis Blues," which they submitted to RCA Phototone. The advent of talking pictures was revolutionizing not only the film industry, but the whole field of entertainment as well. New film companies were springing up overnight, and all were searching for suitable material. Phototone immediately accepted the script and commissioned Dudley Murphy to direct a two-reel short.

At Handy's suggestion Murphy cast Bessie in the lead. She had made the definitive recording of the title tune, and her powerful voice was one of the few that could be heard over the projected accompaniment of a forty-two-voice mixed choir, jazz band, and strings.[4]

The seventeen-minute short was filmed in Astoria, Long Island, during late June 1929. The plot was thin; the main ingredient was Bessie's singing of Handy's song. She portrays a woman named Bessie who is driven to drink by her handsome, opportunistic, unfaithful boy friend. Stepping over a crap game on the ground floor of what appears to be a rooming house—supposedly in Memphis—she opens the door to her room and catches her boy friend Jimmy (played by Jimmy Mordecai) in a compromising situation with a young lady (played by Isabel Washington, who four years later became Adam Clayton Powell, Jr.'s, first wife[5]). After a brief struggle she throws her rival out of the room and is herself thrown to the floor by her boy friend. Still on the floor, she grabs a bottle of liquor, gulps it down, and proceeds to sing the verse to "St. Louis Blues" *a capella.*

As James P. Johnson's piano joins in, the scene shifts to a smoke-filled dive. Bessie is now leaning against the bar, singing into her drink with plenty of support from the huge choir, members of which are strategically seated at tables throughout the room. There follows a hot instrumental passage during which the band is seen briefly, customers get up to dance, and waiters perform acrobatic twirls with their trays. Bessie's boy friend makes a reappearance, accepts Bessie's radiant embrace, and they dance a slow grind together. A happy ending? No. Dazed by the unexpected reunion, Bessie does not see him remove a small bankroll from her stocking. Money

4. The choir is conducted by J. Rosamund Johnson and the orchestra, consisting almost entirely of members of the Fletcher Henderson band, is under the direction of James P. Johnson.

5. Mrs. Powell recalls auditioning for the part and being rejected because her complexion was too light. "I can be dipped," she told the man, who agreed and signed her up.

in hand and a gleam in his eye, the boy friend pushes Bessie back to the bar and struts out of the joint. Staring into her drink, she sings until the final fade-out.

Stories still circulate of how *St. Louis Blues* was originally banned because it was considered too controversial, or "lost" until the mid-nineteen-forties, when someone found a print in Mexico. But theatre advertisements and reviews attest to the fact that the film was shown fairly often between 1929 and 1932. Nowhere is there any indication that *St. Louis Blues* was ever considered too racy to be released. It may have been forgotten for fifteen years or so, but it certainly was never lost.[6]

(In 1950, a group of white liberals petitioned the N.A.A.C.P. to buy what they believed to be the only existing copy of Bessie's film and destroy it. Taking understandable offense to the film's stereotypical portrayal of dice-shooting, eye-rolling blacks, they seemed to lose sight of the fact that the film industry had traditionally stereotyped virtually every ethnic group—*St. Louis Blues* was but a drop in the ocean—and, more important, that those seventeen minutes represented the only footage extant of one of the greatest performers America had produced. Without it Bessie Smith's movements and the effect of her animated facial expressions would have died with the people who saw her in live performance.)

As the talkies put show business through some major changes, Bessie experienced a few of her own. She was still making good money, so the state of the entertainment industry did not worry her. What did occupy her mind was the jealousy she felt every time she thought of Jack, who was still working with—and romancing—Gertrude Saunders. There was no love lost between Bessie and Jack; by this time it was a matter of pride. "People would see Gertrude and Jack together, and they wouldn't tell Bessie because there was no way in the world that Gertrude could ever beat Bessie," recalls Maud. "But Gertrude did know how to handle Bessie—she stayed out of her way." Miss Saunders denies any romantic attachment: "It was strictly a business relationship," she says. "Jack managed my shows, but I never loved him—how could I? He was just an ignorant darkie, but he had a good business head on him, and he was perfect for Bessie; those two belonged together."

6. Although the print found in Mexico was announced as a "discovery," other prints, in superior condition, existed all along, including an excellent one in Dudley Murphy's private collection.

Piecing all the information together, it seems clear that Jack's relationship with Gertrude Saunders was not simply a platonic one. Jack, Jr., recalls that the affair started long before Bessie found out about it: "I've seen times when Mama was on the road and he'd bring Gertrude right to our house."

The hatred between the two women was so intense, especially on Bessie's part, that people predicted Bessie and Gertie would sooner or later have a fatal confrontation. The rivals did have at least two stormy meetings—both of which are said to have been nearly fatal to Gertrude Saunders.

Miss Saunders today confirms Bessie's jealousy and certain details of the incidents, but denies that they ever came to blows. Her claim that Bessie could be dealt with verbally is not convincing. While she is quick to berate Jack Gee, she speaks of Bessie in surprisingly sympathetic, though patronizing, terms: "I really think she loved Jack, but he didn't treat her right, and she would get violent because that's all she understood—neither one of them had any education, and they just didn't fit in with the crowd."

The first encounter took place on the road, shortly after Jack and Bessie had fought it out in the Columbus hotel room. Bessie's show hit a small town in the Midwest, and Gertrude Saunders' show was leaving town that same day.

There had been a bad flood, leaving the unpaved street muddy and partially covered with water. A barge was moored to a pole at one end of the street, ready to take people across a particularly deep stretch.

Bessie and some members of her company were on their way to the hotel, trudging through the slush, when Bessie spotted Gertie and Jack heading toward the barge.

"You motherless bitch!" muttered Bessie, tearing off in their direction like a racehorse, spattering mud in all directions. Before Jack knew what had happened, Bessie grabbed Gertie by her long hair, dragged her through the mud, and started beating her in the face. The two women rolled around in the slush as Jack tried unsuccessfully to separate them. "They looked like two mudpies, you could hardly tell one from the other," said a witness.

"I'm go-ing to make you beau-ti-ful for the show. I am go-ing to make you beau-ti-ful for the show to-night," Bessie said, emphasizing each syllable with a blow to Gertie's bleeding face.

Jack finally managed to pry Bessie loose and push her back into the mud. As she lay there, clutching a fistful of her rival's long hair, Gertie and Jack ran to the barge and pushed it out a safe distance into the deeper water.

"I'm gonna get a gun and kill you," screamed Gertie, hysterically.

"I'll make you eat it, bitch," Bessie roared back, "and every time I see you, you yellow bitch, I'm gonna beat you. One of these days, when you're up on stage, I'm gonna be in the audience and I'm comin' up and grabbin' you off."

Some people say Gertie did apply for a gun permit, purchase a weapon, and carry it around with her as protection against Bessie. Others say that Jack gave her his gun, but Gertie denies ever having had a gun.

The second incident happened much later, in the early nineteen-thirties, when Bessie was living in an apartment on Harlem's West 133rd Street. With equipment supposedly purchased for him by Bessie before their final breakup, Jack had opened a barbershop on Seventh Avenue, near the Lafayette Theatre, almost directly across the street from Bessie's apartment. Gertie owned an adjoining candy and tobacco store, separated from Jack's shop by a rest room that was accessible from either side.

One evening around closing time, Gertie was counting up the day's receipts when she saw Bessie approach the store. The story goes that Bessie, missing some valuable jewelry, learned that Jack had given it to Gertie. She had come to get it back and, during a relatively calm encounter, Gertie told her that the jewelry had been pawned and that Bessie was welcome to the pawn tickets. Bessie took the tickets, and that was that.

Within a half hour an explosive, fiery Bessie Smith returned to the store; the pawn tickets had yielded some cheap costume jewelry, not hers, and it was obvious that this second encounter would be anything but calm.

Gertie reached for the gun in her purse but Bessie was too quick. She jumped over the counter, knocking change in every direction, grabbed Gertie by the hair, and dragged her screaming and fighting out into the street.

"I'm goin' to get you this time, bitch," Bessie said, then beat Gertie until she dropped unconscious to the sidewalk.

Again Jack tried to intervene, but Bessie was in a rage, and it took more than one man to hold her down. The police were quick to arrive on the scene, and Bessie was given a summons. Gertie had had enough; she vowed never to have anything to do with Jack again. It is said that she did not keep her vow.

It's hard to ascertain how much of this story is true. Bessie's police record, and it surely exists, is harder to obtain than her rarest phonograph record. In any case, Gertie's recollection of the incident is certainly less dramatic:

"Jack had bought this barbershop from someone in the South, at a time when he had money, and put it in storage in New York so that he could open it when the show business went bad. He got it all fixed up beautiful on Seventh Avenue, and I took the next-door store myself because my mother was having heart trouble and I had to stay in town and look after her.

"I don't know what Jack had told Bessie, but she just came into my store and started to cuss and raise hell. She was so vicious, but I was always calm, and you know if you stay calm and cool you can handle these people, but if you're going to rant like they do, somebody's going to get hurt. I think she had a reason to do the things she did, I guess, because I think she loved Jack, but she had this other man and it was all a big confusion.

"When she came into my store I told her, 'Bessie, go sit down now and calm yourself, this is my store and I'm busy, so you just sit down.' She cussed me out, but I just went on talking calmly. 'We're not going to fuss, I've got to count my change here—these pennies—want to help me count these pennies?' So she just raised cain, and when she found out she wasn't getting no fight out of me, she walked out. But I was always ready for her because she was drunk, you know, and she was bigger and stronger than me. I figured I was smarter than she was, I could help her and myself by not fighting with her. I had a reputation of being kind of fiery, too, but I wouldn't shoot no woman over no man, unless somebody was going to kill me and I could get to a gun, but I never carried one."

Considering the circumstances, Bessie's attitude toward Gertrude Saunders, and the fact that she was drunk, it is not very likely that she would have passed up a fight.

By the summer of 1929, talkies were firmly established and the demise of vaudeville was already being predicted. It was certainly clear that the great days of the T.O.B.A. were numbered. Although it had provided employment for many black artists, the organization itself had always been considered second-rate. Most of its theatres had been in shameful condition during vaudeville's heyday, but now they were even worse.

Working conditions, too, had become more intolerable. For years performers traveling the circuit had put up with inhumane schedules, bad lighting, and inadequate or even nonexistent dressing-room facilities because the T.O.B.A. was the only game in town. Now the quality of the shows themselves had begun to deteriorate, the public was beginning to complain, and attendance was down. The Chicago *Defender* even ran an article on "The Death Trail of the T.O.B.A."

The Empress of the Blues could still pack them in—even in New York, which had long since ceased to be considered blues territory—but her record sales were falling off, and the talk she heard around town was not encouraging.

Columbia had just exercised its option for twelve more sides, and on July 25 Bessie recorded two more sides with Clarence Williams, "Take It Right Back ('Cause I Don't Want It Here)" and "What Makes Me Love You So?," which was never released. Record companies were now recording many male blues singers (for much less money), and promoting them almost as heavily as they once had Bessie and her female rivals. That and the fact that most theatres were having sound projectors installed were the first indications Bessie had that her profession was taking a major step in a new direction, a step that would affect her tremendously.

In August she opened as a single at the Standard Theatre in Philadelphia. However, the days of Bessie Smith extravaganzas were not over; she soon returned to New York to begin rehearsals for *Late Hour Dancers*,[7] featuring a cast of forty.

*Late Hour Dancers* was such a success at the Lafayette Theatre that it continued the following week at the Lincoln. During that week of September 2, in a world as far removed from Bessie's as any could be, the Big Bull Market reached its peak. Before long the Empress—who rarely read a newspaper and who had not the slightest interest in anything that went on below 132nd Street—would feel the sting of Wall Street's misfortunes.

Columbia picked Friday, the thirteenth of September, to release Bessie's "Nobody Knows You When You're Down and Out." Certainly it was prophetic of Bessie's future. And the way things were heading, it could have served as the national anthem.

---

7. Four days before *Late Hour Dancers* was scheduled to open at the Lafayette, she recorded "He's Got Me Goin' " and "It Makes My Love Come Down" with James P. Johnson.

Male blues singers were not likely to get rich from their records. Peg Leg Howell, a popular artist of the day, did not even receive copyright royalties on his own compositions. *Page from a Columbia Records ledger.*

*I'm gonna straighten up, straighter*
*than Andy Gump;*
*Ain't no use of me tellin' that lie,*
*'cause I'm down in the dumps.*
"Down in the Dumps"

When panic swept through the corridors of America's financial houses in October 1929, the long-range effect of the crash was foreseen by only a relative few. The impact on the average American was not immediate. Fortunes were lost overnight, but, of course, only by those who possessed them to begin with. In the early months of the Depression, not everybody found reason to jump out the window, apples were still something one purchased from a fruit dealer, and naive optimism delayed the broader effects to come.

The October 30 issue of *Variety* bore one of the paper's most famous headlines, "WALL STREET LAYS AN EGG." But the show went on, and it would be some time before the impact of that egg hit the entertainment industry at Bessie's level. Vaudeville—black and white—was still suffering its severest setbacks at the hands of the talkies, and the clearest victims were blacks, whose only alternatives were to stick it out as long as they could, seek another profession, or retire.

White vaudevillians found new doors opening to them: they could turn to Hollywood and join the competition—often portraying black people—or become household words via the three-year-old medium of network radio. Blacks appeared in films, too, but they were mostly low-budget shorts with limited distribution to black theatres. Network radio wasn't ready for blacks, but the old white team of

Gosden and Correll converted their racist Sam 'n' Henry dialogues into a situation comedy, and had millions of Americans from coast to coast laughing at stereotypes Amos 'n' Andy every night. The *Amos 'n' Andy Show* became the country's most popular home entertainment.

For a while, at least, business for Bessie continued as usual. She was touring with her *Midnight Steppers* show and carrying on an affair with one of her performers, blues singer Lonnie Johnson. "It was a constant thing to see Lonnie coming in and out of Bessie's stateroom, and he kept her company on the whole tour," Ruby recalls. "I thought it was strange seeing her messin' around with someone her own age, but they really carried on together." That Lonnie Johnson was a blues singer makes his intimate association with Bessie all the more unusual, but she may not have regarded a male singer as competition. "She was sweet on me," said Johnson in a 1959 interview, "but we never got real serious—Bessie had too many things going for her."

About the only thing Bessie had going for her in the last weeks of 1929 was the fact that she was still in business. The only depression she felt was a personal one, caused by events in her private life. But those who see the Bessie of that period as an anachronism, dejected and bitter, do her an injustice. Her drinking and the public's waning interest in the blues are the reasons generally given for the decline of her career. They are only partially valid. The blues had lost their popularity in New York—although not in the South—long before Bessie's career began to slow down. Her voice was still the strongest in the business, her spirit was unbroken, and her style and repertoire had never been limited to the blues. As for her drinking, it had been going on for years; if anything, she drank less as her career lost momentum.

While Bessie continued bringing her shows to one-horse towns, putting up with woefully inadequate theatre facilities, and cooking her greens in austere theatrical boardinghouses, many of Bessie's colleagues moved on to worldwide fame. Alberta Hunter was a big hit with Paul Robeson in the long-running London production of *Show Boat;* Sam Wooding and his orchestra—who had accompanied Bessie at Smalls' Paradise—made records in Barcelona, and were touring the Continent with great success; Josephine Baker, winding up a two-year world tour, could boast over two thousand marriage proposals, at last count; Ethel Waters was headlining at the London

Palladium, hobnobbing with such notables as Tallulah Bankhead and the Prince of Wales, and considering various offers from Paris.

Bessie kept up with such news from abroad, but she showed no signs of envy—the world of European high society was one about which she knew nothing, and cared even less. People close to her during this period recall that she did not feel left behind, nor did she regard her professional future with anything but optimism.

Her private life was something else again. Bessie made no more attempts at a reconciliation with Jack. In fact, some surviving members of the family maintain that she obtained a divorce, and that she lived to see Jack remarry. "Jack was not the type to stay single," recalls Ruby. "He loved yellow women with pretty hair. That's why every time Bessie saw Gertie, she beat up on her. She said she was going to get her money's worth—and she did, almost."

During the first two years of the Depression, Bessie managed to maintain a comfortable apartment in New York, and a housekeeper who looked after Jack, Jr. She started off the new decade with what was to be her last T.O.B.A. tour. She had sold the railroad car, her salary had gone down from a peak of two thousand dollars a week to half that amount, but in 1930 Bessie was still making what was considered a great deal of money.

It has been said that the T.O.B.A. dropped Bessie, but actually theatre audiences dropped the T.O.B.A. By the beginning of 1930, the deteriorating quality of its shows had led to a virtual boycott of the circuit. White producers—widely and justifiably criticized for underestimating the ability of the circuit's black audiences to distinguish between artists and amateurs—hastily assembled third-rate touring companies. The talkies that now preceded the live shows still lured some people to T.O.B.A. theatres, but boos, hisses, and walkouts were now commonplace. Another reorganization of the circuit took place in mid-February; new officers were elected, policies changed, and improvements planned. But it was too late—the T.O.B.A. was on its last leg.

Nevertheless Bessie's T.O.B.A. show, *Moanin' Low,* with a cast of twenty, was well received. Reviewers praised its "ginger and pep," but beneath Bessie's energy lay a certain sadness: everything she loved seemed to be slipping away from her. Viola, Tinnie, and Lulu, still drinking up a storm, had not taken well to the necessary cut in their allowance and there were times when they were openly hostile toward Bessie. Ruby, through an arrangement made by Jack, was now performing in Gertrude Saunders' show. "Jack made me leave Bessie and threatened me by saying he'd better not catch me with Bessie's show any more. So I had to go with Gertie Saunders, but she couldn't stand me because she knew how close I was to Bessie."

Most heartbreaking of all, however, was the loss of Jack, Jr. Jack Gee had lost interest in his adopted son, but he knew how much he meant to Bessie. His successful effort to separate mother and son can therefore only be regarded as an act of vengeance. Though he was only ten at the time, Jack, Jr., clearly recalls how it happened:

One day, when Mama wasn't home and he was living with Gertrude at her house, he came and got me. He told me to get in the car and said that he wanted to take me somewhere. So I got in the car and wound up at the S.P.C.C. [Society for the Prevention of Cruelty to Children]. They kept me down there for about two weeks—he told the people that Mama let me stay out all night, which was a lie, and that I wouldn't go to school, which was true. She heard about it, of course, so she came down to the court, and they asked her if she ever let me stay out all night. Well, she raised no uncertain hell in that particular court, she said it was a lie. So they eventually let me go on the condition that she would take me and send me to Viola in Philadelphia. Well, she sent me to aunt Vi in Philadelphia that Monday, but I was very restless, and about two weeks later I was making my way back to New York. I was caught in Newark, New Jersey, and taken to this home. They notified Pop and he and Gertrude came over and got me at about four o'clock that morning, and took me back to New York. Gertrude hated me, and she wouldn't let me stay in the house, so they let me sleep down in the basement with her brother. So the brother got me up the next morning, made me clean all the halls, and so on, then gave me a quarter to go get something to eat. I seized the opportunity and ran away from there. As my luck would have it, I wound up at the S.P.C.C. again the next day, and this time they sent me away for good.

The S.P.C.C. sent Jack, Jr., to a home in Valhalla, New York, and for several anxious days Bessie didn't know where he was. Jack Gee was no help; he had achieved what he set out to do. He knew what had happened to the boy, but the rest of the family was in the dark until letters from Jack, Jr., arrived for Bessie, Teejay, Maud, and her brother Johnny Nabors (Bessie's drummer), whom Jack, Jr., liked. Before anyone could reply, the boy had been transferred to yet another home, a farm in Delaware.

If Bessie made any attempt to get her boy back, no one knows about it; if she wrote him any letters, he didn't receive them. At least she knew that he was being taken care of by someone, and she

Paul Robeson, Alberta Hunter (who wrote Bessie's first hit), Edith Day, and Marie Burke on stage of the Drury Lane Theatre during the 1929 London production of *Show Boat*. The cast of the show, which ran for eleven months, also included Cedric Hardwicke. Bessie never traveled further east than Long Island. *Photo courtesy of Alberta Hunter.*

probably realized that there wasn't much of a chance she could get to keep him. Her grief manifested itself not in tears, but in escalated hatred for Jack.

This was the most difficult period in Bessie's life; she was dispirited and lonesome. "She wouldn't cry, she'd just sit there, staring," said a dancer with the *Moanin' Low* company. "It was strange, Bessie used to carry on so when her and Jack were together, but—I don't know, sometimes I just couldn't believe this was the same woman. That man really broke her down, strong as she was."

During those months of being alone, Bessie drowned her personal problems in hard work. When the *Moanin' Low* company played Pittsburgh, Wheeling, and Cleveland, she proved that she was still able to fill theatres with enthusiastic audiences. But something besides Jack, Jr., was missing. When she returned to New York toward the end of March, she told friends that although her tour had been a success, there was too much "worry" out there and she didn't think things would ever be the same again.

Bessie's observation was not unfounded. Tin Pan Alley's latest hit was "Happy Days Are Here Again," but it was wishful thinking. The shadow of hard times loomed over the country: large corporations took drastic economy measures; small businesses went bankrupt; servants were either dismissed or "allowed" to work for room and board instead of salary. With thousands of workers joining the ranks of the unemployed each day, and with those who had jobs saving their money, performers' salaries and ticket prices had to be reduced. The Depression was becoming a way of life.

On March 27 Bessie and Clarence Williams were reunited in the recording studio after five years. She sounds strong and remarkably high-spirited on "Keep It to Yourself" and "New Orleans Hop Scop Blues," but the Depression was also having a devastating effect on record sales.

Bessie's 1929 recordings had been pressed in quantities averaging eight thousand each, a small figure compared to her earlier efforts. Now even that figure was cut in half. Frank Walker later admitted that in 1930 he saw little hope for the future of the recording industry. Whether or not to release a record—the cost of manufacture sometimes exceeded the profits—became a major decision. Such considerations might have been what prevented the release of two doleful sides Bessie recorded with Clarence Williams and Charlie Green on April 12.[1] The Empress, too, was slowly becoming a victim of the Depression.

She made a trip to Philadelphia on May 5, opening for a week at the Pearl Theatre at Twenty-first Street and Ridge Avenue. Billed as a "Record Recording Star" and "Originator of the Blues"—an immodesty she herself would not have been guilty of—she headed a large "get-together show" assembled locally by Quintard Miller. Actually she was appearing as a single; her regular song-and-dance routines were woven into a flexibly staged show.

1. "See If I'll Care" and "Baby, Have Pity on Me" finally reached the market in 1947.

*171*

Improved recording techniques had inspired changes in Bessie's accompaniments over the previous five years, and Frank Walker had experimented somewhat with her repertoire. Her stage presentations, however, had remained basically the same, at least in terms of her style and the type of songs she sang.

Now there was a visual change; she dispensed with the fancy headgear and elaborate costumes. She had loved them, but they were cumbersome, costly, and, by 1930, quite outdated. Now Bessie wore simple but elegant evening gowns, trimmed, perhaps, with a modest sprinkling of sequins. Also missing were the fancy hairstyles and the wigs she had loved to wear. Now she dyed her graying hair, straightened it, and swept it back.

On Bessie's opening day at the Pearl, her movie, *St. Louis Blues,* began a short run at the Alhambra Theatre on Harlem's 126th Street, "in answer to public demand." Twelve days later Bessie herself was at the Alhambra, headlining a small revue. Admission was relatively high for those times, twenty-five to fifty cents, but not too high to discourage Bessie's devoted followers.

During the second week of June, Bessie had what was probably the most unusual recording session of her career: two pseudo-religious tunes with James P. Johnson at the piano and the vocal backing of a slick harmonizing group called the Bessemer Singers. "On Revival Day" and "Moan, You Mourners" are traditionally berated by collectors and scholars, who feel that Columbia took its experiments with Bessie's repertoire too far. But it is interesting to hear the Empress taken out of her usual context, and although the vocal group seems to have stepped right out of Tin Pan Alley, the two sides—with Bessie engaging in mock sermonizing—have a quality that makes them hard to resist.

With that session Bessie completed the twelve selections called for in her annual contract. For the first time since signing up with Columbia, she had not been asked to make more than she had signed for. The handwriting was on the wall, and Bessie read it loud and clear.

The Depression had not yet taken the sparkle out of Harlem's night life. White socialites, movie stars, and foreign visitors still flocked uptown for a good time. One 1930 visitor was the English musical comedy star Gracie Fields, whose report—published in the London *Sunday Dispatch*—received due criticism in the Chicago *Defender.* American racism, said the *Defender,* was spreading to Europe:

Meanwhile, back home, Bessie sheds her horse hair and feathers for a more sophisticated look. *Photos courtesy of Richard Lamparski.*

One evening we went to the famous Cotton Club in Harlem, the colored quarter. They give a marvelous show of dancing and there is a grand orchestra, a real nigger band. It was a place of rather low order and I went there especially for that reason. I wanted to see Harlem in its natural state. There were white women and black men dancing, and black women and white men dancing. If you wanted to dance with a black man you could do so. There were gigolos just waiting to be asked.

The *Defender* excused Miss Fields—who would seem to have confused the Cotton Club with the Savoy Ballroom—in a footnote supplied by singer Ivan H. Browning, its London correspondent. Miss Fields "actually holds no racial animosity," reported Browning, "but picked up her idea of Harlem from white Americans."

The most noticeable change in Harlem was its size; since Bessie's arrival there in the early twenties it had expanded a few blocks south, and 125th Street was becoming the main drag. There, between Seventh and Eighth Avenues, was the Apollo Theatre, owned and operated by the partners Hurtig and Seamon. From Yiddish burlesque shows featuring such performers as Fannie Brice and Sophie Tucker, the Apollo began turning to black vaudeville.

The main attraction at the Apollo over the Fourth of July weekend in 1930 was *The Jail Birds,* featuring the team of Drake and Walker with a cast of sixty. Also on the program, with bottom billing, was Bessie.

It seems strange that she would have accepted such low billing at this time, but black shows were new to the theatre and the only logical explanation is that she saw in the engagement an opportunity to reach a new audience.

A week later she was back in Philadelphia, headlining her own revue at the Standard with a cast of forty-five, including some well-known names. The management of the Standard, fearing that the term "blues" might scare off a Depression audience, billed Bessie as "The Queen of Recording Artists."

As it turned out, the engagement was so successful that the Standard booked Bessie again for August 11. She returned to New York to rehearse an all-new, equally elaborate show for this engagement, calling it *Happy Times.* It was the last big production she starred in.

These were far from happy times at Columbia Records; the company continued to record its established artists, but hesitated to sign new contracts or pick up options. They had obviously not given up on Bessie; she was offered a new contract on the same terms as her previous agreements, except that the fee was reduced from $200 to $125 per selection. Bessie had no choice but to accept the cut.

On July 22, under the new agreement, she once again teamed up with cornetist Ed Allen, who had played so superbly for her on "Nobody Knows You When You're Down and Out." With an obscure pianist, Steve Stevens, they cut "Hustlin' Dan," a tune structured after the widely performed pseudo folk song "Stackolee," and "Black Mountain Blues," a J. C. Johnson composition that describes a most forbidding place:

> *Back in Black Mountain, a child will smack your face,*
> *Back in Black Mountain, a child will smack your face;*
> *Babies cryin' for liquor, and all the birds sing bass.*
>
> *Black Mountain people are bad as they can be,*
> *Black Mountain people are bad as they can be;*
> *They uses gun powder just to sweeten their tea.*
>
> *On this Black Mountain, can't keep a man in jail,*
> *On this Black Mountain, can't keep a man in jail;*
> *If the jury finds him guilty, the judge will go*
>     *the bail.*
>
> *Had a man in Black Mountain, sweetest man in town,*
> *Had a man in Black Mountain, sweetest man in town;*
> *He met a city gal, and he throw'd me down.*
>
> *I'm bound for Black Mountain, me and my razor and*
>     *my gun,*
> *Lawd, I'm bound for Black Mountain, me and my razor*
>     *and gun;*
> *I'm gonna shoot him if he stands still, and cut him*
>     *if he run.*
>
> *Down in Black Mountain, they all shoot quick and*
>     *straight,*
> *Down in Black Mountain, they all shoot quick and*
>     *straight;*
> *The bullet'll git you if you start dodging too*
>     *late.*

*There's a devil in my soul, and I'm full of bad*
    *booze,*
*There's a devil in my soul, and I'm full of bad*
    *booze;*
*I'm out here for trouble. I've got the Black*
    *Mountain Blues.*

Bessie's performance on these sides is magnificent; but, more and more, records were becoming a luxury the average American could ill afford. Frank Walker chose that day to inform Bessie that Columbia was once again on the verge of bankruptcy. The record was ill afford. Frank Walker chose that day to inform Bessie that Columbia was once again on the verge of bankruptcy. The record was released in October with the number of pressings made again cut in half: 2095. Not many years before, Bessie's records had often sold more copies than that in a single day.

New York was the center of black as well as white show business, the home of the big record companies, the great theatres, the big-time black producers, songwriters, and talent. Some of the biggest black stars lived in New York, and by the summer of 1930 many of them were idle because the high salaries they commanded could no longer be met. Taking advantage of the situation, Sam Reevin, now manager of the entire T.O.B.A. circuit, visited New York, hoping to sign up major black talent in a last-ditch effort to save the dying organization. "This will either make us or break us," he told a reporter. Reevin's efforts failed: the T.O.B.A. did not survive the summer.[2]

With the T.O.B.A. dead, Bessie had to make other arrangements for her fall theatre tour. With the help of Frank Walker, Clarence Smith planned a tour through the Deep South into Texas. It was a brave venture: American show business troupes often found themselves stranded in far-off places, but the Depression had made this an everyday occurrence, and Texas was known to be a particularly hard state to get out of.

As "Black Mountain Blues" was shipped to dealers who had managed to stay in business, Bessie and her gang embarked on their long trek, stopping first in Chicago. That stop changed her life.

Paying her traditional visit to Richard Morgan, Bessie was greeted

2. Another unsuccessful attempt was made to revive the T.O.B.A. circuit in 1945.

with open arms and more than the usual warmth. Morgan had heard of her separation from Jack. He told her that he had left his common-law wife, Lucy, and somehow during that visit the two of them decided to turn their long-standing friendship into a much closer relationship. When Bessie and her troupe continued on their journey south, they had a new manager and Bessie had a new lover. It had been quite a while since she had been so happy.

Although at first Bessie had paid little attention to the news of the Depression, she was now experiencing its effects first hand. She began to read the newspapers to keep up with events and trends. What she learned was not encouraging. Many theatres had replaced their stage shows with talking pictures; others had closed altogether. Unable to maintain her latest show, *The Arkansas Swift Foot,* Ma Rainey was touring with Boise De Legge's *Bandanna Babies,* and not doing too well at that. The traditionally successful producer Lew Leslie had to close his *Blackbirds of 1930,* starring Ethel Waters, after five disastrous weeks on Broadway.

Bessie could take some comfort in the fact that she hadn't lost her grip on Southern audiences. From Mobile, Alabama, to the Lincoln Theatre in New Orleans and the Central in Dallas, they came to hear the Empress with all the ardor of earlier audiences. Still, big-money days were over. Bessie could command only five to seven hundred dollars a week for most engagements, and her twenty-five troupers had to be paid out of that.

In spite of the problems, Bessie was happier than she had been during most of her high-income days. Richard Morgan genuinely admired her, both as an artist and as a person. He was certainly not after material gain—his bootlegging business had not suffered nearly as much as Bessie's profession. As things got worse for Bessie, Richard frequently made up the losses from his own pocket.

In Houston Bessie and Richard held Christmas dinner for their gang, which included Clarence and Maud. Hard times could not put an end to Bessie's generosity: she bought presents for all. The Christmas spirit was, of course, somewhat subdued by the absence of Jack, Jr.—who, unknown to Bessie, had now been moved to a home in Easton, Maryland—but Richard helped fill the void.

"She was like a new person," Maud recalls. "Richard was everything that Jack should have been. They got along very well, they both loved a good time, and they respected each other. Richard was very jovial when he'd had a few drinks, but he never got nasty, and when he was sober you had a hard time getting a word out of him. He was a good businessman, he didn't throw money around, but he wasn't tight either. Also, he was tall and handsome, a real sharp dresser. He was perfect for Bessie, he understood her."

Bessie's *Broadway Revue,* as her show was now called, toured Texas in January, appearing in Beaumont, Austin, and San Antonio, and stopping over in Monroe, Louisiana, before heading north. She had not followed Jack's activities since their final separation, but an item in the January 3, 1931, *Defender* indicated that he hadn't exactly become the new Flo Ziegfeld. According to the paper, Jack had left a company stranded in Detroit and taken off with the receipts. With the help of the Koppin Theatre's booking agent, the enraged crew had sworn out a warrant for Jack's arrest.

On May 13 *Broadway Revue* opened at the Pythian Theatre in Wheeling, West Virginia. Booked for three days, the show was so successful that the management asked Bessie and company to stay a week.

On Saturday night Bessie, having just been paid for the first three days, started drinking. An hour before the last show of the evening, she armed herself with a gallon of corn liquor and slipped away from the theatre. She was not trying to hide anything from Richard Morgan; unlike Jack, he was not upset by her drinking, nor did he demand that she account for her time. She simply wanted to look up some old friends and bring along refreshments.

One jug led to another, and by the time she headed back to the theatre Bessie was thoroughly drunk. Unable to get a cab, she roamed the streets in a stupor, occasionally breaking into songs or curses, which apparently disturbed more than the quiet night air. Someone called the police, who arrested and jailed Bessie for violating the Volstead Act.

Meanwhile the last show had gone on without her, and Richard Morgan had been told by an angry theatre manager that a whole day's fee would be deducted from the balance owed them at the end of the extra four days. It was two o'clock in the morning before Richard found out that Bessie was in jail. Some of the performers were still up, and the word quickly spread that Bessie's behavior was going to cost them a day's pay. Having bailed her out, Morgan took Bessie back to the Panhandle Hotel, where the troupe stayed, and told her how much trouble her absence had caused.

The news inspired one of her old tricks. Waking up her sister-in-law and brother, she had Clarence and Richard pack all the costumes and drops they could get on their rented truck. At dawn the four of them drove out of town, leaving the twenty-two other members of the troupe—none of whom had been paid—sleeping in rooms that had not been paid for.

Fortunately for the stranded company, Brother Aberton's *Mose from Birmingham* troupe came to play the Pythian Theatre two days later. Aberton gave them all a week's work and transportation to their respective homes.

By that time Bessie was already working at the Standard in Philadelphia as a single in a show headlined by dancer Peg Leg Bates, and news of her latest escapade was being widely circulated in the black press. The news did not hurt her popularity. It may even have stimulated business—the Standard held Bessie over for another week.

During her second week at the Standard, Bessie shared bottom but prominent billing with Viola McCoy, a blues singer whose career had started with Columbia in 1923, a month after Bessie recorded "Down Hearted Blues." It was a sign of the times—Bessie could no longer demand to be the only blues singer on the bill.

Bessie broke another tradition on June 11 when she recorded four sides with a small band that included drums: Louis Bacon, Charlie Green, Clarence Williams, and drummer Floyd Casey. The recordings of "In the House Blues," "Long Old Road," "Blue Blues," and "Shipwreck Blues"—all her own compositions—are flawed by poor balance; Bacon's trumpet sounds as if it is coming from another room, Green's trombone appears to be swallowing the microphone, and Bessie's voice has a shrill sound to it. Although the ensemble is a little rough, Bessie is singing extremely well. But Columbia's usual technical excellence is not in evidence. Perhaps no one cared any more. Only seven hundred copies were pressed of one record, and four hundred of the other. With figures like that there was no chance of breaking even.

Headlining a cast of forty in *Gossiping Liza,* Bessie returned to the Standard on July 6 for a two-week engagement, following *Trouble on the Ranch,* an all-black musical Western starring Clara Smith and a relative newcomer, Jackie "Moms" Mabley. She was held over again, sharing the stage during the third week with a new accompanist, Hack Back—"The Ukelele Wonder"—a combination that fortunately only lasted the week.

While Hack Back and Bessie were working things out, a mysterious item appeared buried in a *Defender* gossip column: "William W. Christian, trombonist, has just finished recording with Bessie Smith. He grabs his mail at 800½ W. Moore St., Richmond, Va." Her days at Columbia were clearly numbered, and it is possible that Bessie made recordings for another company at this point, but no such recordings have turned up. Quite possibly they were made and never released.

With the second anniversary of the stock market crash, even the most optimistic observers had to concede that the Depression was not going to be over soon. As bread lines became longer, box office lines dwindled: the Lincoln Theatre had now become the Mount Moriah Baptist Church; the Alhambra Theatre, which had dropped live vaudeville shows at the beginning of the Depression, announced its closing as of December 1931.

It has been said that Bessie was "selling chewing gum and candy in theatre aisles,"[3] but there is no truth to the story. Her fees were low, and her voice was affected at times by her hard living, but Richard Morgan's business continued to thrive, and even at its worst, Bessie's voice remained the best in the land. The legion of Bessie Smith fans was still strong, and there was always some place for her to display her talent.

As the Depression entered its third and most devastating year, Bessie found most of her offers—at least (since they didn't involve travel) the most lucrative ones—coming from Philadelphia. She became a regular at the Standard, Pearl, and Forrest theatres, often accompanied by a band led by Maud Smith's brother, Johnny Nabors.

But on November 20, 1931, when she recorded two sides with Fred Longshaw, Frank Walker confirmed what she had already foreseen: Columbia was dropping her. The relationship had lasted almost nine years, during which Columbia and Bessie had helped each other to the top. Now outside circumstances had put Bessie down, and Columbia all but out. It is not surprising that Bessie's voice seems to have lost some of its vigor on "Need a Little Sugar in My Bowl" and "Safety Mama"; she probably did not expect them to be released. As it turned out, they were—just ten days later. But an unusual order accompanied the masters to Columbia's pressing plant: "Ship parcel post only. Manufacture against shipping orders only."

3. *Bessie Smith*, a biography by Paul Oliver (Cassell & Company Ltd., London, 1959).

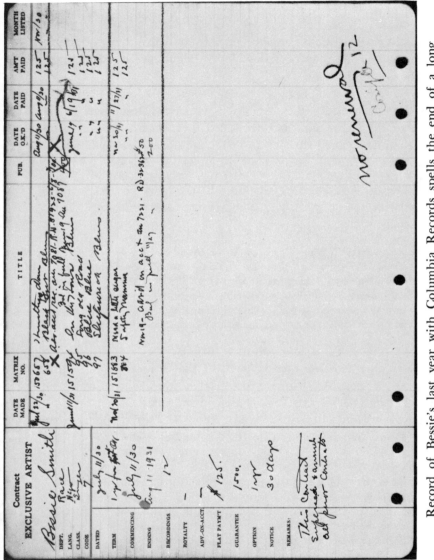

Record of Bessie's last year with Columbia Records spells the end of a long relationship, and shows that she went back to where she started—$125 per side. Notice descriptions in upper left hand corner. *Page from Columbia Records ledger.*

Including this last pair of tunes, Bessie had recorded only eight of the twelve sides called for in her contract, but Columbia found it cheaper to pay her five hundred dollars and forget about the remaining selections. In all her years with Columbia, Bessie never had a royalty agreement. She had been paid a total of $28,575—a fraction of what many young performers of lesser talent receive on signing a recording contract today.

On the road during the last three weeks of December, Bessie found that the Depression had not killed the demand for her brand of entertainment. On February 1, 1932, she opened at the Grand in Chicago, the scene of many past triumphs. A reviewer from the Pittsburgh *Courier* was there:

### BESSIE SMITH AND "GANG"
### CLICK AT GRAND THEATRE

Bessie Smith, herself, is back in town at the Grand theatre. And we don't mean maybe. She's singing "Please Don't Talk About Me When I'm Gone" and "Safety Woman Looking for a Safety Man" ["Safety Mama"]. Bessie has a real humane personality, and when she "puts it her way" it's really put over. She's a scream when she takes full possession of her 200 pounds averdupois [sic] and steps around like a finale-hopper on a ballroom floor.

The review did not mention that Bessie's week at the Grand netted her only two hundred dollars, or that a local critic—a professed fan of Bessie—attributed the packed theatre to the screen offering, *Possessed,* starring Joan Crawford and Clark Gable.

Pianist Art Hodes described one of Bessie's Chicago appearances, an interesting first impression, in the September 1947 issue of *Jazz Record:*

Now comes the big hush. Just the piano goin'. It's the blues. Somethin' tightens up in me. Man, what will she look like? I ain't ever seen her before. Then I hear her voice and, gosh, I know this is it . . . my lucky day. I'm hearing the best and I'm seeing her, too. There she is. Resplendent is the word, the only one that can describe her. Of course, she ain't beautiful, although she is to me. A white shimmering evening gown, a great big woman and she completely dominates the stage and the whole house when she sings the "Yellow Dog Blues."

There's no explainin' her singing, her voice. She don't need a mike; she don't use one. I ain't sure if them damn nuisances had put in their appearance that year. Everybody can hear her. This gal sings from the heart. She never let me get away from her once. As she sings she walks slowly around the stage. Her head, sort of bowed. From where I'm sittin' I'm not sure whether she even has eyes open. On and on, number after number, the same hush, the great performance, the deafening applause. We won't let her stop.

When they returned to New York after a spring tour through Alabama and Louisiana, Bessie and Richard found the situation there worse. Several Harlem clubs had closed; rumor had it that the Lafayette Theatre, Connie's Inn, and the Cotton Club were about to close. Even the Palace Theatre downtown had been forced to reduce its prices.

Jack, Jr., was still at the home in Easton, Maryland. He had written a letter to Frank Walker, inquiring about Bessie. The reply he got was not encouraging; his mother was no longer with the Columbia company, and Walker knew only that her last mailing address was 1139 Kater Street in Philadelphia. Shortly thereafter, Jack, Jr., was transferred to yet another home, in St. Martin, Maryland.

Bessie and Richard moved to Philadelphia around this time. A slight problem had developed with Lucy, Richard's former common-law wife: she wanted him back, and Bessie's reply was "I ain't forcin' him to stay with me." Indeed she wasn't. Lucy died not long after that. "I think she grieved herself to death, just as my uncle Richard grieved himself over Bessie," Lionel Hampton recalls.

Finally, in November 1932, Bessie received a letter from Jack, Jr., who wrote that he was back in New York with his father and that he wanted to be with her in Philadelphia. Bessie immediately assembled a delegation, including Richard, Maud, Teejay, and Maud's brother, Johnny Nabors. They all went to New York, paid a surprise call on Jack Gee, and brought the boy back to Philadelphia. Now Bessie was truly happy. "You could see it in her face, hear it in her voice." She closed out the year at Philadelphia's Lincoln Theatre, sharing top billing with the popular vaudeville team of Butterbeans and Susie in *Hot Stuff of 1933*.

Nineteen thirty-two had been the leanest year for Bessie since she'd achieved stardom, and the outlook for 1933 was worse. In March she took second billing to Jules Bledsoe, the popular singing star of the Broadway production of *Show Boat* at Harlem's Lafayette, which, unlike most of its counterparts, was still in business. It was Bessie's first New York appearance in two years.

Her tours and local theatre appearances had so far kept her fairly busy, but offers were coming in less frequently now, and as spring approached and fees fell lower, Bessie spent more and more time at home. It was in this early part of 1933 that John Hammond, a wealthy twenty-three-year-old jazz enthusiast, met her and decided to record her.[4]

Hammond had heard Bessie perform in a Harlem theatre six years earlier, and he recalls that it was her singing that showed him there was more to jazz than instrumental improvisation. Hammond claims that Bessie was the singing hostess of a Philadelphia speakeasy in the spring of 1933, when he first met her and proposed making the records. "Bessie was amazed to find that someone actually wanted to record her again. She didn't think anyone loved her any more, and I don't think she really believed me."

No one who knew Bessie in 1933 believes Hammond's story of meeting Bessie in a speakeasy, or his claim of having had to pay her fare to New York because she was broke. She probably told Hammond that she was broke, and he probably did pay her fare, but Bessie was simply pulling an old trick—she knew that Hammond needed her in New York for the session, and that her fare was a small price to pay in order to assure her presence.

Neither the declining popularity of the blues, the shift from live to mechanical entertainment, nor prevailing national economic conditions ever left Bessie without money; she was still commanding a decent, if not extravagant, fee when she did work, and Richard Morgan saw to it that she was well provided for. None of the people close to her at the time ever recall Bessie working in a speakeasy, much less as a singing hostess.

As for recording again, Bessie probably didn't believe that Hammond—a total stranger to her—meant what he said. She knew well enough that records had stopped selling and that the status of the record industry had not improved in the year and a half since she had left Columbia. Victor had been absorbed by the Radio Corporation of America; Brunswick had been acquired by Warner Brothers; and the Majestic Radio Corporation, seeking an established worldwide distributorship, had bought the bankrupt Columbia company, which, of course, included acquisition of the Okeh label.

---

4. Hammond's entree to the record industry was its brush with bankruptcy and his inherited wealth. Underwriting the session expenses, Hammond's debut as a producer took place in 1932 when he recorded some solo sides with pianist Garland Wilson.

The larger corporations managed to keep the smaller ones in business, but just barely. Because Columbia records were still selling at seventy-five cents, Hammond decided to record Bessie for Okeh, whose releases at thirty-five cents stood a chance of selling at least a few copies. But neither Hammond nor Bob Miller, Okeh's recording director, looked on the Bessie Smith recordings they were about to do as a potential gold mine—not because they regarded Bessie as a has-been, but because there was virtually no market for anybody's records in 1933. Okeh could not even afford the fee for Bessie and her musicians. That came out of Hammond's own pocket; no royalties, just a flat $150—$37.50 per side.[5]

Bessie's recording session did not take place until several months after her meeting with Hammond. In the meantime Hammond made a trip to England to finalize plans for bringing an all-black satirical revue to London, with music by Duke Ellington. Bessie, after a more or less idle summer, accepted a one-day engagement at Pittsburgh's Roosevelt Theatre.

Pittsburgh audiences had always welcomed Bessie, and her one day turned into three weeks at the Roosevelt. She followed it with a special guest appearance at Mapleview Park, near Little Washington, a celebration of Emancipation Day, on Friday evening, September 22, an event that turned out to be more memorable than intended. Bessie, advertised as accompanied by "her Victor Recording Orchestra," was probably the most emancipated person there.

After singing a few songs and acknowledging her outdoor audience's enthusiastic response, Bessie stepped off the small makeshift stage, slipped, grabbed a pole supporting the canvas roof, and took the entire stage covering with her. As the crowd roared, she emerged from a heap of canvas, helped several local officials uncover the orchestra members, and announced to her audience that things had gone better at rehearsal. The incident must have reminded her of her first electrical recording and the "tent theory."

Bessie spent October at home. Richard's liquor business wasn't making them rich, but it provided enough income to make up for the times when Bessie was out of work. In any case, the days of bootleggers were numbered after the election victory of Franklin D. Roosevelt. The long-awaited repeal of Prohibition was only a month away. The Roosevelt victory was a shot in the arm, the dying embers of hope flared once again, and as the Women's Christian Temperance

Union saw their teetotaling dream deferred, "beer gardens"[6] resounded to the happy tune of the latest song hit, "We're in the Money."

Prosperity had, of course, not returned, but things were looking up for some entertainers. Radio network executives were beginning to eye black talent, and Hollywood was learning that black films need not be for blacks only. Ethel Waters, having scored a tremendous hit in Irving Berlin's *As Thousands Cheer,* signed a radio contract for a reputed $1250 per broadcast, and Dudley Murphy—the man who in 1929 had directed Bessie in *St. Louis Blues*—was enjoying a successful first run of his latest film, *Emperor Jones,* starring Paul Robeson.

Bessie, too, had reason for optimism. She opened at Harlem's Lafayette Theatre on November 18, sharing feature billing with comedian Dusty Fletcher and Mandy Lou, a Fred Waring singer who billed herself as "The Greatest Colored Radio Star." It wasn't top billing for Bessie, but it was more than she had been getting for quite a while.

Then, on November 24, after an absence of two years and four days, Bessie returned to the recording studio with an all-star interracial band, a voice that had lost nothing in the intervening years, and, as far as anyone could see, a reasonably bright future.

6. Legal establishments that heralded repeal, offering light wines and steins of beer for a dime.

# 10

*Picked up my bags, baby, and I tried it again,*
*Picked up my bags, baby, and I tried it again;*
*I got to make it, I've got to find the end.*

"Long Old Road"

When Bessie headed downtown on the subway that Friday morning in November 1933, she could hardly have expected her records for Okeh to do much for her career. But the mere fact that she had been asked to make them had to mean something. People were saying that with Roosevelt in the White House things would soon get better, and anticipation continued to have a good effect. Radio City Music Hall, for instance, was now accepting checks dated three months in advance.

Bessie's week at the Lafayette had been encouraging, and she was to open at the Lincoln in Philadelphia on the following day. The Harlem Opera House—so called because it featured grand opera at the end of the nineteenth century when Oscar Hammerstein built it—was negotiating with Richard Morgan for her to headline a special Christmas show. There didn't seem much doubt about it: the downward momentum of Bessie's career had been reversed.

Columbia and Okeh now had studios at 55 Fifth Avenue, where the entire company was housed on two floors. John Hammond was nervous: this was his first vocal date, and the artist was Bessie, whom he considered without peer. They had argued during the week over using Big Sid Catlett on the date; Bessie was still reluctant to record with drums. She got her way; who was Hammond to argue with the Empress?

Hammond had lined up a formidable band for Bessie's return to recording: trumpeter Frankie Newton, trombonist Jack Teagarden, tenor saxophonist Leon "Chu" Berry, and a rhythm section consisting of guitarist Bobby Johnson, bass player Billy Taylor, and the group's leader, pianist Buck Washington.

At Bessie's request, this was not a blues session. The four selections recorded were written by Leola B. Wilson and Wesley "Socks" Wilson, a husband-and-wife vaudeville team with a long list of Paramount, Okeh, and Columbia records to their credit. Looking back, Hammond has said that the songs in his opinion "do not compare with Bessie's own material of the twenties," and that the band "lacked the special qualities essential to good accompanists," but many critics and collectors regard the session as one of her finest. It differs from her earlier recordings in several important respects: the four selections "Do Your Duty," "Gimme a Pigfoot," "Down in the Dumps," and "Take Me for a Buggy Ride" offer the only opportunity to hear Bessie with swing accompaniment, the flexible rhythm of a string bass, and a saxophonist who doesn't sound like a refugee from a dance hall.

That session was also the only meeting of the Empress of the Blues and the future "King of Swing," although he appears on only one selection and his clarinet is barely audible. Benny Goodman, who happened to be recording with Adrian Rollini's orchestra in one of the two adjoining studios, dropped by Studio A long enough to make his presence known if not felt, on "Gimme a Pigfoot."

"Pigfoot" is a lusty tale about "Old Hannah Brown from 'cross town," who "gets full of corn and starts bringin' 'em down" at one of the illegal rent parties that were popular during the Depression. Bessie delivers the song with appropriate rowdiness, changing her request for "a pigfoot and a bottle of beer" to one for "a reefer and a gang of gin" in the final chorus. The reference to marijuana was common in lyrics and titles of thirties recordings. Tunes like "Reefer Man," "You'se a Viper," "Kicking the Gong Around," and "Viper's Dream" carried messages about drugs that few whites understood, but "Pigfoot" contains the only such reference by Bessie on records. (It is omitted from subsequent versions of the song, made by Billie Holiday in the late forties and Nina Simone in the early sixties, when the use of marijuana became a more widespread concern.)

In the thirties, marijuana smoking was as common in Harlem, Chicago's South Side, and other black ghettos as it is throughout the country today.[1] White society cared very little about what blacks did, as long as it didn't affect whites, but some blacks saw the widespread smoking of "tea" as a threat to the future of their people. The September 9, 1933, issue of the *Defender* carried on its entertainment page an article referring to it as "this deadly puff," and warned that marijuana left young blacks "weak-minded and without will."

Smoking "reefers" was so common in Harlem during the thirties that many older blacks find it hard to believe that today's highly controversial "pot" is the same thing. "No, no," says Ruby, "Bessie didn't smoke pot, not Bessie, nothing like that—just regular reefers."

The session that Friday in 1933 ended with the recording of "Down in the Dumps," which, as it turned out, was Bessie's recorded swan song.

There is an interesting footnote: three days later an eighteen-year-old Bessie Smith—inspired singer nervously entered the same studio to face the same microphone. Just as Bessie was ending her recording career, Billie Holiday was beginning hers.

During Thanksgiving week of 1933, Bessie had every reason to feel festive. The recording session had gone very well, and her appearance at the Lincoln was drawing enthusiastic crowds and reviews. Her repertoire now consisted mainly of popular tunes like "Smoke Gets in Your Eyes" and "Tea for Two," but she still sang the blues when her audience demanded it. The Lincoln featured weekly talent nights in which many children participated, and Bessie spent a lot of time with these children, talking to them and offering them advice.

Juanita Green, who as Baby Allen had first met Bessie around 1930, recalls that the children returned "Miss Bessie's" affection by escorting her to and from the theatre. Later, when she was about fourteen years old, Juanita would go to Bessie's apartment every Saturday and scrub her kitchen floor. Bessie might greet her at the top of the stairs, singing, and would often cook up a meal of chitterlings, boiled with scallions, dipped in flour, and fried.

The Lincoln boasted a "Triple Attraction" Thanksgiving week of

---

1. It seems ironic in retrospect, but marijuana was actually not illegal in the days when liquor was.

1933: Mandy Lou, Bessie, and Jackie Mabley.[2] One critic, completely ignoring Miss Mabley, wrote something that must have pleased Bessie: "Mandy Lou has made a name for herself with Fred Waring's Pennsylvanians, but Bessie Smith, 'Philadelphia's favorite daughter,' will always be the main attraction wherever she appears." Such praise only faintly echoed past accolades, but things seemed to be looking up for Bessie, and Richard Morgan was now talking about another Southern tour.

The Volstead Act was officially repealed within the next two weeks, but this did not mean that bars opened overnight, nor did it put bootleggers out of business. Heavy taxes on alcohol actually prolonged by several years the economic rewards of bootlegging and smuggling liquor from abroad.

Repeal had little effect on Bessie's drinking habits: "She was liking the bad stuff even when the good stuff was in," recalls Ruby. But Bessie did take advantage of the beer gardens.

While preparing for her four-day Christmas show at the Harlem Opera House in New York, some fifty Harlem beer garden patrons saw that Bessie's temper, like her singing voice, was still in fine working order. Seated at a table with Richard Morgan and two friends, Bessie overheard a young, light-complexioned chorine turning on her charm. Having first made sure everybody knew that she would appear in the Lafayette's *Yuletide Vanities*, the chorine sought to hold the attention of her listeners by berating other performers with all the authority of the novice. When the conversation turned to singers, someone mentioned that the Harlem Opera House was going to feature Bessie Smith.

"Bessie Smith!" exclaimed the chorine disdainfully. "Who cares about that old bag, and all them ugly Ma Raineys liftin' their legs."

Her friends were still laughing when Bessie—like a monster out of the sea—rose from her seat at the next table, turned to the chorine, ignored Richard Morgan's advice to sit down, and almost sang her words: "You little yellow bitch. Them Ma Raineys got more high-class movements in their toes than you'll ever have in your whole body, and don't you talk about my girls like that, 'cause you ain't gonna be in *no* show when I'm through with you!"

Then Bessie jumped the girl. Within minutes the beer garden was a free-for-all. Some patrons fled to the street; others remained and

2. On the screen at the Lincoln, Walt Disney's "Three Little Pigs" sang "Who's Afraid of the Big Bad Wolf?"

took sides. The police were summoned, but Richard Morgan managed to get Bessie out before they arrived.

Whether or not the indiscreet chorine appeared in the Lafayette's holiday production the following week is not known, but Bessie, advertised as "Queen of All Torch Singers," launched her *Christmas Revels* at the Harlem Opera House with "twelve dancing mermaids" whose looks scared no one off.

In the early part of 1934 it became apparent that Roosevelt's New Deal wasn't turning things around after all. This killed the 1933 euphoria that had swept Bessie and others into a flurry of promising activity.

After spending January at home, she opened at the Apollo Theatre on February 3. The show, *Fan Waves* (with proceeds going to the Harlem Childrens Fresh Air Fund), was a musical extravaganza featuring Bessie, the dancing team of Meers and Meers, comedians Dusty Fletcher and Gallie De Gaston, "Noma," a fan dancer, and "the Sepia Mae West," a mystery star, said to be "the sensation of Chicago," who appeared in a special production with sixteen chorus girls. It was not uncommon for black performers to be compared with white stars this way.[3] The irony was, of course, that the white stars were actually pale versions of the black performers they imitated—Harlem had its Mae Wests and Sophie Tuckers long before those two ladies made the scene.

One can easily imagine Bessie's surprise at discovering the identity of the Sepia Mae West—it was none other than blues singer Ida Cox, and the whole show was built around her act.

A few years earlier Bessie would have torn down half the theatre, or, at the very least, staged a quick exit at the mere idea of another blues singer sharing the bill with her, much less topping her on the bill. But times had changed her attitude, and Bessie was beginning to regard herself as more than just a blues singer.

"When Bessie saw me at rehearsal, all dressed up like Mae West, she just laughed her head off," said Ida Cox years later. "I thought for sure she would be mad." Bessie was, of course, in no position to be. During the run of *Fan Waves*, the two singers became as friendly as Bessie would allow. Ida had recently toured the South with some success, and it is possible that she provided the encouragement Bessie

3. Such nonsense continues today; a popular rock singer of the early seventies is billed as "the white James Brown."

Advertisement in the *Amsterdam News*, December 23, 1933. The Dancing Mermaids "worked like bitches."

and Richard Morgan needed to implement their touring plans. In any event, it wasn't long before they got some money together, assembled a small group of entertainers, and took to the road.

Her show was called *Hot from Harlem*, but Southern audiences obviously found it lukewarm. Bessie returned to Philadelphia without having made any money on the tour, and for the first time she was depressed by the way her career was going. Until now she had been able to blame the Depression for everything; this trip indicated

Ida Cox—"the Sepia Mae West" —in 1939. *Photo from the author's collection.*

that she might be losing her grip on audiences. The fact that Mamie Smith—no longer singing the blues that had made her famous in 1920—was meeting with tremendous success in the South during the same period further convinced Bessie that she had better change her style to something more up to date, even for her Southern audiences.

If she needed further proof, she got it while appearing at the Harlem Opera House during the last week of October. With a supporting cast of fifty, Bessie headlined the bill with Don Redman, the saxophone player who had accompanied her at the peak of her recording career and now was climbing to the top himself as a band leader. The *New York Age* rated the show one and a half daggers out of a possible five:

> If it were not for the rather clever and different arrangements played by Don Redmond [sic] and his band, the show at the Harlem Opera House this week would hardly rate one dagger . . . the rest of the show is very little out of the ordinary. The chorus rates mention for their performance, especially in what might be called the "production number," in which they put across a nice routine and tableau to the tune of "Out in the Cold Again." . . . Bessie Smith is undoubtedly a good blues singer—but blues singers don't seem to rate as highly as they used to. Her reception by the audience, although warm enough, seemed to be actuated by appreciation of her personality rather than her act. Of course the usual risque lines evoked the usual obscene howls of laughter, but—she wasn't called back àt all.

Most singers who had shifted from pop to blues during the blues craze had long since switched back. Bessie had been a blues singer from the start, but she had always included nonblues songs in her repertoire, giving them blues characteristics by her interpretation.

Out of her blues and that of her contemporaries had evolved the jazz singing of Louis Armstrong and such women as Ivie Anderson, a former dancer with Mamie Smith and now a vocalist with the Duke Ellington orchestra, and newcomer Billie Holiday, who credited Bessie and Armstrong as her major influences. In 1931 Ivie Anderson had sung "It Don't Mean a Thing, If It Ain't Got That Swing," which turned out to be a good prediction of things to come. Benny Goodman's swift rise to the swing throne was only a few months away, and Bessie was already being regarded by many as a living relic.

During the week at the Harlem Opera House, Bessie did receive some encouragement from Will Marion Cook, a distinguished black composer who had studied music in Europe with Anton Dvorak and written numerous successful musicals for the popular team of Bert Williams and George Walker. Cook was now planning *Dusk and Dawn*, an ambitious musical production for Broadway, with a projected cast of two hundred. Its setting was to shift from the shores of Africa to the slave ships and the cotton fields. Cook telephoned Bessie to offer her a featured part.

Bessie accepted, the press made the announcement, and that was the end of that. Ending 1934 with another disappointment, Bessie could look back on it as her worst year. Friends recall that although she was now more depressed than she had ever been—at least as far as her career was concerned—Bessie seemed determined to get in step with the times and make more than visual changes in her performances.

Bessie's personal life was relatively uneventful as the pace of her professional life slowed down. Barely able to support herself, she relied more and more on help from Richard. At about this time Viola's daughter Laura died, and Bessie moved Tinnie and Lulu into the top floor of Viola's house, spending a great deal of money on special plumbing installations and other redecorations to convert the floor into a self-contained apartment.

The arrangement was short-lived. The three sisters fought incessantly, each feeling that the larger share of Bessie's favors should be hers; Viola soon had the house to herself again. "They were mean bitches, those sisters," recalls Ruby, perhaps with a bit of bias. "All they ever did was to try to get as much out of poor old Bessie as they could. They drank up her money and then they had the nerve to call her names behind her back. I can see why Jack didn't like them, there was all this jealousy, but poor Bessie, she didn't know half of what they was doing to her—she was blind to the facts because she just loved her family."

The entertainment pages of the black press carried mixed news during the early months of 1935. The *Defender*, taking a slap at Mae West, proclaimed Ada Overton-Walker, wife of comedian George Walker, the original "Queen of the Curves"; Ma Rainey retired in Columbus, Georgia, on the death of her sister Malissa; Clara Smith died of a heart attack at the age of forty; the bands of Chick Webb and Willie Bryant met in a "savage" battle at the Savoy Ballroom; the Lafayette Theatre, having done away with stage shows a few weeks earlier, closed down;[4] the Apollo Theatre on 125th Street was taken over by Leo Brecher and Frank Schiffman, who vowed to continue the Lafayette tradition of black vaudeville; Louis Armstrong, fresh from European triumphs, failed to show up for an Apollo engagement.

Armstrong had cut short his continental tour—and left his orchestra behind[5]—after a stormy dispute with N. J. Canelli, his European manager. Reports followed that he was ill or even dead, but the truth was that he simply needed a rest, so Bessie was called in for the Apollo show as a last-minute, unadvertised replacement, rating a mere one-line mention from the *Amsterdam News*' disappointed reviewer. Three months later, in the first week of May, she appeared again at the Apollo, this time on a bill headlined by the former Mrs. Louis Armstrong, Lil Hardin.

Lil Armstrong recalled a problem in connection with that engagement: "Bessie Smith was furious because Mr. Schiffman was going to change her show. I had heard so much about her mean temper that I figured I'd better get on the right side of her, so I went out and bought her a chicken sandwich. She didn't say much to me, but she ate the sandwich and I never had any problems with her—she was real mad at Schiffman, though."

Ruby, more directly involved, furnished the details, recalling Frank Schiffman's visit to one of Bessie's rehearsals a week before the Apollo opening.

When the rehearsal was over, Bessie sat down and asked Ruby to massage her shoulders. Schiffman waited for the chorus girls to leave before he spoke. "Bessie," he said, standing in front of her, "you got a dancing bunch of girls with you this time, but they are *so* black that with the makeup on they'll look gray—especially that little one at the end of the front line, she's *exceptionally* dark, and I wouldn't want to bring this bunch into the Apollo."

"A little harder on the left side, baby," said Bessie, her eyes remaining on the floor.

"I have a bunch of girls that we can put in the line," Schiffman continued. "It shouldn't take them long to rehearse up the routine."

Ruby could feel Bessie tensing up. Bessie raised herself to her feet,

4. The Lafayette, as part of the W.P.A. Federal Theater Funds program, soon housed such all-black dramas as *The Hot Mikado* and *Black Macbeth*, produced by John Houseman and Orson Welles.

5. The orchestra continued the tour under the leadership of pianist Herman Chittison.

placed a hand on her hip, and looked Schiffman straight in the eye. "If you don't want my girls, you don't want me."

"Bessie, I—"

"No Bessie nothin'. The only reason those girls look gray out there is because I don't get the proper lighting. We're coming in there, and you get me some amber lights to put on those girls—that is, if you want the show, and if you don't, I don't give a damn, because I'm tired of wearin' myself out. I can go home, get drunk, and be a lady—it's up to you."

Schiffman gave in.

The story spread quickly, with help from Bessie. "Mr. Schiffman had to take all those gals," recalls Ruby. "He didn't mind me, because I was the lightest in the bunch, but all the street cats had heard the story, and they were standing out there on the corners saying, 'I ain't gonna miss the show *this* week, all those Ma Raineys are gonna be there.' So, honey, when we fell in there we stopped the show. You never saw people give applause like they did for us girls—we broke it up! And Bessie told them girls, 'Now the man don't even *want* y'all in here, so don't let me down.' You should have seen us go, we worked like bitches, and each time we went out there, they would applaud for us to come back. We really let them know that we was stewin'—every leg came up together, every smile was turned on just right. All those half-white gals who'd come in there just couldn't work like Bessie's crowd. 'You can say what you want about them Ma Raineys,' Bessie said, 'but they know what they're doin' when they're out there working.' And you can believe that—we worked our asses off."

Frank Schiffman does not recall this particular incident, "But," he says, "that is not to say that it didn't happen."

Schiffman was not the only person to whom Bessie was trying to prove a point; Billie Holiday had made her Apollo debut two weeks earlier, and people were already talking about Ella Fitzgerald, Chick Webb's new vocal discovery, who would make her professional debut at the Apollo a few weeks later. Determined not to let the new trend toward swing music leave her behind, Bessie was updating her material, and *New York Age* gave her a three-dagger rating for her new show:

Bessie Smith of the old blues singing school is probably the first of her clan to modernize her type of singing. She does one number in particular

197

which boasts of 1920 rhythm and 1935 lyrics, employing such phrases as "trucking," "tea," and similar expressions.

Though New York reviewers were somewhat subdued in their praise of Bessie, Frank Schiffman—who since the Lafayette days of the mid-twenties had been one of her most frequent employers—recalls no appreciable waning of enthusiasm on the part of her audience:

"Bessie was sometimes a little shaky, but she never ceased to be a drawing card for us. She was a difficult and temperamental person, she had her love affairs, which frequently interfered with her work, but she never was a real problem. Bessie was a person for whose artistry, at least, I had the profoundest respect. I don't ever remember any artist in all my long, long years—and this goes back to some of the famous singers, including Billie Holiday—who could evoke the response from her listeners that Bessie did. Whatever pathos there is in the world, whatever sadness she had, was brought out in her singing—and the audience knew it and responded to it."

Most reviewers, however, still regarded Bessie as a leftover from the twenties. When, after a three-month absence from the stage, Bessie appeared again at the Apollo on July 26, the *New York Age*—although it acknowledged her "modernization"—placed her historically as far back as 1918:

> Roland Holder, plenty good with the taps, makes his appearance, following which Shelton Brooks turns—musically speaking, of course—the pages of Life back to the days of the Armistice to present a fitting introduction to Bessie Smith, hailed as the Queen of the Blues. Bessie, incidentally, is one blues singer who has ever been a pleasure to hear, and the fact that she has kept step with the times has been all to her credit.

When Bessie returned to the Apollo for Christmas week, making her last appearance of the year, the big silver screen starred Jane Withers[6] in *This Is the Life*. Including that engagement, her performing credits for 1935 amounted to four weeks at the Apollo.

In February 1936, Billie Holiday's future looked as bright as Bessie's looked bleak, but fate played a strange trick. Appearing in *Stars over Broadway* at Connie's Inn—a one-time Harlem spot that had moved downtown to Forty-eighth Street between Broadway and •

6. Now "Josephine the Plumber" in TV commercials.

Seventh Avenue[7]—Billie came down with a case of ptomaine poisoning and had to leave the show. Nat Nazarro, a performer turned promoter, arranged for Bessie to replace her. It was Bessie's most prestigious engagement in several years, and she made the most of it.

Connie's Inn brought Bessie a whole new audience, and what they heard was a new Bessie Smith; gone were the blues—except for an occasional request—and that powerful voice belted out the popular songs of the day with accompaniment that now featured the "modern" swing beat. Bessie had tried to do the same thing at the Apollo, but there she carried the "stigma" of an old-time blues singer and, with her uptown audience requesting one old blues song after the other, she was unable to present as much of her new repertoire as she would have liked to. After her opening night at Connie's Inn, the word began to spread.

Now that Bessie seemed to be getting back on her feet again, "long lost friends" she had sung about in her 1929 recording of "Nobody Knows You When You're Down and Out" reappeared. During the first week of February, Carl Van Vechten invited her to his apartment. This time he wanted to photograph her. She arrived between shows "cold sober and in a quiet reflective mood," Van Vechten later recalled.

"She could scarcely have been more amiable or cooperative. She was agreeable to all my suggestions and even made changes of dress. Of course, on this occasion she did not sing, but I got nearer to her real personality than I ever had before and the photographs, perhaps, are the only adequate record of her true appearance and manner that exist."[8]

The photographs—thirty-six in all—show Bessie in a variety of moods, wearing two different dresses. Van Vechten was justly proud of them. Though posed, they are remarkable studies—the best pictures of Bessie available, and probably the only ones taken in the years of her decline. She smiles, throwing back her head to look at the white plaster face of a Greek god; she looks askance at another prop, a racist's stereotyped Sambo face resting on her shoulder; she dances the "truck" with a mischievous smile for the camera; she stands with her hands clutching the back of a chair, and tells us life has left her with more scars than we see.

---

7. It later became the Latin Quarter, and, in 1971, was converted into "Cine Lido," a movie theatre, specializing in blue movies.

8. *Jazz Record* magazine, September 1947.

"She could scarcely have been more amiable or cooperative. She was agreeable to all my suggestions and even made changes of dress." *The Carl Van Vechten photos, February 3, 1936.*

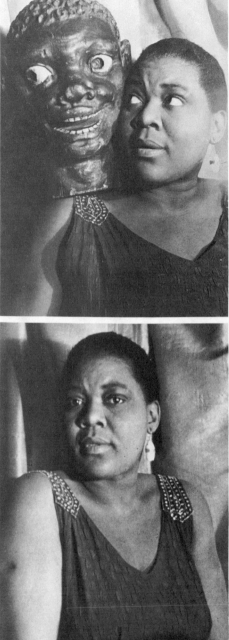

In February, too, she learned that Charlie Green, her favorite trombonist, had been found dead, frozen on the steps of a Harlem tenement, and that Joe Smith was slowly dying in a Long Island sanatorium.

On the more cheerful side, her success at Connie's Inn brought a revival in Bessie's social life. One would have thought Bessie had been in Siberia instead of Harlem, the way people now fussed over her.

Shortly after the Van Vechten photo session, she made her only appearance on Fifty-second Street—"The Street," as musicians would soon call the block between Fifth and Sixth Avenues where a number of small jazz clubs were opening in brownstone cellars. People flocked to these clubs—favorite hangouts for the big names of the Swing Era—in hopes of hearing their favorite sideman, band leader, or singer in an informal jam session. Black and white performers jammed together in these hangouts, but even in midtown Manhattan, racial equality did not go beyond the bandstand; it was not until the mid-forties that Fifty-second Street audiences became totally integrated.

The first jazz spot to open on Fifty-second Street was the Famous Door,[9] a converted speakeasy at 35 West Fifty-second. It was less than a year old by February 1936, but it already had a tradition of Sunday-afternoon jam sessions in an upstairs room. Many great performances took place there; one of those most frequently recalled was the visit paid by Bessie on a cold February afternoon.

"She came in," wrote Robert Paul Smith in the *Record Changer;* "she planted those two flat feet firmly on the floor, she did not shake her shoulders or snap her fingers. She just opened that great kisser and let the music come out." Others recall that she wore a fur wrap and kept it on during her performance. Guitarist Eddie Condon remembers Bunny Berrigan's muted trumpet backing her up on half a dozen numbers from her old repertoire—and singer Mildred Bailey refusing to follow her on the bandstand for fear of breaking the spell. "That's true," agrees guitarist Brick Fleagle, "and I think Mildred was wise not to sing. Bessie left as soon as she was through—no liquor was served at these upstairs sessions—so she just came, sang, and left us all in a daze."

Mildred Bailey and her musician husband, Red Norvo, were

9. So called because many famous jazz musicians had inscribed their names in the small wooden entrance door.

among the people who had recently befriended Bessie and Richard Morgan. "Bessie was crazy about Mildred," Norvo recalled in a 1968 interview with Whitney Balliett for the *New Yorker*. "She and Mildred used to laugh at each other and do this routine. They were both big women, and when they saw each other, one of them would say, 'Look, I've got this brand-new dress, but it's too big for me, so why don't *you* take it?' "

Harlem's latest dance craze was the truck, and trucking contests had become very popular. During the first week of March, Bessie was encouraged by Mildred to attend a contest at the Savoy Ballroom, popularly called "The Home of Happy Feet." The judges were English musical comedy star Beatrice Lillie and Bessie's old rival Ethel Waters. The music was supplied by the bands of Chick Webb and Fess Williams. Mildred and Ella Fitzgerald—then a seventeen-year-old newcomer—sang, and newspapers reported that Bessie did a few numbers accompanied by her old friend James P. Johnson, and that she demonstrated her versatility by executing a few dance steps in the latest style. Was Bessie trucking? Of course. She was certainly no longer being treated as a museum piece.

As her activities increased, so did attention from the press. Allan McMillan had reported in his syndicated column "Theater Chat" that Bessie's Connie's Inn appearance registered a "no click" with Broadway audiences, and that she was being replaced by another singer. Two weeks later he apologized:

> Well, I thought I was right in my report and it didn't exactly mean that La Smith was slipping. Nevertheless, Impresario Nazarro had me know that I must make another visit to Connie's Inn for the express purpose of hearing one of our foremost exponents of blue notes in a cycle of new songs.
>
> So, Sunday night I went to Connie Immerman's hot spot on the Gay White Way and waited for Miss Smith to do her turn. To say the least, I was amply repaid for having waited, because I had an opportunity to see one of the most enthusiastic demonstrations of approval ever recorded in a night club.
>
> The portly blues singer came out and knocked them dizzy and then came back to do W. C. Handy's "St. Louis Blues" for an encore. To Miss Smith I apologize because when any performer is received by a Broadway audience as you were on Sunday night, he's absolutely the tops.

A week after his apology, McMillan reported that Bessie, now in her sixth week, had been held over at Connie's, and the Chicago *Defender* carried a lengthy piece by him in its March 28 issue.

Considering the fact that she had performed almost exclusively, though sporadically, in New York over the past two years, the heading NEW YORK SEES BESSIE SMITH; WONDERS WHERE SHE'S BEEN seems odd, to say the least. The article, which reads like a publicity release, is full of misinformation; and those who knew Bessie also knew that she was handing her gullible interviewer a line of jive, but the important thing was that Bessie was getting attention again:

It's a long way from Tennessee to Broadway, but Bessie Smith made it even though it did take an extra year or so. The highway leading to the glamorous white lights of the gay white way is filled with many disappointments, but the portly delineator of blue notes never allowed such trivials as hard knocks and disillusions to thwart an innerborn desire to reach the top.

Miss Smith is right now in her seventh week of an extended engagement at Connie's Inn and backed by Broadway approval she has taken on new life. "I'm feeling better now than ever in my life," Miss Smith confided in an interview with this writer last week, "and I feel as though I am on the brink of new successes. I am most certainly optimistic concerning the upward trend of the theatre."

### Began Career at Nine

"Things have changed quite a bit," reminisced the jubilant chantress, "and I realize that we are living in an entirely new era of entertainment—far different from the one in which I began many years ago."

It was here that the stylist of blues songs blushed (actresses never like to appear old), but that was because she started her career as a child and has been active in the theater for 27 years.

She was born in Chattanooga, Tenn., April 15, 1898, appeared in school plays, was the champion roller skater of the state, made her first professional appearance at the age of nine at the old Ivory Theatre in her home town . . . used her first weekly salary of $8 to purchase a new pair of ball-bearing roller skates. Got a severe tanning for it from her mother, but it didn't dull that childish enthusiasm. Has since appeared in theatres all over the United States. Also had shows of her own in the old T.O.B.A. days. Her Columbia phonograph records of famous "blues" are played the world over. Very fond of sports but is much fonder of diamonds and fur coats. Once had a box full of genuine sparklers. Plays guitar and piano. Initial inspiration came from Cora Fisher and W. C. Handy. Made the "St. Louis Blues" in a motion picture short for Handy a few years ago. Favorite stage star is Ethel Waters. A lover of pets . . . says she will retire in 1960, maybe (accent on the maybe) and settle down in the country. She's got rhythm in her soul.

With Billie Holiday set to return to Connie's Inn the following night, Bessie closed on April 17, but Nazarro didn't keep her idle for long. A week later she opened at the Apollo as part of a Nazarro package, which also included W. C. Handy's fifteen-piece orchestra, the popular team of Buck and Bubbles—one half of which was Buck Washington, the leader of Bessie's last recording orchestra—and three additional acts. One gets a good idea of Depression fees from the cost of this package: $2,434.40 for the entire week.

Although she was no longer recording, Bessie kept writing new songs. Pianist-composer Eubie Blake remembers being called to W. C. Handy's office on Broadway during Bessie's Apollo engagement. Bessie was there with an idea for a blues, and Handy suggested that Blake set it to music. "They weren't prepared to pay me anything for it, so I said I couldn't do it," Blake says, "but I remember that it was a very good idea—I wish I could remember it—I had never met Bessie before, and I never saw her again."

In the middle of May, Richard took Bessie to the Earle Theatre in Philadelphia, where Lionel Hampton was appearing with Benny Goodman's band. "It was obvious that Bessie and my uncle were very devoted to each other," says Hampton, "and I don't believe there was anything he wouldn't do for her. I introduced her to the members of the band, but she really didn't need an introduction—*she* was the star. I'm convinced that if she had lived, she would have been right up there with the rest of us in the swing music, she would have been a national figure."

STILL TOPS, read the heading over Bessie's photo in the May 30, 1936, issue of the *Defender*. "One need never worry about Bessie Smith holding her own as a blues singer. Although the type of songs she featured have gone out of style, Miss Smith is singing torrid songs which will keep her in the limelight." One wonders how Bessie's singing sounded in this, her "modern" period. The 1933 recordings provide us with only a small hint, and—perhaps because Bessie was always with the times, or ahead of them—no one seems to remember her doing anything different.

Bessie's next engagement, also arranged by Nazarro, was the longest of her career so far. She became the star of a night club show at Art's Cafe, at Twenty-second Street and Ridge Avenue in Philadelphia, from June 18 through September 3, 1935. Since this was her own show—the first one in a very long time—Bessie decided to surround herself with old friends. It was as if Ruby had read her mind, or perhaps she just read the newspapers; in any case, her telegram could not have been better timed. "I had just finished a show with Gertie Saunders and we were going off. Just as the final curtain came down, Gertie said, 'Everybody stay on stage.' She told us to go through a rehearsal, and said, 'Especially you, Ruby. You didn't keep your lines straight. If you were on Bessie's show you wouldn't do that.' She was just trying to embarrass me in front of everybody—that woman really hated me. That night I didn't care if Jack killed me, I sent a telegram to Bessie saying, 'I can't stay on here, Gertie keeps picking on me.' Bessie wired me back, 'Come back with me and let Jack try to stop it.' That's how I went back on Bessie's show."

Bessie seemed more her old self these days. She had her own show; she had bought a car, an old Packard; she was being advertised, however inappropriately, as "that famous radio star"; she was once again meeting life and its pleasures with characteristic excesses, including a bit of philandering.

Romantically, she had her eyes on Eddie Mitchell, a dancer in her show. Young, handsome, a sharp dresser, he was just Bessie's type. It so happened that he was also Ruby's type, and Ruby and Eddie were having an affair.

One of the barmaids had told Ruby that a girl in the chorus had syphilis, and she'd better keep Eddie away from her. One night Ruby walked into a dressing room to find Eddie giving the girl a passionate kiss. Having decided on the spot to drop her boy friend, Ruby cornered Bessie downstairs in the bar, told her what she had heard and seen, and advised her also to stay away from Eddie.

"If he's that common," said Bessie, "what do *you* want with him?"

Unable to convince her aunt that she was expressing concern rather than jealousy, Ruby decided she'd rather not be around when Bessie discovered the truth. She wanted to avoid an embarrassing situation with Eddie. They were at the end of their engagement at Art's, and Ruby felt she might as well return to New York. She later learned that Bessie did have an affair with the young dancer and that he had indeed caught something from the girl, but she never found out if it had been passed on to Bessie.

Bessie's stay at Art's was an unqualified success. She presented three shows nightly, and the attendance was never less than good. She sang new tunes—"It's a Sin to Tell a Lie" and "Pennies from Heaven"—and the old risqué songs—"Kitchen Man," "I'm Wild

About That Thing," and "You've Got to Give Me Some"—which she had recorded in 1929 and now did as duets with Billy McLaurin. "Philadelphia's night life has been enriched," reported the *Tribune* as Bessie did her last show at Art's on September 3.

Jack, Jr., now close to seventeen, was suffering from the effects of his nomadic childhood. "We couldn't keep up with him," says Maud. "He would come home and Bessie would give him any amount of money that he would ask for, she'd dress him up, and the next thing you know he'd be gone. He had a lovely home and everything, but he just wouldn't stay in one place. I think the longest he stayed home was about two months, he'd be all dressed up, Bessie would give him a hundred dollars and goodbye, he was off again."

Confirming his aunt's recollections, Jack, Jr., admits that he never got along in school, and tells how Bessie constantly tried to impress upon him the value of a formal education: "I'll never forget the only time Mama put a hand on me. The truant officer had told her that I wasn't going to school, and she asked me about it. 'You don't want to go to school,' she asked, 'tell me, and I'll take you out of school if you don't want to go.' She was just trying to trick me into telling her the truth, so, like a fool, I said, 'No, I don't want to go.' Well, she beat me up all over the room."

Bessie never gave up trying to get her son interested in school. "Mama was a real bug on education, and I remember when I was about seventeen or eighteen she wanted me to become a lawyer. 'Baby,' she said one day, 'if you go back to school, I'll buy you anything you want. I'll buy you all the clothes you want, pay your tuition, and I'll even buy you a car.' I should have listened to her."

Bessie ended 1936 as she had 1935, with a week at the Apollo, but this time the circumstances were far happier. Jane Withers was on the screen again, sharing honors with Hattie McDaniel in *Can This Be Dixie?,* and Bessie was singing with a new, pulsating band led by trumpeter Erskine Hawkins.

During the week Frank Schiffman made the mistake of refusing Bessie an advance. She stormed out of his office and into the crowded lobby of the theatre, threw her two hundred pounds on the floor, and treated the startled patrons to a performance they had not paid for. Lying on her back, she pounded her heels and fists furiously into the floor, and hollered in a voice that could be heard clear across 125th Street: "I'm the *star* of the show, I'm Bessie Smith, and these fuckin' bastards won't let me have my money." It wasn't long before she got it.

That same week she met Ruby at the Braddock Bar,[10] a favorite entertainers' hangout on the corner of 126th Street and Eighth Avenue. They were having a drink at the end of the long bar when a man walked in and engaged the bartender in conversation.

"You see Bessie Smith at the Apollo this week?"

"No," said the bartender, knowing that Bessie was listening at the other end of the room. "How is she?"

"Oh, that bitch, she thinks she's some big shit. I knew that bitch when she was right down in Atlanta, and don't you know she passed right on by me and didn't even speak?"

"That ain't like Bessie," said the bartender.

"Well, you don't know her like I do."

At this point Bessie got off her barstool. Wearing her dark glasses, she walked up to the man and said, "Hey."

Ruby braced herself.

"Hey, lady," said the man, surprised.

"Have a drink on me—bartender, give this gentleman a drink." She leaned on the bar and smiled. "So, tell me more about Bessie."

"That black bitch, I know her well."

"You really know her, huh?"

"You're damn right I know her—from way back in Atlanta, when she wasn't nothin'."

"And she passed right by you and wouldn't speak—ain't that some shit?" Bessie was obviously enjoying her little game.

"Yeah, that bitch wouldn't even open her mouth."

With that Bessie kicked the man in his most vulnerable spot. "That bitch opened her mouth *this* time," said Bessie, "and the next time I see you, you black bastard, I'll do the same damn thing. C'mon, Ruby."

Just like the old days, Ruby thought, as they walked out of the bar. It was the last time she ever saw her aunt.

On February 4, 1937, Bessie began another night club engagement in Philadelphia. She was supposed to appear for only three weeks at the Wander Inn Cafe on Eighteenth and Federal Streets, but her stay stretched into the summer.

In his autobiography Sidney Bechet recalls dropping into the Wander Inn around that time. He had married since he last saw Bessie, and his wife was with him: "Bessie just showed up and came

10. Now the Venus Lounge.

over to our table and sat down. She'd been drinking and she wasn't too careful about how she'd do things. She just came over and sat down and started fooling around with me, talking in a way that could lead on to things.

"My wife was one of those real pretty girls and she wasn't having any of this. The way it was, Bessie must have known how much my wife had been hearing about me and Bessie, all what people had been telling her about our going together; 'Bessie this and Bessie that' whenever old friends meet. Bessie must have known that pretty well; it was the kind of woman-knowing she'd been born with. And she started in deliberate-like, needling my wife. Only my wife got to needling right back and it seemed like she was a little better at it because before long I could see that Bessie was ready to haul off and pull hair. She wasn't one to stand for anything, Bessie. She was really a hell of a woman.

"Lucky though, before anything really happened, the woman who owned the place, who liked my wife, came over and got Bessie to go with her. She brought her into the back of the club and got her calmed down. . . . That night at the club, it was the last time. That woman led Bessie away to the back of the club and I never saw her again."

As the summer of 1937 drew to a close, Bessie faced a busy schedule. The record industry had recovered from the near-fatal wounds of the early Depression years; as far as race records were concerned, the resumption of recording in the mid-thirties concentrated on the big bands, and—in the blues field—on such singers as Leadbelly, Leroy Carr, Big Bill Broonzy, and Charley Patton. Now swing was the thing and a renaissance of older jazz forms, including the classic blues, was yet to come. A new generation of blues women was lining up, but Bessie was not interested in re-creating her past. She had transcended the idiom and slipped gracefully into the Swing Era.

"I had planned to record her for Columbia's Brunswick series, the lower-priced pop label," recalls John Hammond. "I was going to use Jo Jones, Walter Page, Buck Clayton, Jack Teagarden, and Hershal Evans or Chu Berry—I was even going to sneak Basie in on piano."

Hammond's was not the only such plan afoot: "We were going to make records," says Lionel Hampton. "I told everybody in the Goodman band about Bessie being tight with my uncle, and Benny said, 'Oh, man, we *gotta* make some records with her. And I had just signed a contract with Victor Records to do a lot of small-band dates with people like Johnny Hodges, Nat King Cole, and all those guys, so Eli Oberstein of Victor told me, 'Be sure to get Bessie,' because she was just coming back into prominence then. You know, what she sang was so relaxed, the stories she sang became so true—this was reality. She always adapted the 'now' sound, whatever that became, but we never got around to recording it."

Bessie was also scheduled to make another film, this time in Hollywood. It was 1923 all over again. Into her forties, her huge frame scarred by two decades of reckless living, Bessie still radiated vitality. She had weathered the storms of her personal and professional life, and now she was defying those who were ready to relegate her to the past. Bessie felt that life had been good to her, and she had remarkably few regrets.

Although she had felt the love of millions whom her artistry profoundly affected, she had not always found love at home, where she sought it most. She had inspired performers who now stood where she had stood fourteen years earlier, but rather than sit back and observe, Bessie Smith was prepared to break new ground. "I never saw so much life left in someone who had lived so much," said one gospel singer who frequented the Wander Inn when she was there. "I don't think anybody or anything could break that woman's spirit."

In September Bessie accepted a feature spot with Winsted's *Broadway Rastus* show, touring the South. Jack Gee has said that she paid him a surprise visit in New York to ask him if he thought she should accept the *Broadway Rastus* engagement. He recalled the alleged meeting in the 1965 *down beat* yearbook:

"The last time I saw my wife living, she was at 48 West 127th Street in New York. I was out late that night, when I came home I stumbled over some bags in the hall. I asked my mother what it was all about, and she told me my wife was in my room. I went in and Bessie was in bed. She said she come to talk to me about doing a carnival show. I went out and bought a half dozen Cokes which Bessie was a lover of a long time before then.

"We decided that night to let bygones be bygones and get back together as before, and I agreed with her to accept the carnival show at $250 a week. We figured after the season we'd reinstate ourselves back to normal. This never happened, I'm sorry to say."

Not surprisingly, those who knew Bessie well during this period say that this "last visit" with Jack never happened. Jack, they contend, invented such clandestine meetings with Bessie in order morally to justify his rights to her estate. One family member commented: "Yes, she loved Coca-Cola, but that's the only truth in that statement."

Bessie did go on the tour, and she took Richard Morgan with her—a fact that hardly supports Jack Gee's story. Morgan had, of course, remained quite astonishingly faithful during those years when Bessie faced hard times with hard liquor and hope. She decided to travel in her own car, the old Packard, with Richard driving—that was something Bessie had never learned to do.

The show, which had done good business in the Memphis area, was scheduled to open in Darling, Mississippi, on Sunday afternoon, September 26. Early that morning after the last Saturday-night performance, Bessie felt restless and suggested that she and Richard get a head start on the troupe, drive down to Clarksdale, and spend the night there.

According to Richard Morgan, who related the story to Bessie's family, he insisted on staying in Memphis because he wanted to get into a card game with some of the boys, but—after a heated argument—he gave in when Bessie threatened to get someone else to drive the car.

They left Memphis at about one in the morning and headed south on a straight stretch of road called Route 61. They had driven about seventy-five miles. The heat of the argument had produced an aftermath of painful silence. Richard was tired. The road was dark and seemingly endless. There was a huge truck—it was too late.

# II

The Associated Press report of Bessie's death that appeared in white newspapers across the country was brief and inaccurate, but it represented more attention than the white press had ever given Bessie in her lifetime.

Stories in the black press were more detailed and, of course, more prominent, but no more accurate. The Chicago *Defender* ran a headline across the top of its front page: BESSIE SMITH, BLUES SINGER, KILLED. Capsule biographies and accounts of Bessie's final hours were wildly contradictory. It was obvious that reporters knew little about Bessie's life and even less about how it ended.

Her funeral a week and a half later inspired more write-ups and photos in newspapers that for six years had all but forgotten her existence. There were fragmentary and inaccurate references to the accident—most papers merely pointed out that it had occurred—but there were long stories describing Bessie's accomplishments, real and imagined: the *Afro-American* told its readers Bessie had made 1023

*215*

records for Columbia, "including many with accompaniments by white orchestras," and that she had spent seventy-five thousand dollars cash in the course of a few weeks; the Philadelphia *Tribune* claimed she "pulled the Columbia Recording Company back to its feet after it had collapsed on the verge of bankruptcy" and that George Gershwin "refused to write the final score of *Porgy and Bess* until he had sought her opinion."

The widespread controversy over the circumstances surrounding Bessie's death did not arise until the following month, when *down beat* magazine[1] printed an article by John Hammond. Hammond's story, under the provocative heading "Did Bessie Smith Bleed to Death While Waiting for Medical Aid?" contained the first published hint that Bessie might have been the victim of Southern racism:

> A particularly disagreeable story as to the details of her death has just been received from members of Chick Webb's orchestra, who were in Memphis soon after the disaster. It seems that Bessie was riding in a car which crashed into a truck parked along the side of the road. One of her arms was nearly severed, but aside from that there was no other serious injury, according to these informants. Some time elapsed before a doctor was summoned to the scene, but finally she was picked up by a medico and driven to the leading Memphis hospital. On the way this car was involved in some minor mishap, which further delayed medical attention. When finally she did arrive at the hospital she was refused treatment because of her color and bled to death while waiting for attention.
>
> Realizing that such tales can be magnified greatly in the telling, I would like to get confirmation from some Memphis citizens who were on the spot at the time. If the story is true it is but another example of disgraceful conditions in a certain section of our country already responsible for the killing and maiming of legitimate union organizers. Of the particular city of Memphis I am prepared to believe almost anything, since its mayor and chief of police publicly urged the use of violence against organizers of the CIO a few weeks ago.

Hammond ended his extraordinary piece with an ill-timed pitch— the first harvest of Bessie Smith's death was about to be reaped:

> Be that as it may, the UHCA [United Hot Clubs of America] is busy sponsoring a special Bessie Smith memorial album . . . the album will be released by Brunswick-Columbia around the middle of November with pictures of the performers and details about each of the discs. Take it from one who cherished all the records that this will be the best buy of the year in music.

1. In 1937 *down beat* was a monthly news publication, very pop-oriented, and more widely read than today. It was called "the musician's bible," and its format resembled that of *Variety* and *Billboard*.

Dr. Hugh Smith in 1957. Twenty years earlier, tragedy made him part of the Bessie Smith legend. *Photo courtesy of the Campbell Clinic, Memphis.*

There had been plenty of talk in jazz circles about racial injustice in connection with Bessie's death,[2] but the *down beat* article spread the rumors far afield and—Hammond's admitted lack of evidence notwithstanding—gave them credence.

Considering the temper of the times and Hammond's involvement in what was then a very disorganized and far from popular fight for the civil rights of black people, the irony of Bessie's dying at the hands of Southern bigotry provided the perfect *cause célèbre*. From a writer's point of view it made a fascinating story: Bessie Smith, the great blues singer who had moved millions of Southerners to tears with her songs of misery, killed by Southern prejudice.

Thirty-four years later John Hammond admits with some embarrassment that his article was based entirely on hearsay and that a few phone calls, made at the time, might have curbed the circulating rumors. Once the article appeared, however, it was too late to change the story; people refused to accept any other version.

2. The black press, usually quick to point out incidents of racial injustice, carried no such story in connection with Bessie Smith's death until after the publication of Hammond's *down beat* piece.

The attack on Memphis in Hammond's article drew angry protests from the city's hospital authorities. In response *down beat* published a second article stating that Bessie had been taken directly to the black hospital in Clarksdale, Mississippi, where she had died due to loss of blood. There was no mention of her having been refused admittance to a white hospital, but no one paid attention when this contradictory story was published.

Twenty years later, in the October 17, 1957, issue of *down beat*, the late George Hoefer noted that the truth about the accident and its aftermath was still being ignored by writers. He quoted the Hammond article and set the record straight; once again, it made little difference. In 1960 Edward Albee's play *The Death of Bessie Smith* opened in West Berlin; based on the same rumors that had inspired the Hammond article—and perhaps on the article itself—it perpetuated the myth. Bessie Smith became better known for the way in which she had allegedly died than for what she had done in life.

Richard Morgan, who survived the accident, died around 1943. No reporter ever asked him what actually happened on the morning of September 26, 1937. Only he could have described the circumstances that led to the accident.[3] The highway patrolmen who handled the case were reported dead by the mid-fifties, and if there are any records of the accident in the files of the Clarksdale Police Department, they seem unwilling to make them public—letters of inquiry remain unanswered.

Virtually nothing would be known of the circumstances leading up to Bessie Smith's death were it not for the arrival on the scene, moments after the accident occurred, of Dr. Hugh Smith[4] and his fishing partner, Henry Broughton. Mr. Broughton has long since died, without anyone's having interviewed him, but Dr. Smith—referred to by *down beat* only as "a Memphis surgeon who came upon the scene of the accident and attended Bessie Smith"—was contacted by that magazine in the early nineteen-forties for a published interview. Further details of Dr. Smith's recollections appeared in a 1969 *Esquire* article entitled "The True Death of Bessie Smith," but that

3. The only other person who might have shed some light on the circumstances, the driver of the truck, has never been found or identified. Morgan's account of the accident was only given to the family. It appears at the end of this chapter.

4. A past president of the American Academy of Orthopedic Surgeons, Dr. Smith has been an orthopedic surgeon on the staff of the Campbell Clinic in Memphis since 1936.

piece revealed little more than the fact that Dr. Smith was still alive, and contained such misinformation as the detail that Bessie's car was traveling north instead of south.

We will never know the whole story, but the truth probably lies somewhere between the two following accounts based on Dr. Smith's detailed recollections for this book, and a 1938 interview with Jack Gee, Jr.

Smith and Broughton were in the habit of leaving Memphis around one o'clock every other Sunday morning and driving south into Mississippi for two or three hours to go fishing in a lake there before daybreak.

On Sunday, September 26, 1937, they left home at one-thirty and headed down Route 61 as usual. Dr. Smith had just finished his training at the Campbell Clinic and was recently married. To celebrate he had traded in his old Model A Ford for a small new Chevrolet. The fishing tackle was on the back seat and the weather conditions seemed perfect: a warm, humid night, no moon, no wind stirring.

They were about seventy miles south of Memphis when they spotted something on the road ahead. Dr. Smith had been driving at fifty to fifty-five miles per hour, but now he slowed down and stopped fifty feet from the wreck of a big car, lying on its left side diagonally across the narrow highway. Illuminated by the bright headlights of Dr. Smith's car was the large figure of Bessie Smith, lying lifeless in the middle of the road. A man moved out of the darkness, waving his arms frantically as he approached the doctor's car—it was Richard Morgan, who was unhurt. In the distance Dr. Smith could see a pair of red tail lights disappearing into the night, heading in the direction of Clarksdale.

The tail lights belonged to the truck Bessie's car had struck; in previous accounts it has been described as belonging to the National Biscuit Company or the U-Needa-Biscuit Company, but Dr. Smith believes it was a truck leased to the U.S. Post Office during the week and used to deliver the Memphis *Commercial Appeal* on Sundays.

According to information Dr. Smith received in the days following the accident, the driver, fearing that his tires were overheated, had pulled up and parked on the side of the road. The shoulders were only two feet wide on this particular stretch, so it was impossible for him to pull completely off the road. Most of the truck had to rest in the right lane, making it necessary for any passing car to pull into the northbound lane. The truckdriver checked his tires, found them to be all right, and climbed back into the cab of his vehicle. He had just started moving at the time of the impact.

Dr. Smith's theory of how the accident happened is certainly a plausible one:

> If you've ever driven down a two-lane highway in the middle of the night, you know that it's almost impossible to estimate the distance of a pair of tail lights—they can be a mile, four miles, or four hundred and forty yards away. I would assume Richard Morgan realized there was a truck up there, but didn't realize that his depth perception extended only to his head-lights. . . . It would be natural to assume he expected those tail lights to be moving at about forty-five to sixty miles per hour down the highway when, in fact, the truck had just pulled back on the highway and hadn't gone two hundred and twenty yards at the time of the accident. So the tail lights and the depth perception all came together just at the instant that Richard Morgan realized he was about to plow into the back of a slowly moving truck on the east side of the highway.
>
> From the skid marks, I don't think there is any question but that he tried to go to the left side of the truck and miss it, but at the same time he applied his brakes, which made it go into a skid and probably almost a 90° angle at the time of impact. It ricocheted backwards and then flopped on its left side. The impact of Morgan's car was on Bessie Smith's side and she had "side swipe" injuries.[5]
>
> So one of two things happened. Either she was asleep with her entire arm out of the car, or else just the point of her elbow was out of the car—I suspect that was true—and it hit the tail gate of the truck as the top of Bessie's old Packard was sheared off. It was a real old car, for instead of a metal roof or metal struts supporting the roof, it was all wood—it was literally splintered like an old piece of dead kindling wood.

Dr. Smith jumped out of his car, rushed toward Bessie, and began a preliminary examination:

> All the bones around the elbow were completely shattered; there was a complete circumferential interruption of soft tissues about the elbow, except, miraculously—despite the fact that she had almost had her forearm torn loose from her upper arm at the elbow—the three nerves were intact, lying there like telephone wires. The two major vessels, the artery and the nerve were intact. What that boils down to is that hemorrhage from the arm did not cause Bessie Smith's death.

5. Many Mississippi roads, built during the Depression, were so narrow that two wide trucks could barely pass each other. Drivers often rode with an elbow protruding from the car's window, and it was not unusual for the bed of a passing truck to hit the elbow of a driver going in the opposite direction. These were called "side swipe" injuries—usually a combination of a compound fracture dislocation of the wrist, both bones of the forearm broken, and the elbow itself completely crushed.

It was a horrible mess, lying out there in the open with maybe a half a pint of blood on the highway. But if that had been her only injury, she would have survived—there's no question in my mind about this at all. In this day and time we might even have saved her arm, but in that day and time there wouldn't have been any question; you'd just amputate, she'd have a seven-inch stump below the shoulder and probably be out of the hospital in twelve or fourteen days. However, that was not the case—she had sustained severe crushing injuries to her entire right side.

I don't recall if Bessie Smith ever uttered a word, I don't think she answered any questions. She was moaning and groaning from excruciating pain and she was having a lot of trouble getting her breath. She was just breathing on the left side of her chest, all the ribs on her right side had been crushed pretty bad, and she probably had some interabdominal injuries. She was probably bleeding in her abdomen, because it was very stiff and rigid.

Whether or not she had a head injury is a moot question, she wasn't conscious enough to talk. In the available light and without tools, I could not examine her pupils—at this stage it would have been too early to know if she had an intercranial hemorrhage, but she did have only minor head lacerations. Suffice it to say that Bessie Smith was in very critical condition.

As Richard Morgan watched in silence, Mr. Broughton and Dr. Smith moved Bessie onto the road's grassy shoulder. They covered the major wound with a clean handkerchief, and Dr. Smith asked his friend to go to a house some five hundred feet off the road and call an ambulance. About ten minutes had lapsed since the accident, and another fifteen passed before Mr. Broughton returned. By this time Bessie was in shock.

The scene of the accident was still quiet; a few crickets and the voices of the two men seemed loud in the humid night. Richard Morgan, who had remained quite calm, just stood there—there was nothing he could do to help Bessie at this point. It has been suggested that Morgan was intoxicated at the time of the accident, but Dr. Smith recalls that he was completely sober.

As time passed without a sign of an ambulance, Dr. Smith suggested that they remove the fishing tackle from the back seat of his car and take Bessie into Clarksdale. They had almost finished putting the tackle in the car's trunk when they heard the distant sound of another car approaching at high speed. Dr. Smith's car was in the middle of the road, making it impossible for the approaching car to pass on either side, and it didn't sound as if it were slowing down. At Broughton's suggestion, Dr. Smith climbed onto the left running board of his car and proceeded to blink his lights manually as a warning to the other driver:

> I'll never forget this as long as I live. Mr. Broughton was on the right side hollering "Smith, you'd better jump—he ain't checkin'." Well, I jumped and Broughton jumped just as this car barreled into the back of my car at about fifty miles per hour. It drove my car straight into the wrecked Bessie Smith car and made a real pretzel out of it—it was a total loss. He ricocheted off the rear of my car and went into the ditch to the right. He barely missed Mr. Broughton and Bessie Smith.

Riding in that car was a young white couple who had obviously been partying. Dr. Smith had his hands full:

> Now, my God, we had three patients on our hands. A young lady, curled up under the instrument panel on the right, screamed at the top of her voice, hysterical, scared to death. There was a man draped over the steering wheel, which had broken off completely. Well, we got them out in the grass and started to check them. As far as I could tell, the young lady didn't have any major injuries, but the man had a chest injury and that was about all. It turned out later that he had multiple fractures of his ribs, but fortunately he didn't have any lung injury, he wasn't in shock and he wasn't critical.

Dr. Smith was examining the young couple when an ambulance, a deputy sheriff, and several officers of the law appeared on the scene. They carried Bessie to the ambulance, and Richard Morgan accompanied her in it to Clarksdale. Almost simultaneously a second ambulance arrived and picked up the injured couple.

One of the ambulances had been summoned by Broughton. The other, it turned out, had been sent at the request of the truck driver, who had gone straight to Clarksdale and reported the accident.

It is at this point that the story of Bessie's death becomes controversial: was she refused admittance to a white hospital? After answering that question with an emphatic no, Dr. Smith explains:

> The Bessie Smith ambulance would *not* have gone to a white hospital, you can forget that. Down in the Deep South cotton country, no colored ambulance driver, or white driver, would even have thought of putting a colored person off in a hospital for white folks. In Clarksdale, in 1937, a town of twelve to fifteen thousand people, there were two hospitals—one white and one colored—and they weren't half a mile apart. I suspect the driver drove just as straight as he could to the colored hospital.

The driver of the ambulance, Willie George Miller—a black man—confirmed this twenty years later. He remembered taking Bessie straight to the G. T. Thomas Hospital, Clarksdale's black hospital. He also claimed that Bessie was dead on arrival. "I can't remember for certain," he told a reporter, "but I don't think she died instantly. But she did die within a few minutes after putting her in the ambulance, before we could get her to the hospital."

That part of Miller's statement is almost certainly not true. According to the official death certificate issued by the Mississippi State Board of Health, Bessie Smith died in Ward 1 of the Afro-American Hospital, 615 Sunflower Avenue, Clarksdale, September 26, 1937, at 11:30 A.M. "The principal cause of death and related causes of importance in order of onset were as follows: *Shock. Possibly internal injuries. Compound, comminuted fractures of rt. humerus, radius and ulna.* Contributory causes of importance not related to principal cause: *Rt. humerus, radius and ulna.* Name of operation: *Amputation rt. arm.*"

As Dr. Smith points out, in 1937 it took an hour to draw a pint of blood from a donor. Then, too, both Clarksdale hospitals were country hospitals, neither of which was as well equipped as the ones in larger cities, like Memphis. Given the same situation today, says Smith, Bessie would have stood only a fifty-fifty chance of surviving the accident—she certainly would never have been able to sing again.

Of course, none of this can excuse the neglect on the part of the truck driver, who should have transported Bessie to a hospital at once, nor Dr. Smith's failure to do so in his own car before wasting time summoning an ambulance.

Much later Dr. Smith found out who the woman he had attended that night in Mississippi was. The name Bessie Smith meant nothing to him in 1937,[6] and he did not see Hammond's article when it first appeared. Not long after it was brought to his attention, he found himself in New York on a business trip, and decided to look up Frank Walker. "I wanted to give him the full details as to what actually happened down there in Mississippi," Dr. Smith recalls. "Well, he wasn't very interested and I could tell that he couldn't care less about Bessie—and that was the end of that."

Richard Morgan may well have colored his account of what happened at the scene of the accident and in the hours that followed. Some members of the family felt he was holding something back.

---

6. A strange fact, considering that Dr. Smith even then was a part-time jazz pianist with a Fats Waller–inspired style.

15284

BUREAU OF VITAL STATISTICS   STANDARD CERTIFICATE OF DEATH   State File No.

MISSISSIPPI STATE BOARD OF HEALTH

**1. PLACE OF DEATH**

County Coahoma

Voting Precinct ................................ or Village

or City Clarksdale, Miss. No. 116- 4th St., .......... Ward

(If death occurred in a hospital or institution, give its NAME instead of street and number)

Length of residence in city or town where death occurred Afro-American Hospital, 615 Sunflower Ave., Clarksdale d.

**2. FULL NAME** Bessie Smith 520

(Write or Print Name Plainly)

(a) Residence: No. 7003 12th St., Philadelphia, Pa. Ward

(Usual place of abode) (If nonresident give city or town and State)

| PERSONAL AND STATISTICAL PARTICULARS | MEDICAL CERTIFICATE OF DEATH |
|---|---|
| **3. SEX** Female  **4. COLOR OR RACE** Negro  **5.** Single, Married, Widowed, or Divorced (write the word) Married | **21. DATE OF DEATH** (month, day and year) Sept. 26, 1937 |
| **5a.** If married, widowed, or divorced HUSBAND of (or) WIFE of  Jack Gee | **22. I HEREBY CERTIFY,** That I attended deceased from Sept. 26 1937 to Sept. 26 1937 I last saw h alive on Sept. 26 1937 Death is said to have occurred on the date stated above, at 11:30 A.M. |
| **6. DATE OF BIRTH** (month, day, and year) | The principal cause of death and related causes of importance in order of onset were as follows: Date of onset |
| **7. AGE** Years 42 Months Days If LESS than 1 day, hrs. or min. | Shock, Gastly internal injuries. Compound comminuted fracture. |
| **8.** Trade, profession, or particular kind of work done, as spinner, sawyer, bookkeeper, etc. Artist | Contributory causes of importance not related to principal cause: 1-2 10 |
| **9.** Industry or business in which work was done, as silk mill, saw mill, bank, etc. | |
| **10.** Date deceased last worked at this occupation (month and year) 9/26/37 **11.** Total time (years) spent in this occupation 25 | Was there an operation (if any was done) Hugu Laceration R. arm. Date of Sept 26, 1937 |
| **12. BIRTHPLACE** (city or town) (State or country) Chattanooga, Tenn. | What test confirmed diagnosis? |
| **13. NAME** Unknown | Was there an autopsy? No |
| **14. BIRTHPLACE** (city or town) " (State or country) " | **23.** If death was due to external causes (violence) fill in also the following: Accident, suicide, or homicide? Auto accident |
| **15. MAIDEN NAME** Unknown | Date of injury Sept 26 1937 |
| **16. BIRTHPLACE** (city or town) " (State or country) " | Where did injury occur? Highway 61 between Lyon & Mem Specify city or town, county, and State Public road |
| **17. INFORMANT** (and Address) Richard Morgan Philadelphia, Pa | Specify whether injury occurred in industry, in home, or in public place Manner of injury Auto struck parked truck Nature of injury |
| **18. BURIAL, CREMATION, OR REMOVAL** Place Philadelphia Date Oct. 3 1937 | **24.** Was disease or injury in any way related to occupation of deceased? No If so, specify |
| **19. UNDERTAKER** Afro-American Burial Ass (and Address) Clarksdale, Miss. | (Signed) W. H Brander M.D. (Address) Clarksdale, Miss |
| **20. FILED** Sept 26 19 Registrar | |

# CERTIFIED COPY OF RECORD OF DEATH

I, Hugh B. Cottrell, M. D., State Registrar of Vital Statistics, hereby certify this to be a true and correct copy of the death record of the person named therein, the original being on file in this office.

Given at Jackson, Mississippi, over my signature and under the official seal of my office, this the | 13th Day April, 1971 |

Hugh B. Cottrell, M. D.   State Registrar

*Paul Burnell Hawkins*

Paul Burnell Hawkins, Deputy State Registrar

Mississippi State Standard Certificate of Death #15284.

"He used to talk about Bessie, and he'd start crying," says Maud Smith. "I never would ask him exactly what happened, but there were many times when he would start crying in my company. Richard and Bessie were *very* close, he was good for her, and he was never the same after she died. Richard sent for me before he passed, but I wasn't able to come to him in time—he said he had something to tell me, but I have no idea what that could have been."

Rather than rely on his memory, Jack Gee, Jr., produces a newspaper clipping from an early 1938 issue of the *Afro-American* to give his version of his mother's death. It is, he says, based in part on Richard Morgan's account to the family.

"My mother and her chauffeur were on their way to Clarksdale, Mississippi, where she was to fill a singing engagement. It was on Saturday night, September 25. About 3 A.M., Sunday, just ten miles out of Clarksdale, her car ran into a parked truck belonging to the National Biscuit Company, which was standing on the side of the narrow highway without any lights.

"Before the chauffeur, Richard Morgan, had a chance to stop, or turn out, he ran into the left corner of the truck, wedging my mother between the truck and the car.

"Her left arm was cut almost off, and was hanging just by the skin. She was knocked unconscious. Moore (sic) jumped out of the car and went up to the driver of the truck, a white man, and said: 'What have you done? Pull up your truck.' The truck driver pulled up, but pulled away and had to be run down by State troopers and arrested. He was released on bail and is still free.

"A white physician, a Dr. Smith, came along about this time. He stopped to administer first aid, while Moore (sic) hiked to town to get an ambulance. My mother was still unconscious.

"While the doctor was administering first-aid to my mother, another motorist came along and hit his car. A white woman passenger in the car was hurt in this second accident. One of the spectators asked the doctor why he didn't take my mother to town in his car, but he replied that his car would get too bloody.

"About this time Morgan came back with the ambulance. As the men were about to take the stretcher out to take my mother, somebody in the crowd said: 'Wait, let's see what's the matter with this white woman first.' The doctor then administered first-aid to the white woman, and then put her in the ambulance, and sent her back to town. Morgan protested but could do nothing.

"We have never found out accurately yet how my mother was taken back to town, but we do know that she was first taken to a white hospital, which refused to administer first-aid or take her in. She was then taken to the Afro-American Hospital, a colored institution. This hospital didn't have the proper equipment with which to operate. Physicians had to run all over town to get the proper equipment.

"It was about 11:30 A.M. before they administered ether to her. She died at 11:45 A.M. No reason was given as to why she died, but we know clearly that she died from loss of blood and neglect. I believe that if the ambulance had taken my mother back to town, as it was proper for the doctor to have instructed the driver, since the ambulance was sent for her case, she might be alive today."

While it behooved Jack Gee, Jr. and the day's liberal press to keep alive the story sparked by John Hammond's article, it contained too many inconsistencies not to also produce some serious skepticism. Among the early disbelievers was folk-lorist John Lomax, who in 1941 wrote several letters of inquiry and received some interesting and—in one case—significant responses.

"Sadly, the Country is infested with negro communists who seek to poison their own people against their best friends," wrote the mayor of Memphis, Walter Chandler, "and I am glad to have the opportunity to join in establishing the facts, which I am sure will disprove the story." In a subsequent letter, dated September 8, 1941, the mayor referred to Hammond's *down beat* article, saying that the writer "either lied maliciously, or is an irresponsible writer desiring to foment trouble between white and colored people." If a racial incident had played a role in the death of Bessie Smith, the setting was not Memphis, he concluded. The most significant letter came a month later, from Dr. W. H. Brandon, the man who had treated Bessie and signed her death certificate:

October 7, 1941

Dear Mr. Lomax:

I am very glad to have your letter with reference to Bessie Smith.

Bessie Smith was injured in an automobile accident several miles out from Clarksdale and was brought to Clarksdale in a colored ambulance. The car in which she was riding was smashed and she was in shock when brought to the hospital.

She died some eight or ten hours after admission to the hospital. We gave her every medical attention, but we were never able to rally her from the shock.

She was badly broken up, having many fractures of her limbs and internal injuries.

The man who was driving the car was apparently very drunk. As I remember it, he received very few injuries, as is often the case.

You may brand the statement that she was refused treatment as an absolute untruth.

If there is any further information that I can give you on this subject, I will be glad to do so.

Very truly yours,
(signed) W. H. Brandon, M.D.

# EPILOGUE

*"That woman must be weeping in her grave—*
*poor Bessie, even after she died, people*
*wouldn't let her be."*

Ruby Walker

Bessie Smith's impact was far too great for her story to end on that Mississippi road in 1937. Her musical influence, direct and indirect, has carried over into the seventies; the magic of her name continues to ring cash registers.

By its very nature, the entertainment industry thrives on publicity. Vast amounts of money are spent creating stars and keeping them in the limelight. To this end, ingenious devices and gimmicks are dreamed up by promotion men—and few sales weapons are as effective as the premature death of a major star, even a onetime major star.

As was the case with Bessie Smith, record companies traditionally "pay tribute" to their late artists by rushing out reissues of their stellar performances,[1] or hitherto unreleased performances which— sometimes due to artistic or technical imperfection—were originally rejected. Since this often makes more money for the company than it does for the artist's estate, it does not take much cynicism to regard it as cashing in on a tragic event, playing to the consumer whose interest in the artist is heightened by death.

Bessie's recording debut and her immediate success in 1923 had

1. Louis Armstrong's death, in 1971, was anticipated by at least two companies, which had "memorial" albums ready for release at a moment's notice.

227

been a lifesaver for the near-bankrupt Columbia company. Her death was equally timely, since it virtually coincided with the renaissance of traditional jazz that began in the late thirties and eventually also revived interest in the classic blues singers—suddenly, Columbia would remain the sole owners of Bessie Smith recordings. In 1938, the year Columbia released the first Bessie Smith reissues, a new generation of blues women began to record, and Bessie was already becoming a legend.

The Bessie reissues sold reasonably well, not only because of her death but also because the enormous popularity of swing music—the spark that ignited the renaissance—stimulated an almost fanatic interest in older jazz forms among whites. The new jazz fan appeared—large numbers of young white people listened seriously, carefully noted who played what and how, and delved into the music's past.

They found that the roots were often more interesting than swing music; they made a game of tracing them back to such "colorful" figures as Ma Rainey, King Oliver, Jelly Roll Morton, and Bessie Smith—performers whose exploits, real and imagined, made good subjects for after-dinner conversation. They found a history riddled with social inequities and racial injustices that they deplored and romanticized at the same time. The jazz fan was ready to bemoan past injustices—when he recognized them—but he did little or nothing to correct present ones. White jazz followers readily embraced a black performer's output as art, but they rarely accepted him as a man.

This renewed interest in jazz brought work and a measure of recognition to many black artists whose careers had been going downhill, but it was more materially lucrative for the promoters, impresarios, and record companies than it was for the performers. What passed for admiration and benevolence was often simply further exploitation, but on a grander, less obvious scale.

Like any new movement, this one needed its martyrs, and it found them in people like Joseph "King" Oliver, Louis Armstrong's early boss and lifetime idol, who ended his days as a janitor, chronicling them in a series of moving letters to his sister; in Bix Beiderbecke, a white cornet player who had died at twenty-eight in 1931, the victim of artistic frustration and alcoholism; and in Bessie, whose premature death—allegedly because of racism—qualified her. Oliver, Bix, Bessie, and a handful of other jazz performers became legends, and the myth surrounding them so ingrained—because it was tailor-made—that the truth continued to be ignored. (Some truth did surface: it was clear that Paul Whiteman was anything but the "King of Jazz," and—in more recent times—people are discovering that Benny Goodman was equally mislabeled the "King of Swing.")

The largely unrecognized black musician of the twenties became the darling of the late thirties' and early forties' left-wing liberal. Socialists and Communists found in America's black population the proletariat to suit their cause—what better way to show social concern than to have a "colored" man play for your gathering of friends! Carl Van Vechten was way ahead of the game. In this milieu many of today's established, old-ward jazz writers, record collectors, promoters, and recording executives made their fortunes. Beneath their interested smiles, the relish with which they greeted the rhythms and musical creativity of the black man, their patronizing attitude did not often escape the notice of most performers.

This kind of writer-performer relationship accounts to a great extent for the lack of accurate reporting that until recently has characterized nearly all books on the subject of black music and its creators. The writers believed only what they wanted to believe, and their sources told them only what they wanted them to hear. Sadly enough, this communications gap has resulted in the increasing distortion of Afro-American music history such as the overly simplified and not entirely true Africa-to-New-Orleans-and-up-the-river story. The theme of many concert presentations, it formed the basis for John Hammond's successful "From Spirituals to Swing" concert at Carnegie Hall in January 1938, a concert which was to have starred Bessie, but was instead dedicated to her memory.

Ruby Walker—who had now changed her name to Ruby Smith— represented Bessie at Hammond's concert, and, according to the evening's program notes, was being groomed by him to replace her famous aunt. Ruby made her first recordings four months later for the Blue Bird label, and continued over the next years to record for Vocalion, Decca, Harmonia, and Victor. She made frequent club and theatre appearances into the sixties, gradually abandoning the imitation of Bessie's dress and mannerisms which her promoter had forced on her.

In the early seventies—with that long-promised "big break" yet to materialize—Ruby continues to sing in public whenever the opportunity arises, often dipping back into her aunt's repertoire. Ruby did not sing while Bessie was alive, but their long and close association prepared her well for the task. Bessie's influence on Ruby went much beyond music. It gave her a spirit and sense of humor that has not diminished. Ruby Walker grew from girlhood to womanhood in the shadow of Bessie Smith's triumphs and tribulations, but, unlike Bessie, she could not cope with the exploiters who inherited her.

In the final analysis, Richard Morgan may well have been the one true love of Bessie's life. One thing seems certain: wild as she was, Morgan was her true friend to the end. They say he never recovered from her death, that he began to age prematurely. "I saw Richard on the street shortly after Bessie passed," says Ruby, "but I didn't recognize him until he came up and spoke to me—it was hard to believe that he could have gotten old that fast." Lionel Hampton concurs: "My uncle grieved himself to death, he loved that woman so."

Gertrude Saunders survived her eventful relationship with Jack. "She was always a smart woman," recalls Alberta Hunter. "She was investing in real estate long before the rest of us thought of investing in anything." In the thirties Gertrude continued her career success-fully in Hollywood as a voice for animated cartoons. A woman of youthful spirit, she has long since retired from show business to lead a quiet life as the landlady of a Bronx apartment house.

At the time of Bessie's death, Clarence Smith had retired from show business to operate a beauty parlor in Philadelphia, and, by the end of the forties, he and virtually all of Bessie's closest kin were dead. The remaining nieces and nephews died prematurely, before the end of the sixties, and only Jack Gee, Jack Gee, Jr., and Clarence's widow Maud survive at this writing.

Jack Gee, Jr., had received no love from his father during Bessie's final years, and her death did not change that. In fact, a $250,000 lawsuit against the National Biscuit Company served to end once and for all any semblance of kinship between Jack Senior and the rest of the family.

The lawsuit, instigated by Jack Gee, Jr., was filed in Clarksdale on behalf of him and his father shortly after Bessie's death. "I've always been looked upon as a sort of black sheep by my family," Jack, Jr. told a reporter at the time, "and that's why I want to fight this thing through. I believe it will in a way help to make up to my mother for some of the trouble I caused her while she was alive. I intend to fight this case all the way. I don't know what luck I'll have, because I know, that despite the fact that we have a good case against the company and the doctor too, the case will come up in Clarksdale, Miss., sometime this month [January, 1938], and I feel that it will be hard to get justice down there."

According to the *Afro-American,* the National Biscuit Company offered to settle out of court for $80,000[2] but "the family is holding out for $250,000, and the establishment of justice in this case."

"As far as I know," recalls Jack Gee, Jr. some thirty years later, "my father collected the money—some $58,000, I believe, but we were on the outs then and, in fact, the whole family had a falling out about this." Following the lawsuit, Jack Senior maintained some form of relationship with his son with constant promises of financial rewards, but all he actually did was to lead Jack, Jr. into a life of petty illegal activities that often resulted in jail sentences and built up an understandable bitterness. While his father continued to fabricate the myth of a close bond between himself and Bessie, and to collect whatever monies the estate produced, Jack, Jr., entered middle age without receiving as much as a penny from his mother's legacy. In fact, his father saw to it that no writer knew of his existence. Both these errors will be corrected with the publication of this book. Although Bessie left no will, Jack Gee, Jr., should—by moral rights—be a wealthy man today; his mother's labors have never ceased to make money.

In the forties, Columbia (which had been acquired by the Columbia Broadcasting System in 1938) continued to reissue Bessie's records or authorize their reissue by such private labels as the United Hot Clubs of America. These releases also included some selections that had originally been rejected,[3] and for which neither Bessie nor her accompanists were paid. Through these recordings, Bessie continued to influence young singers whose following often regarded Bessie's own records as ancient history.

For many years the stigma of Uncle Tomism was attached to the music of Bessie and her contemporaries, scaring off young black would-be followers. Fortunately, that has changed, and a new recognition of the old can be heard in much of the music performed by contemporary rock and soul groups.

2. Documentation of the alleged settlement is not possible as the National Biscuit Company's files from that period have been destroyed.

3. Twenty of Bessie's rejected selections have never been found, but it is rumored that some of them are in the hands of a New Jersey collector who is unwilling to make them available for release despite a no-questions-asked offer from Columbia Records.

This change of attitude is perhaps most dramatically reflected in the sales of Bessie Smith reissue albums. In 1951, George Avakian produced for Columbia a reissue of forty-eight of Bessie's recordings on four long-playing albums. This fine series was a slow but steady seller which the company kept in its catalogue for nineteen years. In 1970 Bessie Smith became the subject of Columbia's most ambitious reissue project to date: five double albums containing her entire available recorded output, to be released over a period of two and a half years, the time it took to produce them. By the summer of 1972, the first four albums of the new series had sold a total of two hundred thousand copies, or four hundred thousand records, exceeding by about 90 percent the combined sales of the four 1951 albums over the nineteen-year period.

In all fairness it should be pointed out that the 1951 reissues were given limited promotion, while Columbia's publicity department went to work on the 1970 series six months prior to the release of the first album. Press releases and telephone calls resulted in unprecedented advance publicity for reissues with articles and photos appearing in major newspapers and magazines across the country and overseas.

The secret of Columbia's success with the new series was that it geared its publicity to the young, placing advertisements in the so-called underground press—the rock publications—and skillfully couching the advertising copy in terms that are usually reserved for contemporary albums. Such tactics would have been of little use had not the timing been right, and it was right: a new interest in the old blues was stimulated by such popular groups as the Rolling Stones, who openly admitted their debt to Robert Johnson, Skip James, Furry Lewis, and other blues pioneers.

Within weeks of the release of the first album in the new Bessie Smith series, her name was being bandied about on inane daytime TV quiz shows; a Philadelphia organization voted to strike a silver coin in her honor; contemporary performers were recording tributes; Edward Albee's *The Death of Bessie Smith* enjoyed some revivals; her film, *St. Louis Blues*, was shown on TV for the first time; she became the subject of innumerable term papers. The Bessie Smith albums won two Grammy awards; critics awarded the first album the Grand Prix du Disque at the 1971 Montreaux Jazz Festival; *Billboard* magazine's "Trendsetter of the Year" award was given to the producer of the series, and the series came out on top in all jazz critics' polls.

With all this publicity, it was inevitable that someone should discover that Bessie Smith's grave was still unmarked. This was not the first time the matter had been brought up: newspaper clippings describe successful benefits held during the forties and fifties to raise funds for Bessie's gravestone, but fail to account for the fact that the grave remained unmarked,

"I never saw three cents of all that money," Jack Gee replied when he was asked why *he* didn't purchase a stone, but other surviving relatives support claims that proceeds of such benefits were turned over to Mr. Gee on at least two occasions. Ruby recalls performing at such an event in New York's Town Hall during the forties: "Jack showed up and demanded the money. He said he'd have his lawyers stop the concert if he didn't get it. He got it, but knowing Jack he spent it on something for himself."

Maud Smith may have been referring to the same event: "When Jack went to New York, he made enough money to buy two stones, but he used the money for something else." She also points out that Bessie's funeral did not absorb all the insurance money, and tells of a benefit that took place at Philadelphia's Blue Note Club in the early fifties: "Jack Fields gave the benefit, and the place was packed full of stars and people from Philadelphia and New York, including Juanita Hall. I remember it was a Saturday morning when William Upshur came to the house and gave me a check from the benefit at the Blue Note. I got into Mr. Upshur's car and we went to Jack on South Street. I gave the check to him and we were supposed to go and pick out a stone for Bessie, and that's the last time I saw the check, and every time I would ask him about the stone he said he was busy, that he was waiting on his lawyers, or waiting on somebody. I don't remember the amount on the check, but it was more than enough to buy a stone—and that's what the money was for."

All this time, Jack Gee could well have afforded to purchase a stone on his own, even if the story of his settlement with the National Biscuit Company wasn't true. He has consistently received composer's royalties for Bessie's tunes—many of which have been recorded by top artists through the years—and over the years he has invested money in several small businesses and real estate. Affluent "close friends" and admirers of Bessie have likewise remained unperturbed by her anonymity at Mount Lawn Cemetery.

In July 1970, following the rash of publicity given the records, Mrs. Barbara Muldow, a black Philadelphia housewife, in a letter to the Philadelphia *Inquirer*'s Action Line, recalled the unmarked grave.

The *Inquirer* immediately set out to correct the situation. Prepared to contact a number of people for donations, Action Line reporter Frank Coffey was able to complete his fund-raising with only two telephone calls. Each pledging to pay half the cost, whatever it might amount to, were Janis Joplin, the rock superstar who had made her admiration for Bessie well known, and Mrs. Juanita Green, the little girl who had scrubbed Bessie's kitchen floor on Saturdays, and was now a registered nurse, owner of two Philadelphia nursing homes, and president of the North Philadelphia chapter of the N.A.A.C.P. Armed with those pledges, the *Inquirer* contacted a monument firm which agreed to let them have a stone at cost—five hundred dollars.

The unveiling of the stone took place Friday, August 7, 1970.

John Hammond's raincoat covers the gravestone of Bessie Smith as the Reverend Wycliffe Jangdharrie (wearing dark suit and sun glasses) and the Reverend W. E. Cook prepare for the August, 1970, "unveiling." Onlookers include (center foreground) John Hammond, Juanita Green, and pianist John Brown. The lady with the flowers is Mrs. Barbara Muldow, whose letter to the *Philadelphia Inquirer* prompted the event. *Photo courtesy of Columbia Records.*

Jack Gee, Jr., was not there; no one connected with the event knew that he existed. Jack Gee wasn't there either, but for different reasons: Mrs. Green had called him with an invitation and the offer of a car to pick him up, but her call was greeted with verbal abuse and threats of legal action against all involved. Later, claiming to have misunderstood her intentions, Jack Gee sent Mrs. Green a letter of apology.

Miss Joplin was absent due to prior commitments, but, as she had made it a point to stress that her involvement was a reflection of her personal admiration and debt to Bessie Smith, rather than a publicity gimmick, there are those who believe she did not attend the ceremony for fear that her presence might detract attention from the event itself. In a phone conversation with Mrs. Green she expressed the hope that they might soon meet to discuss plans for a proposed Bessie Smith scholarship fund, but that meeting never took place—two months later, Janis Joplin herself was dead. John Hammond was present in an unofficial capacity, but Columbia Records was represented by a professional photographer and its Philadelphia distributor, both of whom had been summoned at the last minute by Robert Altshuler, the company's director of publicity.

The ceremony itself combined a sincere tribute with irreverence that bordered on the farcical: as a small group of about thirty people gathered in a semicircle around the modest gray stone, someone pointed out that a covering would be needed if an unveiling was to take place. There followed a moment of confusion before an old blue raincoat was retrieved from the trunk of John Hammond's car, thrown over the stone, and lifted off again for the "unveiling."

Two ministers, one of whom was running for local office and obviously posing for the cameras, offered a few sanctimonious words, flowers were handed out and put on the grave, and the ceremony was over. However, the press and publicity photographers, not having expected that things would go quite as fast as they did, had not been able to get the shots they wanted. A brief conference was held, and the principal characters were asked to pick up their flowers from the grave and throw them again in a reenactment.

Afterward, at an informal gathering in her home, Mrs. Green announced the foundation of a scholarship fund in Bessie Smith's name "to help a student in a career of music and science." Donations from those present started the fund off with three hundred dollars, a figure that remained intact until a year later when Columbia Records contributed one thousand dollars, with John Hammond adding a personal contribution of fifty.

On the evening of the grave-marking ceremony and the following day, the quiet event received widespread publicity in newspapers across the country and on the television networks. Most media emphasized Bessie's alleged death because of Southern racism, and the involvement of Janis Joplin in the purchase of the stone.

Columbia's publicity department put out a press release on August 17, 1970:

### COLUMBIA PARTICIPATES IN
### TRIBUTE TO BESSIE SMITH

*After Thirty Years, a Marker Is Put on Empress's Grave*

Janis Joplin, Columbia Recording Artist, Juanita Green, a registered nurse from Philadelphia, and John Hammond, Director of Talent Acquisition, Columbia Records, among others, shared the cost of a gravestone for legendary blues singer, Bessie Smith, whose grave had lain unmarked since her death in an auto accident in 1937. About fifty fans of the late Miss Smith were present at the unveiling of the stone last week at her grave-site in Sharon Hill, Pennsylvania, near Philadelphia.

Robert Altshuler, Columbia executive and long-time admirer of her recordings, was responsible for the inscription on the stone, which reads, "The Greatest Blues Singer in the World Will Never Stop Singing—Bessie Smith—1895–1937."

The epitaph, at least, was true.

The epitaph came from Columbia Records' publicity
department. *Photo courtesy of Columbia Records.*

# SELECTED DISCOGRAPHY

The following long-playing albums relate directly or indirectly to Bessie Smith. All are available at time of publication.

*BESSIE SMITH*

The World's Greatest Blues Singer (Columbia GP-33): *Down Hearted Blues; Gulf Coast Blues; Aggravatin' Papa; Beale Street Mama; Baby Won't You Please Come Home; Oh Daddy; Tain't Nobody's Biz-ness If I Do; Keeps on a-Rainin'; Mama's Got the Blues; Outside of That; Bleeding Hearted Blues; Lady Luck Blues; Yodeling Blues; Midnight Blues; If You Don't, I Know Who Will; Nobody in Town Can Bake a Sweet Jelly Roll Like Mine; See If I'll Care; Baby Have Pity on Me; On Revival Day; Moan, You Mourners; Hustlin' Dan; Black Mountain Blues; In the House Blues; Long Old Road; Blue Blues; Shipwreck Blues; Need a Little Sugar in My Bowl; Safety Mama; Do Your Duty; Gimme a Pigfoot; Take Me for a Buggy Ride; Down in the Dumps.*

Any Woman's Blues (Columbia G 30126): *Jail House Blues; St. Louis Gal; Sam Jones Blues; Graveyard Dream Blues; Cemetery Blues; Far Away Blues; I'm Going Back to My Used to Be; Whoa, Tillie, Take Your Time; My Sweetie Went Away; Any Woman's Blues; Chicago Bound Blues; Mistreating Daddy; Frosty Morning Blues; Haunted House Blues; Eavesdropper's Blues; Easy Come, Easy Go Blues; I'm Wild About That Thing; You've Got to Give Me Some; Kitchen Man; I've Got What It Takes; Nobody Knows You When You're Down and Out; Take It Right Back; He's Got Me Goin'; It Makes My Love Come Down; Wasted Life Blues; Dirty No-Gooder's Blues; Blue Spirit Blues; Worn Out Papa Blues; You Don't Understand; Don't Cry Baby; Keep It to Yourself; New Orleans Hop Scop Blues.*

Empty Bed Blues (Columbia G 30450): *Sorrowful Blues; Pinchbacks—Take 'Em Away; Rocking Chair Blues; Ticket Agent, Ease Your Window Down; Boweavil Blues; Hateful Blues; Frankie Blues; Moonshine Blues; Lou'siana Low Down*

Blues; *Mountain Top Blues; Workhouse Blues; House Rent Blues; Salt Water Blues; Rainy Weather Blues; Weeping Willow Blues; The Bye Bye Blues; I Used to Be Your Sweet Mama; I'd Rather Be Dead and Buried in My Grave; Standin' in the Rain Blues; It Won't Be You; Spider Man Blues; Empty Bed Blues (Parts I and II); Put It Right Here; Yes Indeed He Do!; Devil's Gonna Get You; You Ought to Be Ashamed; Washwoman's Blues; Slow and Easy Man; Poor Man's Blues; Please Help Me Get Him off My Mind; Me and My Gin.*

The Empress (Columbia G 30818): *Sing Sing Prison Blues; Follow the Deal on Down; Sinful Blues; Woman's Trouble Blues; Love Me Daddy Blues; Dying Gambler's Blues; St. Louis Blues; Reckless Blues; Sobbin' Hearted Blues; Cold in Hand Blues; You've Been a Good Ole Wagon; Cake Walking Babies; Yellow Dog Blues; Soft Pedal Blues; Dixie Flyer Blues; Nashville Woman's Blues; Mean Old Bedbug Blues; A Good Man Is Hard to Find; Homeless Blues; Looking for My Man Blues; Dyin' by the Hour; Foolish Man Blues; Thinking Blues; Pickpocket Blues; Muddy Water; There'll Be a Hot Time in the Old Town Tonight; Trombone Cholly; Send Me to the 'Lectric Chair; Them's Graveyard Words; Hot Springs Blues; Sweet Mistreater; Lock and Key.*

Nobody's Blues But Mine (Columbia G 31093): *Careless Love Blues; J. C. Holmes Blues; I Ain't Goin' to Play Second Fiddle; He's Gone Blues; Nobody's Blues But Mine; I Ain't Got Nobody; My Man Blues; New Gulf Coast Blues; Florida Bound Blues; At the Christmas Ball; I've Been Mistreated and I Don't Like It; Red Mountain Blues; Golden Rule Blues; Lonesome Desert Blues; Them "Has Been" Blues; Squeeze Me; What's the Matter Now?; I Want Ev'ry Bit of It; Jazzbo Brown from Memphis Town; The Gin House Blues; Money Blues; Baby Doll; Hard Driving Papa; Lost Your Head Blues; Hard Time Blues; Honey Man Blues; One and Two Blues; Young Woman's Blues; Preachin' the Blues; Back Water Blues; After You've Gone; Alexander's Ragtime Band.*

## MA RAINEY

The Immortal Ma Rainey (Milestone MLP-2001): *Jealous Hearted Blues; Cell Bound Blues; Army Camp Harmony Blues; Explainin' the Blues; Night Time Blues; 'Fore Day Honry Scat; Rough and Tumble Blues; Memphis Bound Blues; Slave to the Blues; Bessemer Bound Blues; Slow Driving Moan; Gone Daddy Blues.*

Blame It on the Blues (Milestone MLP-2008): *Chain Gang Blues; Wringing and Twisting Blues; Dead Drunk Blues; Ma Rainey's Black Bottom; New Bo weavil Blues; Moonshine Blues; Deep Moanin' Blues; Daddy, Goodbye Blues; Tough Luck Blues; Blame It on the Blues; Sweet Rough Man; Black Eye Blues.*

Down in the Basement (Milestone MLP-2017): *Mountain Jack Blues; Broken Hearted Blues; Down in the Basement; Trust No Man; Morning Hour Blues; Blues, Oh Blues; Oh Papa Blues; Black Cat Hoot Owl Blues; Hear Me Talkin' To You; Prove It on Me Blues; Victim of the Blues; Sleep Talking Blues; Runaway Blues; Leaving This Morning.*

Blues the World Forgot (Biograph BLP-12001): *Booze and Blues; Toad Frog Blues; Louisiana Hoo Doo Blues; Stormy Sea Blues; Levee Camp Moan; Titanic Man Blues; Broken Soul Blues; Weeping Woman Blues; Misery Blues; Blues the World Forgot (Parts I and II); Traveling Blues.*

Oh My Babe Blues (Biograph BLP-12011): *Jealousy Blues; Shave 'Em Dry; Farewell Daddy Blues; Oh My Babe Blues; Soon This Morning; Don't Fish in My Sea; Countin' the Blues; Sissy Blues; Log Camp Blues; Hustlin' Blues; Ma and Pa Poorhouse Blues; Big Feeling Blues.*

Queen of the Blues (Biograph BLP-12032): *Sad Luck Blues; Boweavil Blues; Barrel House Blues; Those All Night Long Blues; Moonshine Blues; Last Minute Blues; Southern Blues; Walking Blues; Lost Wandering Blues; Dream Blues; Honey, Where You Been So Long?; Ya Da Do; Those Dogs of Mine; Lucky Rock Blues; South Bound Blues; Lawd, Send Me a Man Blues.*


## IDA COX

Blues Ain't Nothin' Else But . . . (Milestone MLP-2015): *I've Got the Blues for Rampart Street; Chattanooga Blues; Chicago Monkey Man Blues; Blues Ain't Nothin' Else But!; How Can I Miss You When I've Got Dead Aim; I Ain't Got Nobody; One Time Woman Blues; How Long, Daddy, How Long; Pleading Blues; Seven Day Blues; Cold and Blue; Booze Crazy Man Blues; Broadcasting Blues; Fogyism.*


## ETHEL WATERS

Oh Daddy! (Biograph BLP-12022): *Oh Daddy!; Down Home Blues; One-Man Nan; There'll Be Some Changes Made; At the New Jump Steady Ball; Oh, Joe, Play That Trombone; Memphis Man; Midnight Blues; That Da Da Strain; Georgia Blues; You Can't Do What My Last Man Did; Ethel Sings 'Em; Sweet Man; Craving Blues.*

Jazzin' Babies' Blues (Biograph BLP-12026): *The New York Glide; At the New Jump Steady Ball; Dying with the Blues; Kiss Your Pretty Baby Nice; Jazzin' Babies' Blues; Kind Lovin' Blues; Brown Baby; Ain't Goin' Marry; You'll Need Me When I'm Long Gone; I Want Somebody All My Own; Black Spatch Blues; One Sweet Letter from You.*

On Stage and Screen 1925–1940 (Columbia CL-2792): *Dinah; I'm Coming Virginia; Am I Blue?; Birmingham Bertha; You're Lucky to Me; Memories of You; You Can't Stop Me from Loving You; Stormy Weather; Heatwave; Harlem on My Mind; Hottentot Potentate; Thief in the Night; Taking a Chance on Love; Honey in the Honeycomb; Cabin in the Sky; Love Turned the Light Out.*

Women of the Blues (RCA Victor LPV-534): Includes tracks by Mamie Smith Spivey; Alberta Hunter; Sippi Wallace; Margaret Johnson; Lizzie Miles and Victoria Spivey.

The Sound of Harlem (Columbia C3L-33): Three-record set including tracks by Bessie Smith, Mamie Smith, Gertrude Saunders, Alberta Hunter, Clara Smith, Buck and Bubbles, Billie Holiday, Ethel Waters, Eubie Blake, Clarence Williams, and James P. Johnson.

Stars of the Apollo (Columbia G-30788): Two-record set including tracks by Bessie Smith, Mamie Smith, Buck and Bubbles, Butterbeans and Susie, Jackie "Moms" Mabley, Ida Cox, Ruby Smith, and Bill "Bojangles" Robinson.

Spirituals to Swing (Vanguard VRS–523/4): Two-record set of recordings made during John Hammond's 1938 and 1939 Carnegie Hall concerts, the first of which was a memorial to Bessie Smith. Artists include Ida Cox, Sidney Bechet, Fletcher Henderson, Helen Humes, James P. Johnson, and Joe Turner.

# SUGGESTED READING

Bechet, Sidney. *Treat it Gentle.* New York, Hill and Wang Inc., 1960.

Bradford, Perry. *Born With the Blues.* New York, Oak Publications, Inc., 1965.

Chilton, John. *Who's Who of Jazz.* London, Bloomsbury Book Shop, 1970.

Handy, W.C. *Father of the Blues.* New York, The Macmillan Company, 1941.

Schuller, Gunther. *Early Jazz.* New York, Oxford University Press, 1968.

Schiffman, Jack. *Uptown—The Story of Harlem's Apollo Theatre.* New York, Cowles Book Company, Inc., 1971.

Shapiro, Nat and Nat Hentoff. *The Jazz Makers.* New York, Rinehart and Company, Inc., 1957.

Shapiro, Nat and Nat Hentoff. *Hear Me Talkin' To Ya.* New York, Rinehart and Company, 1955.

Stewart-Baxter, Derrick. *Ma Rainey and the Classic Blues Singers.* New York, Stein and Day Publishers, 1970.

Waters, Ethel and Charles Samuels. *His Eye Is on the Sparrow.* New York, Doubleday and Company, Inc., 1950.

Jones, LeRoi. *Blues People.* New York, William Morrow and Company, 1963.

Oliver, Paul. *The Story of the Blues.* New York, Chilton Book Company, 1969.

n addition to the above books, information pertaining to Bessie Smith and the show business milieu of her era can be found in the entertainment pages of the following newspapers (editions printed between 1915 and 1937), many of which are available on microfilm in the Schomburg Collection of the New York Public Library, and in various other libraries around the country:

*The Afro-American* (Baltimore)
*The Amsterdam News* (New York)
*The Chicago Defender*
*The Commercial Appeal* (Memphis)
*The Interstate Tattler* (New York)
*The Journal and Guide* (Norfolk, Va.)
*The New York Age*
*The New York Clipper*
*The Philadelphia Tribune*
*The Pittsburgh Courier*

# Index